CIVIL WAR GHOST TRAILS

CIVIL WAR GHOST TRAILS

Stories from America's Most Haunted Battlefields

MARK NESBITT

STACKPOLE
BOOKS

Published by
STACKPOLE BOOKS
5067 Ritter Road
Mechanicsburg, PA 17055
www.stackpolebooks.com

Printed in the United States of America

10 9 8 7 6 5 4 3 2 1

FIRST EDITION

Cover design by Caroline Stover

Library of Congress Cataloging-in-Publication Data

Nesbitt, Mark.
Civil War ghost trails : stories from America's most haunted battlefields / Mark Nesbitt. — 1st ed.
p. cm.
Includes bibliographical references (p.) and index.
ISBN 978-0-8117-1061-9 (pbk.)
1. Ghosts—United States. 2. United States—History—Civil War, 1861–1865—Battlefields—Miscellanea. 3. Historic sites—United States—Miscellanea. I. Title.
BF1472.U6N46 2012
133.1'22—dc23

2012006395

Contents

A Note About EVP

Electronic Voice Phenomena, also known as EVP, is one of the more interesting aspects of investigating the paranormal. EVP is thought by many to be the voices of the dead recorded on audio devices. In the past, writing a book and including examples of EVP has been problematic: Without including some kind of storage device—a tape or a compact disc—how does the reader get to examine EVP?

The now-ubiquitous presence of the personal computer and the Internet has solved this problem. This book has been written with the realization that most will be reading it within arm's length of a device with access to the Internet.

Examples of EVP gathered at the Civil War sites are mentioned in many of the chapters, along with my subjective interpretation of what is being recorded. The reader may access these recordings by going to www.marknesbitt.info.

The recordings are listed under the name of the historic site where they were gathered.

Introduction

> When all those legs and arms and heads, chopped off in battle, shall join together at the latter day and cry all "We died at such a place"; some swearing, some crying for a surgeon, some upon their wives left poor behind them, some upon the debts they owe, some upon their children rawly left. I am afeared there are few die well that die in battle.
>
> —*King Henry V*, 4.1

What is a ghost? By the age-old definition, a ghost is a disembodied soul that after the life of its body is over goes on to live an existence apart from the visible world. That particular definition says a lot: That we are more than just physical, flesh-and-blood bodies, that we also contain an intangible soul; that after the death of the physical body, the soul lives on and may be immortal; that it lives on in a place invisible to us, another world, another plane, another dimension, that may exist alongside the one in which we exist.

A more sinister twist is found in the famous ghost hunter Hans Holzer's definition: "Ghosts are the surviving mental faculties of people who died traumatically." So, according to Holzer's studies, if you want to come back as a ghost, it's going to hurt.

But it is Holzer's definition that would seem to apply to just about every soldier who died in the American Civil War, whether by bullet or shell, or slow, painful, wasting disease. And it may at least partially explain why the battlefields of the Civil War are such fertile ground for hauntings.

Why would ghosts be associated with the Civil War? Like most wars, the Civil War began with naïve expectations of a quick victory—on both sides. Men enlisted for ninety days and prayed that the war wouldn't end before their enlistment. Parties and celebrations sent young men off to glorious war, and girlfriends could not really be serious when they told their beaux to bring home their uniforms without any holes in them.

Tragically, after four years, more than 620,000 of those young men would never come home. Half of that number would die wasted from disease. Hundreds of thousands more would return missing a limb. These figures, however, are slightly misleading. America in the nineteenth century had less than one-tenth the population it does today. So we need to multiply those figures by ten to get the same impact they would have today. Imagine if, in just four years of war today, America lost more than 6 million young men and millions more came home missing an arm or leg or both. The outcry would be overwhelming.

Analyzing just a few of the major battles gives insight into how horrifying the fighting really was. At Gettysburg, for example, while the battle lasted three days and cost 51,000 casualties, the actual fighting only consumed about twenty-four hours. Simple division tells us that in that time, 2,125 men were struck by hot lead or jagged iron every hour. That divides down to 35 men struck per minute. This means that every two seconds a man was being struck by a projectile.

Near Fredericksburg, Virginia, four of the Civil War's bloodiest battles consumed 100,000 casualties. In December 1862, the town itself was the scene of savage street fighting; a dozen Federal assaults upon Marye's Heights made the grass slippery with blood. Four thousand men fell in one hour in those charges.

Many of the casualties from Chancellorsville in 1863 and the Wilderness and Spotsylvania in 1864 were brought back to Fredericksburg, again filling the same churches, public buildings, and homes with wounded and dying as during the first combat there. If the Wilderness and Spotsylvania were counted as one battle (and they logically could since there was only one day of maneuvering between them), the 60,000 casualties would make it the bloodiest battle in all of American history.

The dubious distinction of being the bloodiest single day falls to the Battle of Antietam (or Sharpsburg) in Maryland. Some 23,000 men were killed, wounded, or missing in the hours between the sunrise and sunset of September 17, 1862.

The Western Theater of the war produced as much agony as the Eastern Theater. Chickamauga, in Georgia, became the second-bloodiest battle of the war. During the siege of Vicksburg, Mississippi, civilians resorted to living in caves to avoid the Union cannon fire. Sherman's March to the Sea across Georgia brought the war to the doorsteps of the Southern civilian population; when Sherman turned north, his march across South Carolina was even worse.

The last year of the war brought horror upon horror while prison pens, like Johnson's Island in Ohio, Point Lookout in Maryland, Elmira in New York, and Andersonville in Georgia filled to overflowing with malnourished, sick, and poorly dressed prisoners who were forced, in some cases, to provide their own shelter from the elements.

The explosion of raw human emotions as men were shot, bayoneted, clubbed to death, or liquefied in the burst of an artillery shell (which may account for those listed as "missing") may not be the only reason our Civil War battlefields remain haunted. Many of the fields themselves have been preserved as national parks, and the houses, farms, and barns where the wounded suffered and "shuffled off this mortal coil" are still in existence. Many of the towns have kept and restored the Civil War–era buildings that once saw horrors beyond belief. Of the 400 buildings in 1863 Gettysburg, 200 remain; Fredericksburg retains 350 of its original 500 Civil War–era structures.

Even when structures are burned to the ground, spirits may still abide. Sherman's March to the Sea stripped that section of Georgia. Why would it be haunted? According to Valerie V. Hunt in her book *Infinite Mind*, raw human emotions exude a force: "Emotion is aroused energy." Certainly, the experience of a people watching their homes and possessions stolen or consumed by fire elicits strong emotions that linger to new generations; mention to virtually any Georgian today the name "Sherman" and listen to the reaction. Some paranormalists believe that emotional energy can remain embedded in certain elements of the environment and result in a particular kind of haunting called "residual."

Scientific Explanations for Ghosts

In the search for a cogent analogy for just what reality is, physicists have theorized many models to attempt to illustrate how things happen in the universe. Originally, it was thought that the very nugget of matter, the atom, looked like a tiny planet with electrons whirling around a nucleus.

Since then, dozens of theories about the nature of reality have emerged and been discarded. Others seem to have a longer shelf life. Whatever the theory, it would have to take in all realities: the macrocosm and microcosm; the visible and the invisible; the potential that several realities exist simultaneously on different planes or in different dimensions; that time does not move in just one direction; that life and the finality of death is an illusion. Physics has become more akin to philosophy than science.

One theory in physics that may apply to the intertwining of dimensions is the concept of multiverses (as opposed to one universe). Numerous universes exist side-by-side upon malleable membranes (or "branes"). These branes can flex and bend and bulge so that, periodically, they intersect and information is passed between them. Perhaps we exist on a brane that occasionally intersects and passes information (in the form of energy—light, sound, heat) with another brane upon which exists the spirit energy of former living humans. When they intersect, we experience what we call ghosts, the vision or voice or touch of someone who has passed over to that other brane.

Perhaps a simpler explanation for why the physical energy remnants remain attached to a specific site is a geological one. Joe Farrell, a paranormal investigator from the Gettysburg area, was the first to bring this idea to my attention. Paranormal investigator Richard Felix, from England, also had the same thought, and we tossed it around on a recent visit of his to Gettysburg. It seems that a great many paranormal encounters occur where there is a lot of granite. Granite is one of the most plentiful types of rock on earth and contains quartz crystal. Quartz (or silicon) is known to capture or resonate to electricity in its environment. We have been keeping time using quartz watches for close to half a century, and silicon quartz is what the main operating systems in computers use. We also know that when humans die, they release an explosion of photons, or a "light shout," as Polish physicist Janusz Slawinski called it in the *Journal of Near-Death Studies*. While studying the Shroud of Turin, Slawinski discovered that a dying organism emits photons more than a thousand times greater than the electromagnetic field it gives off during its usual resting state. As cells die and genetic material begins to unravel, as it does at death, a powerful charge of electromagnetic energy is released. As well, when bones are broken (as when struck by a bullet), it creates a piezoelectric effect, releasing electricity into the surroundings. This occurs, of course, thousands of times during a battle and during its surgical aftermath. Perhaps this electromagnetic energy is captured in the quartz, then released under certain environmental conditions—conditions that may include an interface with living humans.

Types of Hauntings at Civil War Battlefields

Paranormalists classify hauntings into several types.

- **Intelligent, or interactive.** In this type of haunting, the ghost acknowledges the presence of the living percipient and sometimes attempts to communicate. One story from Devil's Den at Gettysburg is of a female photographer who, early one morning, was out at the site alone, standing on top of one of the rocks about to take a picture. Suddenly she got the feeling she was being watched. She turned and saw a man behind her. "What you're looking for is over there," he said, and then pointed past her head. She looked where he was pointing, but then turned immediately back to him and he was gone. The fact that he acknowledged and spoke to her classifies this as an intelligent haunting.

- **Residual.** These sightings are scenes that play out over and over, much like a video. The phantom battalion at Gettysburg, which marches out, does a few maneuvers, and then disappears without ever acknowledging the observer, is an example of a residual haunting. Another is the Woman in White at Chatham Manor in Fredericksburg; she wanders the grounds apparently without seeing anyone from the present. Closely related is a warp, which is a rip in the fabric of time, a vision into the past. There is a story of a woman in Fredericksburg who hanged herself at the top of some stairs. Periodically, someone will glance up and see a misty figure swinging back and forth, a vision of what once occurred in that space many years before.

- **Poltergeist.** Poltergeist means "noisy ghost." The activity is manifested in slamming doors, lights flickering on and off, levitation, and generally disruptive behavior. Silverware flying off tables in some of the restaurants in Fredericksburg is an example of poltergeist activity.

- **Ghost lights.** These are unexplained illuminations. Phantom campfires have been seen near the Wilderness Battlefield and in the Wheatfield at Gettysburg; when they are investigated, there's no evidence of a fire. The mysterious orbs caught on digital cameras at haunted sites are also examples.

- **Crisis apparitions.** These occur only during emergencies, apparently to inform the living. They seem to happen at night when most people are sound asleep. The typical crisis apparition awakes you in the middle of the night. For instance, you would recognize the figure standing by your bed and ask, "Uncle Joe, what are you doing here?" He answers, "I just came to say goodbye," and vanishes. You look at the clock: it is 2:00 A.M. and you figure you just had a strange dream and so you go back to sleep. The next morning Aunt Mary calls to tell you that your Uncle Joe died this morning at about 2:00 A.M.

So what should you expect from a battlefield haunting? Most people never see a ghost. Only about 10 percent of all ghost manifestations are visual. A good 60 percent are auditory. So you are

more likely to hear a ghost than see one. But all the senses can be involved—smell, touch, and taste, as well as sound and sight. There is also that intangible sense, the feeling that something is different or something is there.

On battlefields people have smelled rotten eggs. Why? Sulfur was a main component of black powder, the main propellant used during the nineteenth century—and sulfur smells like rotten eggs when it burns.

People have been touched—caressed or pushed—on Civil War battlefields and in buildings that were in existence on or near those sites. Others have experienced cold spots. The reenactors who played in the movie *Gettysburg* felt them when they were marching across the field of Pickett's Charge. It was a warm summer day, in the high 80s, but when the men descended into one of the swales in the field, it became immediately icy cold. They claimed they could see each other's breath condensing in the cold. When they went up and out of the swale into the summer heat, they were totally confused about what happened.

People have heard things on Civil War battlefields that hearken back to the most famous moments in history: cannons firing, musketry, cheers of large bodies of men, orders being shouted, drums, fifes, and cries and screams of the wounded.

Why Do Spirits Linger?

Paranormalists have listed a number of reasons why they believe spirits remain or return to visit the living. The conditions below are all present during a battle-related death. In many cases, several are present for any one individual killed in combat. In other words, battles are the "perfect storm" for creating ghosts.

- **Abrupt death.** Death didn't get any more abrupt than when a soldier was charging artillery loaded with double or triple canister, the anti-personnel projectile that turned the cannon into a giant shotgun. In an instant, a man was blown to atoms.
- **Youthful death.** Most of the soldiers in the Civil War were in their early twenties, perhaps younger if a large number of them

lied about their age in the heady early days of the war in order to enlist. Most of those who died in the Civil War were young and perished far too soon.

- **Unexpected death.** This is closely related to an abrupt death. Men and women enter combat hoping, praying, and fighting to live through the experience. That's why suicide soldiers are so rare and horrifying to the normal person's mind. Although the thought of death in battle can never be far from the average soldier's thoughts, actually *seeking* death is not the norm. Therefore, when death comes to the soldier, it is usually unexpected.
- **Drawn to the living.** Ghosts seem to be attracted to people. Some mediums I know tell me that when asked by people if their house is haunted they reply, "No, but you are." Each year, tourists visit the battlefields where thousands died. The attraction to humans may be a reason why ghosts are seen so often at places of mass death like the Civil War fields of conflict.
- **Bringing a message.** Some spirits are said to appear as harbingers, or forecasters of future events, whether for good or bad. Other ghosts may intend to send other messages. Perhaps what the dead have learned about war is the message they wish to pass on.
- **Drawn to the grieving.** Tourists flock to battlefields literally by the millions. Gettysburg, for example, sees annually 1.5 million people, who wander the site in awe of what the young soldiers did there. We Americans visit our Civil War battlefields and ponder the deeds done on them. In other words, we mourn this entire generation of young soldiers every time we visit. The mourning has gone on for a century and a half.
- **Unconsecrated burial.** Many soldiers killed on Civil War battlefields were buried at least twice. First they were interred where they fell on the field, with no family or clergy to consecrate the ground. In some of the earlier battles, like Shiloh, the dead were gathered together and buried in mass graves. In later battles, too, the dead spent some time in hasty, shallow graves where they fell, then were exhumed and reburied in the

new national cemeteries established near the battlefields. Ceremonies like those surrounding Lincoln's Gettysburg Address consecrated the grounds. Still, not all the dead from our Civil War rest peacefully. Only five of the dozen or so mass graves at Shiloh have been identified. Individual remains still are found periodically, like at Gettysburg as recently as 1997. If an unconsecrated burial is criteria for lost, wandering souls, again, our battlefields are filled with them.

The Evidence

EVP, or electronic voice phenomena, was discovered when magnetic tape was invented, although some sources say it had been recorded on older wire recording devices. Voices were recorded on the tape when no one was speaking, in total silence. In the summer of 1959, Frederick Jurgenson was audiotaping bird calls alone in a field when he discovered that he had picked up voices. Later, he recognized the voice of his deceased mother calling him by a pet name. Convinced he was capturing the voices of the dead, he continued to record and in 1964 wrote a book called *The Voices from Space.* Modern paranormal investigators rely on digital recorders set on "voice activation," so they should not record anything if no one is talking. In the field, investigators ask a pertinent historic question, such as "What state are you from?" and then pause in silence. Suddenly, the player starts recording with no discernable sound present. When played back, the results are sometimes remarkably clear, like the answer I got in the cellar of the Cashtown Inn when we contacted Andrew, a Confederate soldier. Asking the question about his provenance, I got the answer, "Mis-sis-sip-pi," in four distinct syllables.

Photographs and videos have been taken of strange mists, circular lights called "orbs," and even full-body apparitions. These photos have been taken at night and during broad daylight. Near-infrared cameras seem to capture more spirit energy than regular film did. Most digital cameras can "see" farther into the extreme ends of the light spectrum than film cameras. Some paranormalists believe that ghosts are visible in the infrared or ultraviolet wavelengths, beyond what the mature human eye can perceive. One caveat: The human brain is structured to "connect the dots," or fill in the blanks to form a full image inside the brain of what we see in pieces. This phenomenon is called apophenia, and it sometimes works against us when we try to analyze what we think are ghost photos with a matrix background. Apophenia occurs with sound as well, and in analyzing EVP.

Small children's eyes and animals' eyes often have perception in the higher and lower areas of the spectrum, which may account for domestic animals' reactions to things unseen by their owners and why children sometimes have "imaginary" friends.

Video cameras now come with an infrared ability to tape in the dark, and have captured everything from orbs moving in apparently intelligent ways to mists floating by. Often, when set up on a tripod and left alone to tape in a known paranormally active site, the camera will go in and out of focus a number of times without anything visible appearing on the tape. Whatever caused the camera to change disrupted the infrared focus but it was invisible to the human eye.

Infrared game cams, or trail cams, have been used successfully in a number of night investigations to capture spirit entities when no one living is in the area. These are particularly helpful in "lockout" investigations, where an area can be evacuated completely, leaving only the ghosts around to have their picture taken.

And, of course, there are the witnesses to paranormal phenomena. While many may scoff that this is merely anecdotal evidence, what is all history before it is published?

At the least, a large collection of ghost stories from eyewitnesses provides a mass of information from which data can be extrapolated. For example, analyzing my stories from Gettysburg tells us that at least half of them occurred in the daytime, giving the lie to the age-old fable that ghosts only come out at night. It is through this analysis that we determined that only 10 percent of all ghost-related experiences are visual, while some 60 percent are auditory. The other 30 percent involve all the other human senses: taste, touch, and smell. More analysis may tell us if ghostly encounters occur more frequently during certain times of the year or month, or to men, women, or children. All the data gathered and analyzed will hopefully lead us to better understand just what it is that is happening, seemingly consistently, on our Civil War battlefields.

First and Second Manassas

Like a number of sites in nineteenth-century America with key crossroads, railroad junctions, and strategic terrain features, Manassas in Virginia was unfortunate enough to be the scene of more than one bloody conflict.

Located less than two days' march from the Federal capital of Washington, D.C., the junction of the Manassas Gap and the Orange & Alexandria railroad provided a supply of rations and ammunition to the rebel army encamped in the area.

First Manassas, or First Bull Run

After the fall of Fort Sumter in April 1861, the North was filled with cries to advance "on to Richmond." While the Union blockade of Southern ports began to be established, President Lincoln directed Union general Irvin McDowell to come up with a plan to take the 35,000 troops around Washington and oust the nearly 21,000 Confederates ensconced around Manassas Junction under the command of the hero of Fort Sumter, Gen. P. G. T. Beauregard. A relatively large Union force was to prevent some 11,000 Confederates under Gen. Joseph E. Johnston from leaving the Shenandoah Valley and reinforcing their comrades at Manassas.

McDowell began his march to defeat the smaller Confederate force and capture the railroad junction at Manassas on July 16, 1861. His plan was to have part of his force demonstrate towards a stone bridge and Blackburn's Ford on Bull Run while sending a large flanking force to Sudley Ford to attack the Confederate left and rear.

By the time McDowell's men reached the battlefield, however, the 11,000 Confederates under Johnston had slipped away from the Federals in the Shenandoah Valley and climbed aboard railroad cars that took them directly to their comrades at Manassas Junction. It was the first time in warfare the railroad had been used to transport troops to the battlefield. Now the two sides were of even strength.

In the early morning of July 21, the Federals began their demonstration at the stone bridge. Facing them was the Confederate brigade of Col. Nathan G. Evans. Though the Union troops approached the bridge, they made no effort to force a crossing.

About 9:00 A.M. Evans received an urgent message from Confederate signal officer E. P. Alexander, using the wig-wag method of flag communication: "Look to your left. You are turned." Leaving part of his force at the bridge, Evans marched the rest to Matthews Hill to confront the two flanking enemy divisions.

Fortunately, Confederate general Barnard Bee, after hearing the firing earlier, began moving his and another brigade toward Henry Hill. As the Union flank attack began to threaten Evans's hold on Matthews Hill, Bee marched the two brigades to support him. While fighting continued on Matthews Hill, another officer whose reputation would be made in the next two years led his brigade across Bull Run and toward the rear of the Confederates on Matthews Hill. Col. William Tecumseh Sherman and his troops made the Confederate position on the hill untenable and the three rebel brigades began to withdraw.

The Federals paused in their assault. The break allowed a Virginia Military Institute professor-turned-colonel to find an excellent position behind the retreating Confederates and establish a new defensive line. General Bee saw the brigade and proclaimed, "There is Jackson standing like a stone wall," exhorting them to "Rally behind the Virginians!" Never again would Thomas J. Jackson teach under the students' nickname "Tom Fool," but would fight under the nom de guerre of "Stonewall."

At this early stage in the war, it was not the Blue versus the Gray. Uniforms from prewar militia units were used, or new, gaudy uniforms were supplied by home states. Some Northern units wore gray; some Confederate units wore blue; some units on both sides wore red.

The now-familiar St. Andrew's cross Confederate battle flag was not yet in use, and the Confederate flag was similar to the United States flag; in fact, it was mistaken in the smoke and haze of the battle. Because of this, there were several instances of "friendly fire" casualties.

By mid-afternoon Confederates had solidified their line on Henry Hill. McDowell attempted another advance to Chinn Ridge, but it was anticipated by the arrival of two Confederate brigades. He then ordered a withdrawal back across Bull Run.

What started out as an orderly withdrawal soon became a rout. Rumors swirled that the Confederates had reserved the Black Horse Cavalry to swarm down on the retiring units to capture—or worse, slaughter—the men on foot. A wagon crossing the Cub Run Bridge overturned, clogging that route and producing panic. To make things worse, civilians and congressmen from Washington had ridden out to watch the "show" from the safe side of Bull Run. As they began to head back to the capital, the traffic jam increased.

Yet, some Federal units maintained enough composure to discourage a full Confederate pursuit. They had all been marching and fighting since before dawn and were played out. Despite rampant rumors, the Confederates, disorganized in victory, were in no shape to advance upon Washington.

When the final roll of casualties came in, they were higher than in any other battle fought by an American army. According to the National Park Service's figures, Confederates suffered 1,750 casualties and the Union army, 2,950. Another casualty was elderly Judith Henry, who refused to leave her house on the hill that bore her family's name. She was killed by an artillery shell that exploded in her bedroom.

The real casualty, however, was American innocence. Suddenly those citizen-soldiers who signed up for ninety days hoping to get in a battle before it was all over were being asked to reenlist for three years. Everyone began to finally realize how costly–in both treasure and blood–this war might be.

Second Manassas, or Second Bull Run

After the defeat at Manassas, Lincoln put George B. McClellan in command of the new Army of the Potomac. McClellan's unsuccessful Peninsula Campaign in the spring of 1862, in which the Confederates drove the Union army from the doorstep of Richmond, led the Federal War Department to organize troops around Washington into an army and brought Gen. John Pope from the west to command it. Gen. Robert E. Lee, now in command of the Confederate Army of Northern Virginia, decided to use Stonewall Jackson's troops to contest Pope's movements. A battle was fought at Cedar Mountain on August 9. Although Jackson held the field at the end of the day, he did not administer a decisive blow to Pope.

On August 12, Lee received intelligence that McClellan was heading to the area by water from the Peninsula. The next day Lee sent Gen. James Longstreet to join with Jackson, and Lee followed on August 15. Lee's plan was to attack Pope before he could be reinforced by McClellan. Fortunes of war would dictate otherwise.

Gen. J. E. B. Stuart, Lee's renowned cavalry commander, was nearly captured by Yankee troopers at Verdiersville on the morning of August 18. Stuart had been expecting other Confederate forces that morning, and when he heard approaching hoofbeats, he sent out some of his staff to meet them. Then he heard shots. Federal forces had surprised Stuart and his staff, who barely made it out of the yard where they had been encamped. As it happened, the Federals captured some of Stuart's personal items, including his cloak and his famous plumed hat. More importantly, they got his haversack with Lee's orders in it. Now Pope knew some of Lee's aggressive plans and acted to withdraw north of the Rappahannock River.

Pope covered well the several fords across the Rappahannock, and heavy rains swelled the river so that it was virtually impassable.

Stuart approached Lee with a plan that could dislodge Pope from the Rappahannock line, but yielded something more valuable.

In a raid on Catlett's Station, Stuart missed capturing Pope, but got his dress uniform (which went on display in Richmond) and Pope's dispatch book with marching orders and troop strengths. Lee now had some valuable information.

Splitting his army in the presence of the enemy seemed to be one of Lee's tactical trademarks. On August 25 he sent Jackson and his 27,000 men and 80 pieces of artillery on a 50-mile march around Pope's right flank. In just two days of marching, Jackson struck behind Pope's lines and seized his supply depot at Manassas Junction. The hungry Confederates ate everything they could, and then burned the rest of Pope's supplies and went into position behind a crossroads near Manassas Junction called Groveton.

Pope realized that Confederates had turned his right flank and attacked his base of supplies in his rear. His response was to become aggressive and march on Jackson's men at Manassas, hopefully being able to hold them up until McClellan arrived from disembarking his troops at Alexandria and before Lee and Longstreet could cross the mountains to the west. It was what Lee feared.

Pope decided to concentrate his army at Centreville. As part of it marched along the Warrenton Turnpike through Groveton late in the afternoon on August 28, 1862, Federal officers saw a lone Confederate horseman ride out and observe the column. At least one Federal commander wanted someone to take a shot at him, but was unsuccessful in his efforts. As quoted in David G. Martin's book *The Second Bull Run Campaign*, the lone rider returned to the woods near the Brawner Farm and told his subordinate officers, "You may bring up your men, gentlemen." The single horseman making a personal reconnaissance was Stonewall Jackson himself.

Jackson knew Longstreet was on the march and would rejoin him by the next day; he also knew there were only a couple of hours of daylight left in case the battle went poorly for him; and finally he knew he wanted to hold up Pope from uniting his forces. In Jackson's mind, they were circumstances good enough to risk an attack.

What ensued was the large-scale equivalent of an old-fashioned duel. Two of the most vaunted units in either army were involved:

Jackson's own Stonewall Brigade and some tough Midwesterners who would soon earn the cognomen Iron Brigade. Civil War shoulder arms were quite accurate and deadly at 300 yards; the Northerners' first volley was fired at 150 yards, yet the Confederates continued to advance to within 80 yards before they fired their first volley. For twenty minutes the first units in the battle volleyed toe-to-toe, suffering horrendous casualties.

As the sun slowly sank, more units were thrown into the fight by both sides and blasted away at each other from practically point-blank range: one Union colonel called the participants "crowds" of men firing at each other from 50 yards; the right flank of the Union line was fired upon from 30 yards away; and famed Confederate artillerist John Pelham drove his guns to within 100 yards of the left flank of the Federals and opened up. Neither side wanted to withdraw. Finally, darkness forced an end to the first day of one of the most intense battles—for its duration—in the war to that date.

Jackson pulled his men back to an abandoned railroad bed, which made for fine entrenchments and defensive breastworks. He placed his artillery on Stoney Ridge behind his 20,000 infantry and secured his flanks with Stuart's cavalrymen. Now, all he had to do was hold off twice as many Yankees until Longstreet and Lee arrived.

The Federal advance against Jackson began at 5:30 A.M. on August 29. Pushing their way through dense woods, they engaged the Confederates along the railroad bed. By mid-morning, more Federals began advancing westward, past Groveton to the battlefield of the day before. Suddenly they were confronted by a large number of the enemy right before them: Longstreet had arrived.

Longstreet's line hooked up with Jackson's right flank, completing an L-shaped line. Connecting to Jackson were Gen. John B. Hood's division of infantry and the famous Washington Artillery from New Orleans. Lee wanted to attack Pope immediately; Longstreet wanted to reconnoiter. While Longstreet, Stuart, and finally Lee himself examined the Union dispositions, Jackson's position was under attack.

Fortunately for the Confederates, Federal assaults between 1:30 P.M. and 4:00 P.M. were not coordinated. Even so, several Northern

A headless solider has been seen in the vicinity of the unfinished railroad on the Manassas battlefield.

units broke through Jackson's front line. Unsupported, they were driven back by second and third Confederate lines.

Pope sent confusing orders to one of his commanders, Fitz John Porter, who stood idle just a few miles away with his 10,000-man Fifth Corps. Even a discussion with Gen. Irvin McDowell did little to solve the confusion. When a second order arrived at 6:00 P.M., Porter believed it was too late in the day to make an attack and remained where he was. He would later be court-martialed for his role—or lack thereof—in the battle.

Pope, in the meantime, believing Porter to be moving into position to attack, ordered another assault at 5:00 P.M. It resulted in the Federals being driven back yet again.

If Pope was having trouble with subordinates attacking, so was Lee. A third time Lee requested Longstreet to attack, but was disappointed. A small-scale fight took place with some of Hood's troops in the dusk. Nightfall ended the fighting of August 29.

Sometime that night Pope received a message that his cavalry had spotted numerous regiments of Confederates marching through Gainesville toward the battlefield, but for some reason, he dismissed it. Jackson was his obsession and he would continue his attacks the next day.

Before noon on August 30, Pope began to receive erroneous reports that Jackson was in retreat. By early afternoon he had convinced himself that all he needed to do was pursue and destroy a retreating column of Confederates. As his troops advanced toward the railroad bed, they were met by volleys from the enemy, obviously not in retreat but as determined as ever to hold their position. Fighting was particularly fierce in the lowest section of the railroad embankment known as the "Deep Cut," and Federals nearly broke through a gap in the Confederate line at a place called "The Dump," where the defenders ran out of ammunition and hurled rocks at the Union troops.

While Jackson's men doggedly resisted Pope's onslaught, Longstreet still held off on his attack. In the meantime, McDowell mistakenly withdrew a portion of the Union troops in front of Longstreet, leaving a lone unsupported battery of artillery to defend the Federal flank.

Lt. Charles Hazlett, the commander of the battery, realized the extreme danger and sent an aide to find some troops. Two infantry regiments, the 10th New York and the 5th New York, dressed in their gaudy Zouave uniforms—red pantaloons, white gaiters, and tasseled fezzes—hurried to their doom. They arrived in position just in time to face Longstreet's massive assault.

Twenty-eight thousand Confederates bore down on the New Yorkers, approximately 1,000 strong. In five minutes the 5th New York lost 123 men. After all the horror and slaughter of the Civil War was finally tallied, the Zouaves held the grisly record: They lost the highest number of killed in any infantry regiment in any battle of the entire war.

Longstreet's men pushed on toward Henry Hill, landmark of the first battle of Manassas in 1861. Atop the hill were two brigades of the Pennsylvania Reserve Division, Gen. John F. Reynolds commanding, and two more brigades and other assorted troops.

Reynolds, who would meet his death in less than a year at Gettysburg, ordered the Reserves forward.

The opposing lines met at the Sudley Road. The Yankees seized the washed-out depressions as cover. More troops from both sides arrived and the Union troops, after having stalled Longstreet's attack, began to withdraw. Finally, mercifully, sunset brought an end to the fighting.

Casualties were high. According to the National Park Service, of the 70,000 Union troops present, 1,750 were killed, 8,450 wounded, and 4,250 missing; the 55,000 Confederates engaged lost 1,550 killed in action, 7,750 wounded, but only 100 missing in action.

Undeterred by the 9,400 casualties, Lee turned his army's marching columns northward and began his first invasion of the enemy's territory.

Manassas Ghosts

With two bloody battles occurring on the same ground, surely Manassas would be the site of numerous ghost stories. During the first battle, the newly recruited soldiers marched into their initial fight as if going to a picnic; death, in all its hideous forms, took them by surprise. One paranormal theory as to why ghosts linger at one spot is that death comes too quickly for a person to even realize he is dead. Another theory is that a person, even after death, cannot believe that the state he is in is death. Both of these could apply to the naive soldiers of First Manassas.

Second Manassas, on the other hand, was a battle of hardened veteran soldiers who slugged it out, toe-to-toe, and knew the risks and sudden consequences of combat all too well.

The Headless Zouave

I can't remember the first time I heard the story about the headless Zouave, who has been seen in the area where the unfinished railroad crosses the battlefield of Manassas. It was most likely in the mid-1970s, when I was a ranger at Gettysburg and would visit friends at Manassas.

First, some historical background: Zouave units were formed at the very beginning of the American Civil War. In the mid-nineteenth century, anything and everything French was in vogue, from women's garments to military style. The common kepi headgear, used by both sides, was of French design. Some military units took the fashion statement to extremes and outfitted themselves, head-to-toe, with the uniform of the French forces in northern Africa. With Middle Eastern influence, the uniforms featured ballooning pantaloons tucked into gaiters; short, waist-length jackets with looping embroidery; waistbands that were yards long; and, to top it all off, tasseled, turbaned fezzes. The worst part, at least to soldiers who would do much of their fighting in woods and fields, is that the uniforms were brightly colored—red sashes or jackets, yellow piping, and blue-striped pantaloons—making them perfect targets.

Others claim to have seen the ghost of a Zouave at or near the New York Monument on New York Avenue. The headless Zouave I had always heard about had been seen near the unfinished railroad.

Stories abound of out-of-place sounds, intense cold spots, and weird smells like rotten eggs and a smoky odor of something "charred."

Sullivan Ballou and the "Charred" Smell

L. B. Taylor Jr., in his *Civil War Ghosts of Virginia*, may have an explanation for the "charred" odor that people smell at Manassas. Taylor recounts a story printed in *Washington Magazine* in the early 1990s that refers to people on the battlefield reporting the smell of black powder and burning flesh, as well as localized cold spots. A park ranger confirmed that visitors have randomly reported the weird, out-of-time smells. Taylor wrote about the ranger's explanation of the smells.

One of the more moving moments in Ken Burns's classic series *The Civil War* was when a letter from Maj. Sullivan Ballou to his wife in Rhode Island was read. In flowery, Victorian prose he promises if he should die in the coming battle (First Manassas) that he will return to her as a ghost and watch over her. While the sentiment is beautiful, reality is far more brutal.

After he was wounded, Ballou and a colonel were taken to Sudley Church, where they died and were buried in shallow graves nearby. In the spring of 1862, the Confederate army left the area and orders came down from the governor of Rhode Island to locate and recover the bodies of the two heroes. As the parties were digging near the church, a local girl told them that the Confederates had already emptied the graves and took the body of the higher-ranking officer to a ravine, mutilated it for ghastly souvenirs, and burned it. The exhumation party located the decapitated remains. But she was wrong about the identity of the body: It wasn't the colonel but Major Ballou whose body had been partially cremated. Could this then be the source for the consistent reports of the "charred" smell? Could it be the soul of Major Ballou calling out from the desecrated grave he once occupied?

The Stone House

The Stone House is a battlefield landmark with a sordid past and mysterious happenings associated with it. Literary references to the Stone House go back to 1866, when Confederate veteran and novelist John Esten Cooke referred to it in his book *Surry of Eagle's Nest*. Cooke referred to it as "The Old Stone House of Manassas," or more ominously, "The Haunted House." After the turn of the twentieth century, a story emerged of a curse put on the house and the family that lived there after the war. The family lost at least six of its members to death in a relatively short time.

The pre-Civil War history of the house is checkered. It was once a tavern and inn for western traders on their way to Washington. According the National Park Service's brochure, it was never a fancy place but catered, rather, to rough-and-tumble, liquor-drinking cattlemen and teamsters. Park historians have documented that, as well as a private home, the building was used as a parole station and as a hospital during both battles. Wounded men left their names carved in the woodwork of the house.

David Roth, in *Blue & Gray Magazine*'s *Guide to Haunted Places of the Civil War*, wrote about the negative energy in the house that is felt by many people. In a story dated 1986, he wrote that visitors

Witnesses claim to have seen the Stone House at Manassas National Battlefield Park disappear and then reappear.

sometimes feel a distinct pressure from invisible hands pushing them down the stairs from the second floor.

I received a letter in July 1994 from a gentleman who wrote of his similar experience at the Stone House. He recounted what he had heard about the house's history as a tavern with hard drinking and fistfights. The day was hot, but while he was walking through the house he became the victim of one of those inexplicable cold spots. As he was leaving, he was "hit hard" from behind and fell out of the house to the ground, injuring his knee. In physical pain, he was also upset, because coming from the house he heard laughter, as if a group of people were gloating over his being thrown to the ground. He turned to ask for help only to find that no one was inside or outside of the house. He was alone.

A friend and former park ranger told me the story of a couple of other rangers who were working in the basement of the locked Stone House. As they paused from their work, they heard footsteps on the floor above their heads. Thinking that somehow a visitor had gotten into the house, they went upstairs to find all the doors still locked.

Taylor also quotes a ranger as saying that people driving through the park at night report seeing lights on in houses that have been torn down long ago. The antecedent to that story was told to me in September 2010 by a young woman who lived near Manassas and was familiar with her "neighborhood." One night she was driving to an appointment and passed through the intersection where the Stone House sits. She was astounded. The house wasn't there. She almost panicked. Was there some calamity that forced the park service to tear the historic building down? Had there been a recent fire that she hadn't heard about? Before she could comprehend what could have happened to the famous old building, she was through the intersection and on her way. After her appointment, she returned the same way, perhaps thinking she might be able to stop and examine whatever remains of the structure were left. As she approached the intersection, she was struck by one incredible thing: The house was there again.

Later she related the story to some friends. They were silent just a little too long. When she asked if they thought she was crazy, they answered that the same thing had happened to them. The old Stone House had vanished only to reappear a while later.

In paranormal studies there is a phenomenon known as a *warp*, defined as a rip in the fabric of time wherein a percipient sees into the past and looks at a scene that was once at that spot but has changed. Is there some sort of warp in the area of the Stone House that occasionally allows us to see the site before the house was built in 1828? Is there a rip in time there that opens and closes according to some as yet unknown natural—or should I say, unnatural—law?

Broken Machinery

After a speech about ghosts I had given once, a man approached me and said that he was working for a consulting firm in Manassas that was helping with construction around the area. The project was halted because they had discovered human remains, which they determined had come from one of the battles there. He was working with the machinery to exhume what was left of the soldiers after many years in the soil. Suddenly, as they were about to unearth the remains, the machinery broke down. They had to stop and send the machine back to the shop for repairs.

They scheduled another time to begin to remove the soldiers. Again they were working at the site when the backhoe broke down. Chalking it up to bad luck, they again returned to the shop for repairs.

Once again they were on site, continuing where they'd left off before. It's plausible to blame bad luck for a mechanical breakdown twice. But once the repairs are done, there should no longer be a problem—unless there's something else involved, like in this case.

A third time the hoe broke down. This time they covered the remains and gave up.

EVP Findings

A brief visit I made to the unfinished railroad in September 2011 yielded several recordings of EVP. In the first I asked if would the highest-ranking officer would speak with me and what is your name? At 4 seconds I heard the word "DeHeiser" or "DePeyster." Interestingly enough, there was a Union officer, a Maj. J. Watts De Peyster Jr. on the staff of Maj. Gen. Philip Kearny. Kearny's division made an attack on the Confederate line at the unfinished railroad on August 29, 1862.

A second recording was made at 2:49 P.M. First, there's some loud noise that cannot be recognized as words; then, at 10 seconds, a voice says, "Most definitely." At 14 seconds there is a strange "clink," sounding like a railroad spike being hit with a sledge hammer, that could not have come from any piece of equipment or clothing I had. With EVP this is not unusual: clinks, raps, clicks (like fingers snapping), bits of song, roars, and whispers are often heard in the background. Where the "clink" in this recording came from is a mystery. Finally, at 16 seconds, very quietly, as if they do not want me to hear, a voice says, "You can't talk to him."

A final recording was made that day at 2:57 P.M. I say "Men of the 63rd you can talk to me." At 10 seconds a quiet voice says, "He can hear us."

Shiloh

Confederate general Albert Sidney Johnston was held in high esteem by his president Jefferson Davis. "If Sidney Johnston is not a general," Davis said in defense of him, "we had better give up the war, for we have no general." But because of the fall of Fort Henry and Fort Donelson in February 1862, Johnston's reputation had suffered, and he was forced to abandon Kentucky and much of middle and western Tennessee. He concentrated his 42,000-man army at the major rail junction of Corinth, Mississippi. From there he and his commanders planned an offensive to retake the important state of Tennessee.

Union general Ulysses S. Grant was sent to Pittsburg Landing on the Tennessee River, there to expect reinforcements of some 35,000 men that would bring his army to 75,000. From there the Federals would launch an attack on Johnston at Corinth. The Confederates beat them to the punch.

In spite of delays in their march from Corinth toward Pittsburg Landing, the Confederates arrived on April 5, 1862. Johnston was warned by his subordinates that Grant may have already been reinforced (which he hadn't been yet) and that he should call off the attacks scheduled for the next morning. Johnston summed up his fighting spirit by telling them, "I would fight them if they were a million."

Grant, too, would show his aggressiveness by refusing to have his men construct breastworks, reasoning that they might lose their fighting spirit if they were put to work digging defensive works. Besides, his plan was to attack the Confederates at Corinth. Offensive thinking on the part of Grant and William Tecumseh Sherman, commanding a division in Grant's army, in this case courted disaster.

Sherman was told more than once by front-line officers that something was brewing in front of their position. Sherman dismissed it merely as pickets firing. On the morning of April 6, he would see how wrong he was.

Heavy skirmishing preceded the main Confederate attack past a small country church called Shiloh, whose name in Hebrew, ironically, meant "place of peace." But Sherman was finally convinced a Confederate offensive was underway when a Confederate volley ripped through his camp, killed his orderly, and wounded him in the hand. He finally conceded, "My God, we're attacked!"

Grant heard the firing nine miles away at his headquarters in Savannah, Tennessee. He immediately boarded a boat and steamed to disembark at Pittsburg Landing by 9:00 A.M. But even Grant's presence on the field did little to stem the panicked retreat of his inexperienced soldiers.

Luckily for Grant, the Confederates were just as green. In spite of their success, there were Southern units that retreated in disorganization. Grant rode the battlefield, organizing a defensive line along a ridge west of the landing. Johnston, too, was at the front, rallying and organizing his men. Bullets clipped his uniform and tore a sole off a boot. At about 2:15 P.M., Tennessee governor Isham G. Harris, acting as a volunteer aide, rode up to Johnston and thought he appeared unusually pale. Harris asked Johnston if he had been wounded. "Yes," replied the Confederate army commander, "and I fear seriously."

Johnston had been struck by an Enfield rifle ball in the back of the right knee. The .577-caliber, soft-lead projectile opened an artery, but Johnston apparently didn't feel it at the time. He had been shot in a prewar duel that caused some loss of feeling. Within a few minutes, Albert Sidney Johnston, who had sent his personal surgeon to help some wounded Union prisoners, bled to death. Afterward,

The modern reconstruction of Shiloh Church, the building from which the battlefield took its name.

a potentially life-saving surgeon's field tourniquet was found in his pocket. Aides wrapped his body so the soldiers wouldn't know they had lost their commander. Gen. P. G. T. Beauregard of Fort Sumter and Manassas fame took over command of the Confederate Army.

While Northern troops continued to retreat, Grant ordered the troops in his center along what they later called the Sunken Road to hold the position "at all hazards." Some 4,500 Federals held back a dozen Confederate assaults on their position along the road. From the point of view of the 18,000 rebels who advanced upon that Union position, it became "The Hornet's Nest."

Frustrated Confederate commanders ordered fifty-three cannon to concentrate their fire on the area. The half hour to forty-five-minute barrage silenced many of the Union cannon defending the Hornet's Nest. Union troops on the left withdrew; then support on the right retreated, leaving the men in the Hornet's Nest to fend for themselves. By 5:30 P.M., they were nearly surrounded and individual officers began to surrender their commands rather than have them slaughtered. Only 2,250 Federals remained to be captured after some six hours of tenacious fighting. But they bought time for the rest of the army, allowing Grant to establish a new line closer to the river under the protection of massed Union artillery and the huge cannons of the Union gunboats.

In postwar years, a controversy would emerge as to why Confederate commander Beauregard called a halt to his troops' advance instead of driving the Federals into the Tennessee River. The argument, like many in the years following the war, was made to bolster or defend reputations. The fact is that Beauregard, by 6:00 P.M., commanded exhausted, disorganized troops who would be attacking at dusk a solid, reorganized Federal line supported by field artillery and naval guns. The Confederates, in their minds, had already won a stunning victory and captured the Yankees' camps, thousands of prisoners, and forty artillery pieces. The next day, after resting, they would mop up. Grant, however, had other plans.

Late in the day, the future author of *Ben Hur*, Maj. Gen. Lew Wallace, finally arrived on the Shiloh battlefield with his division. For years after the war, controversy would surround the six-mile march, which should have taken two hours but instead took seven. Don Carlos Buell's Army of the Ohio was ferried across the Tennessee River all night long in the pouring rain to swell the number of fresh troops in Grant's army by some 25,000. Before dawn on April 7, Grant was ready to attack the still-disorganized rebels.

As Grant's troops marched, they were shocked by the sight of the mutilated dead and groaning wounded, soaked by the night's storms. By 10:00 A.M. Confederates had become somewhat reorganized and their defense stiffened about a mile and a half from the Tennessee River. As the Federals advanced, determined pockets of Confederates held out, sometimes engaging in hand-to-hand fighting, stopping and driving back portions of the Union attack.

On all parts of the Union line fierce fighting raged throughout the morning and early afternoon, gradually pressing the rebels back until the Northerners had regained their camps from which they were driven the day before. After they thought they had won a complete victory the day before, Confederate morale plunged, a condi-

Union reinforcements arriving at Pittsburg Landing on the Tennessee River helped turn the battle in favor of the Federals.

tion obvious to even Beauregard. A final rear guard was established by the Southerners at 3:00 P.M. By 5:00 P.M., much of their army had retreated toward Corinth.

Again, over the years, hindsight would plague the combatants with questions. Grant was nearly removed from command by critics questioning why he did not pursue the defeated enemy. He had his reasons, not the least of which was lack of cavalry, necessary to garnering information on enemy ambushes during any pursuit. Later, Northern newspapers clamored for Grant's removal because he had been "surprised" by the enemy. Lincoln silenced critics by reportedly saying simply, "I can't spare this man. He fights."

The country was stunned by the massive casualties. There were more soldiers killed, wounded, and missing in just two days of the Battle of Shiloh than in all of America's previous wars added together. Beauregard listed his casualties as 10,699; Grant's losses were recorded at 13,047.

Shiloh Ghosts

Both sides buried their dead in mass trench graves. In 1866, Union soldiers were removed and reburied in the newly established National Cemetery overlooking Pittsburg Landing. Only five of the several mass burial sites for the Confederates were discovered and marked. To this day, the bodies remain buried on the field of Shiloh. Many believe the spirits of these men remain as well.

The Phantom Drummer Boy

Perhaps the most famous ghost story about Shiloh is that of a phantom drummer boy. There have been reports of drums heard on the battlefield when no drummer is present. The sounds are attributed to a youth that won a victory by mistake.

Shiloh was fought fairly early in the war. By April 1862, the armies and their commanders were still learning their deadly trades. Drummer boys were no exception. Many boys had to learn to play the drum before they could learn the meaning of the different beats as commands to the soldiers. And battles wait for no man . . . or boy.

In a particularly critical moment at Shiloh, the drummer was told to sound the beat for the advance, which he did. The soldiers advanced and fought gallantly until they were outnumbered. The commanding officer then told the drummer boy to tap out the drumbeat meaning retreat. Instead the drummer pounded out "advance" again. The commander was horrified. His men began to attack rather than retreat. He commanded the drummer to beat out "retreat," but the boy could only apologize. He hadn't had time to learn "retreat." The commander was frantic. His men were advancing into the jaws of death. Suddenly, the enemy began to withdraw before his men and his attack was successful, thanks in part to the drummer boy's ignorance of the drumbeats.

The story goes on that in the ensuing advance, the drummer boy was killed, his drum smashed to pieces. Still, however, these many years later, his cadence can be heard rolling from the distance across the fields of Shiloh.

Some say that the drummer was John Clem, the famous "Drummer Boy of Shiloh," whose spirit roams the fields tapping out rhythms. But that must be a case of mistaken identity. Though John Clem was indeed associated with the Union Army, he first served with the 22nd Michigan, which hadn't even been formed when Shiloh occurred in April 1862. Clem, however, did ride an artillery caisson into the Battle of Chickamauga, carrying a musket cut down to fit his stature. With it he shot a Confederate colonel who had the temerity to demand the boy's surrender. For his action Clem was promoted to sergeant and became the youngest soldier to attain the rank of noncommissioned officer in the U. S. Army.

After the Battle of Chickamauga, a Civil War song was written called "The Drummer Boy of Shiloh." Many later assumed that Clem was the subject of that song, in which the drummer boy died. But the "Drummer Boy of Chickamauga" was alive and well. He would be captured in October 1863, relieved of his miniature Union uniform, and then exchanged to participate in several other battles with the Army of the Cumberland. He would be wounded two times before being discharged in 1864. He later rejoined the Army, finally retiring as a brigadier general. So while the ghost drummer boy of Shiloh plays on, his identity remains unknown.

Bloody Pond

Another haunted site is Bloody Pond. During the battle wounded soldiers and horses congregated at the small pond to quench their thirst. After a while, so many wounded men had used the pond that it was tinted red.

There's a legend that permeates the history of the battlefield of Shiloh that, at certain unpredictable times, the water in the pond turns crimson again, as if to remind those in this and future generations of the horror of war.

Those trying to explain the phenomena contend that it is the sunset reflecting in Bloody Pond that makes the water appear red; but then it would be stained red every night with the setting sun, and it clearly isn't. Perhaps, others say, it's the clay around it that tints it when it rains particularly hard; but apparently it happens when there has been no rain. One final theory is that there is a particular type of algae that grows in the pond at certain times of the year and paints the water the color of blood. But the water is bloody

The Bloody Pond at Shiloh, where the waters are said to turn red on occasion.

for only a few hours, and there is no algae that grows, dies, and disappears in that short amount of time.

The Vanishing Man in Gray

A visitor to the park reported a strange event on the website *Off the Beaten Path* (www.offthebeatenpath.ws/Battlefields/GhostsOfShiloh Battlefield). He and a friend were parked near the Bloody Pond. The park was deserted and so they felt a little uneasy when they looked in the rearview mirrors and saw a man dressed in gray approaching their car from behind. They were slightly confused, as well, because they had just driven down that stretch of road and hadn't seen anyone. Had he hidden so that he could "ambush" them? They wanted to get a picture and the driver stepped out of the car while the passenger continued to watch the man approach. When the driver got out, he looked back to keep an eye on the man but could not see him anymore. Even using his camera's zoom lens, the man had disappeared from his sight. But the passenger could still see the man in the rearview mirror. Looking over to the driver and encouraging him to get back in the car, the passenger looked back into the mirror and the man had vanished.

They later compared notes and figured they both observed the man in the mirrors for three to four minutes. Even though the man was walking, he never seemed to get closer to them and they realized that while he was visible in the mirrors, he could not be seen once the driver got out of the car.

The Caretaker's House

Then there is the old caretaker's house in the park. Although the happenings there might seem bizarre to some, those who follow the supernatural will find the events are all too common, if unexplainable. They seem like the work of a poltergeist, because they consist of the sound of footsteps roaming about the floor when no one can be seen, doors opening and closing by themselves, and disembodied voices being heard. As well, there are the sounds so common on all battlefields: gunshots and cannons in the distance, the sounds at night of a marching column of men, and the hoarse shouts of masses of men going into battle emanating from uninhabited woods.

EVP and Dowsing Rod Findings

The burials at Shiloh were, for the most part, in mass graves. At this stage in the war, no one had ever seen this many dead men in one place, let alone knew what to do with them all. At Shiloh they gathered the dead together and buried them in common graves. According to the National Park Service there were something like ten or twelve mass gravesites filled to capacity after the battle with the bodies of the slain. Today, the locations of only five are known. Using dowsing rods, my wife Carol may have found at least one more.

We were at one of the mass gravesites for Confederate soldiers on the battlefield and she began to walk back and forth around and behind it. The rods were crossing periodically, both on either side of the marked area and behind the marked mass grave, indicating that there may be soldiers buried outside the marked boundaries of the grave.

Confederate dead at Shiloh were interred in mass graves such as this one.

I also had several opportunities to attempt to gather EVP. In recording #1603, after I ask any soldier to shout his name, at 5 seconds I hear a soft voice say, "Paxton Knuble," or "Knugle," a Germanic-sounding name. Later, in recording #1626, I attempted the same technique of asking someone to shout out his name. At 3 seconds I hear a soft voice say "Joe King," and then at 5 seconds into the recording, I hear the name, "Murphy."

Descending into the little swale where Gen. Albert Sidney Johnston was taken after a bullet clipped an artery and he bled to death, I began to address the Confederate commander. In recording #1642, I ask the general if he's still here and, at 4 seconds, I hear the words, "Now, the vein." Was he describing his own wound that killed him? Then, in the same recording, at 11 seconds, I hear what sounds like a female voice saying, "You hurt me."

Finally, I record another one of those mysterious clicks at 3 seconds. The remarkable thing is that I actually heard it live. I ask the general if that was him, and at 5 seconds, I get the answer, "It could be."

Finally, we had lunch at a local establishment just a mile or so away from the park. There is a legend about a grave on the bank of the Tennessee River at the far end of the restaurant's parking lot. Sometime prior to the Civil War, a body washed up in this vicinity. He had no identification, but the man who owned the property buried him near where he found him. Apparently, the spirit of the dead man has interacted with some of the early and more recent patrons. Later, someone named him "Elmo" and made sure that he had a stone marking his grave. At the grave I attempted to capture some EVP from Elmo and got recording #1453. I asked Elmo if he still likes to haunt this place. At 3 seconds into the recording, I hear a soft voice say, "I hate this place."

The Peninsula

In the spring of 1862, the Virginia Peninsula was central in Union general George B. McClellan's plan to strike at Richmond and end the war. He would land an amphibious force at the tip of the Peninsula and march his army straight towards the Confederate capital. The campaign was the largest and most intricate of any campaign to that point in American military history. Assembling a flotilla of 389 ships, on March 17, McClellan began transporting his army over three weeks down the Potomac River from Alexandria to the Chesapeake Bay, disembarking at Federal-held Fort Monroe.

Once he began the overland part of his campaign, he realized that the roads in that part of Virginia were not going to cooperate with his plan of "rapid marches" toward Richmond. The rural dirt roads soon became quagmires from the heavy use an army demanded; mud sucked at the shoes of the men and bogged down the artillery.

As he advanced up the Peninsula, he ran into the Confederate fortifications along the Warwick River near Yorktown, the old Revolutionary War siege site. His scouts and officers reported some 100,000 rebels in those works, which extended from the York to the James River. McClellan decided they were too strong to take by assault and began planning a siege. Little did he know that he had been the victim of a Confederate ruse.

Confederate general John B. Magruder commanded only 13,000 men to man the Warwick defensive works, but marched them around in full view of McClellan's scouts so that they counted the same rebel soldiers several times over. McClellan taking time to bring up and mount his heavy guns for the siege gave Confederate general Joseph E. Johnston time to bring his troops from above Richmond to support Magruder.

By the end of April, McClellan's siege lines were ready. On May 4, after a heavy nighttime bombardment from the Confederates, Union skirmishers inched forward in silence and made an incredible discovery: the Confederates were gone.

It had been Johnston's plan to withdraw from the Warwick line because of its vulnerability to flank fire from Union gunboats on both the York and the James. As well, he wanted to establish a defense closer to the capital, within supporting distance of other Confederate forces moving toward Richmond's defense. As Johnston retreated, Union troops attacked his rearguard at Fort Magruder and fought in the streets of the old colonial capital of Williamsburg.

In the meantime, thanks to the Union Army's advance up the Peninsula, the Federal Navy was sailing up the James River toward Richmond. As Confederates abandoned the eastern Peninsula, Gosport Navy Yard was also given up and the famous Confederate ironclad *Virginia* (the U.S. Navy ship *Merrimac* captured and converted to ironclad), which had terrorized the Union fleet since March, had to be scuttled, freeing the James to U.S. gunboats.

The danger to Richmond from naval bombardment was clear, and while telling the populace to remain calm, politicians sent their own families inland. Frantic Confederate sailors sank obstructions in the river, but at 7:30 A.M., May 15, the Federal flotilla rounded the bend and engaged with Confederate artillery on Drewry's Bluff. After three hours of plunging artillery fire and sharpshooters picking off sailors, the gunboats retired. Richmonders rejoiced.

But there was still the threat of McClellan's land force advancing up the Peninsula. On May 16, Johnston established battle lines at a crossroads called Seven Pines using the Chickahominy River, which was prone to flooding into a swamp, as part of his defense. Though Johnston had spent the previous three weeks withdrawing, he had in mind the strategy to draw McClellan farther from Fort Monroe; should the Yankees be defeated, they would have a long retreat, dogged every step of the way back down the Peninsula by the Confederates.

Meantime, Stonewall Jackson's "foot cavalry" was making swift marches up and down the Shenandoah Valley, covering some 600 miles and engaging the enemy in five pitched battles. His actions accomplished what the Confederate high command wanted: Jackson drew Union troops away from McClellan's threat to Richmond.

By the end of May, McClellan had established a base of supplies at White House Landing on the Pamunkey River, a tributary to the York and railhead for the Richmond & York River Railroad. In order to protect this base and attack Johnston, McClellan had to stretch his army across the Chickahominy, effectively splitting it before the enemy. As long as the river remained low, both wings could support one another via the few bridges across the river.

Johnston realized that, at least south of the Chickahominy, he outnumbered the Federals significantly. On May 31, he attacked. The two-day battle of Seven Pines (called Fair Oaks by the Federals) was complicated by the torrential rain the night before the battle and by confusing Confederate orders that were altered by subordinates before the battle had begun. Nevertheless, the Confederates stopped the Yankee movement on Richmond for the time being, but with a cost. Some 6,100 Confederates (and 5,000 Federals) became casualties in the battle. One significant Southern casualty was their commander, Joseph E. Johnston, who was wounded. President Jefferson Davis sent Robert E. Lee to replace him and command the army in the field.

Lee immediately ordered the fortifications around Richmond to be strengthened and had his men dig in whenever they halted. There was concern that he might not be aggressive enough to command an army in the field; however, his first decision, upon consulting with Davis, was to attack the Yankees.

McClellan, on the other hand, had halted his offensive up the Peninsula and called on Washington for more troops. Though 30,000 were sent by mid-June, he felt he needed more.

Lee also needed something more: information. He sent his twenty-nine-year-old cavalry commander, J. E. B. Stuart, to locate McClellan's right flank. Once he found it, Stuart realized that the Union cavalry was expecting him to return the way he had come and was organizing to stop him. Instead of retracing his hoofprints, he rode completely around the Federal army and returned to Lee, his command virtually unscathed, with the information he needed.

Lee met with his generals, including Stonewall Jackson, who rode 50 miles ahead of his own men. The council decided that the attack would begin on June 26 when Jackson's men arrived. Jackson then returned some 40 miles to his columns.

The Confederate attacks would shift from east of Richmond to north of the city near Mechanicsville. Union troops were dug in behind Beaver Dam Creek and, after waiting for Jackson to attack all the morning of June 26, A. P. Hill launched his division at the Federals. The results of Confederates assaulting entrenched positions were horrifying: 1,500 Southern casualties to only 360 Federal.

Though McClellan reported a complete victory, he began a retreat to high ground near Gaines' Mill, four miles to the south. He couched his moves from then on as a "change of base" from White House on the Pamunkey River to Harrison's Landing on the James. On June 27, Lee attacked him at Gaines' Mill.

Jackson again was not his aggressive self. Again, A. P. Hill fought nearly alone. Throughout the hot afternoon Confederate assaults were uncoordinated. Late in the day, John Bell Hood and his Texans finally broke through the Union line, but Yankees arriving from across the Chickahominy plugged the gap and acted as a rear guard. The Federals continued their retreat toward the James, leaving some 6,800 casualties. Confederates, again on the offensive, suffered around 9,000 casualties.

The armies fought again on June 29 at Savage's Station, a depot to which the Federals had brought some 2,500 wounded for evacuation. The battle began at 9:00 A.M. in a peach orchard on Allen's Farm about 2 miles west of Savage's Station on the Richmond & York River Railroad. Confederates brought up a 32-pounder Brooke naval rifled cannon mounted on a railroad car with sloping sides for armor and lobbed shells at the Yankees. The infantry fighting approached a ferociousness that compared to any battle in any theater of the war. The Fifth Vermont Infantry, in only twenty minutes of fighting, lost over half its numbers. But again the Yankees escaped Lee's grasp.

On June 30, Jackson passed Savage's Station and was ordered by Lee to continue the pursuit of McClellan's retreating columns, although McClellan was no longer with his army. After placing seven divisions around the Glendale crossroads and issuing vague orders to protect the intersection while the rest of the army retreated, he took a skiff out to the gunboat *Galena* and spent the rest of the day and part of the next ostensibly trying to find a safe place for his army to occupy. He, in essence, left his army without a head for two days while vital rearguard battles took place.

When Jackson found the bridge on his route through White Oak Swamp destroyed, the fight at White Oak Swamp became predominantly an artillery duel with Jackson unsuccessfully attempting to find an alternate route through the morass. Again in the campaign, Jackson demonstrated an uncharacteristic lack of initiative, which allowed the Federals to successfully protect their army on its retrograde movement and prevented Jackson from connecting with the rest of Lee's army at Glendale.

Glendale, about two miles west of White Oak Swamp, was fought to protect an intersection that proved vital for McClellan's retreat. Confederates under James Longstreet seemed to realize that the place was tactically important and launched themselves recklessly at the enemy. The rebels were at first successful, but Union counterattacks stabilized their lines. The battle became a seesaw affair: Alabamians captured a six-gun battery from Federal forces; infantry and the angry Federal gunners recaptured it in hand-to-hand fighting; Virginians retook the guns in more savage fighting. The fighting cost the Confederates some 3,600 casualties. The Union forces lost 2,800, but successfully defended their retreating army.

By the next day, July 1, Lee realized that McClellan's army was nearly to the James, where the Navy's gunboats could help protect it. By the time the Army of Northern Virginia was prepared to attack, McClellan's army was in a nearly perfect defensive position on top of a broad plateau near the James called Malvern Hill. Three steep sides funneled any Confederate attack onto a plain swept by artillery lined up almost wheel hub-to-wheel hub. The gunners were supported by 18,000 infantry. Worse for the Confederate attackers, they were within range of the huge naval guns firing from the James River.

One Confederate general realized the danger. A. P. Hill, whose men had done the lion's share of the fighting on the Peninsula so far, cautioned against an assault. But Lee, whom the army once thought defensive-minded, and Longstreet, who would later gain the reputation of being reticent to attack, personally scouted the terrain and felt they had found some good artillery positions for their gunners to neutralize the Federal advantage and allow for frontal assaults.

The attacks were to be preceded by the artillery bombardment, but the guns were spread out along the road back to Glendale as the army marched to Malvern Hill. Not enough artillery arrived on the battlefield and the preliminary bombardment never happened. Instead, the few guns that arrived were quickly put out of action by the more numerous Union cannons.

Confederate infantry advanced against massed Federal artillery firing canister—antipersonnel rounds of small iron and lead balls encased in tin, which disintegrated upon firing and turned the cannons into giant shotguns—and case shot, which exploded into fragments above the attackers like large, long-range hand grenades.

Worse, the Confederates never launched a coordinated, massed attack. The small, piecemeal attacks were easily driven back by the Northern gunners, leaving the torn, bloodied bodies of the rebels strewn across the plain. Yet more Confederate assaults continued, the attackers leaping over the bodies of the fallen, soon to become casualties themselves. The infantry of Confederate general D. H. Hill, who had warned of attacking Malvern Hill earlier, suffered some of the most horrendous casualties: the Third Alabama, one of John B. Gordon's regiments, in just fifteen or twenty minutes, had lost more than half its men along the attack route. Attack after attack continued, but only one Confederate assault ever threatened the Union line. Darkness brought an end to the horrific slaughter.

The results of the Seven Days' Battles for the Confederacy were bittersweet: Richmond was saved, but at a cost of nearly 20,000 casualties, highly visible lying in the churches, public buildings, and private homes of the capital. While McClellan lost some 15,000 men, his Army of the Potomac was far from destroyed or demoralized and he began plans to resume another offensive—as soon as Washington sent him more men. It was a refrain they had heard all too often in the Federal capital.

McClellan's army was ordered to evacuate the Peninsula, and by mid-August, ships had brought him and his army back to Washington to fight on the battlefields of northern Virginia.

Peninsula Ghosts of Fort Monroe

Fort Monroe on Old Point Comfort, at the eastern end of the Virginia Peninsula, was built on the site of the 1609 Fort Algernourne and has been occupied and garrisoned longer than any other post in U. S. Army history. Some of America's most prestigious military men have served there—or were imprisoned there.

The fort was designed by an aide to Napoleon I and construction was partially supervised by Robert E. Lee and mostly completed by 1834.

In March 1862, soldiers at Fort Monroe watched with great interest the ending of an era in naval warfare when the Confederate ironclad *Virginia* destroyed or damaged a number of all-wood vessels, then herself was stopped the next day by an odd-looking, turreted iron ship named *Monitor*. Standing on the parapets today, one can watch yet another era in naval warfare pass as nuclear submarines and aircraft carriers steam out to sea.

With all that history, it would seem a natural—or *super*natural—thing that ghosts would choose to remain and haunt the historic fort. And indeed they do.

Quarters Number One

Jane Keane Polonsky and Joan McFarland Drum collected some of the stories in *The Ghosts of Fort Monroe* and have documented several sightings. Old Quarters Number One seems to be where some of the more famous ghosts appear. Originally built for the commandant, it has been the quarters for visiting presidents, including Andrew Jackson, Franklin Pierce, and Abraham Lincoln. Future Confederate president Jefferson Davis stayed in the quarters when he was U. S. Secretary of War, and future president Ulysses S. Grant resided here as a general while he planned the climactic campaign of the Civil War.

Tunnels in the lower floor of the house were rumored to be used by escaping slaves during the antebellum years. The sounds of shuffling feet are attributed to these slaves, still trying to find their freedom decades after it was won for them and decades after they've died. Other sounds of boots and the rustle of crinolines are commonly heard in Quarters Number One. One resident, after trying to sleep through a night of the sounds of a distant party, complete with boot steps and swishing silk, came down to find fresh flower petals on the hall floor below the stairs. The guest was confounded by the fresh flowers since the season was midwinter.

Some poltergeist activity has also been reported: Lights will go on and off of their own accord, cupboard doors will open and slam shut, and the water will be turned on, all accomplished by unseen hands.

The Ghosts of Lincoln and Grant

And there are reports of the rarest kind of ghostly encounter: the visual apparition. Who is it that has been seen? Abraham Lincoln, whose specter has most often been observed and documented in the White House, apparently will appear upon his whim in Quarters Number One. He reveals himself in the former guest room, now named the Lincoln Room, wrapped in a casual dressing gown near the fireplace, engrossed in the weighty problems of a country at war with itself. Perhaps he is reenacting, in spirit form, his visits to Fort Monroe during the ironclad crisis of 1862 and during the Hampton Roads Peace Conference of 1865. Both were fraught with tension and Lincoln, no doubt, expended a great deal of emotional energy, perhaps still trapped within the building, during both periods.

General Grant, though characterized as one who was incredibly cool in battle and under fire, must have somehow left his imprint in Quarters Number One, because his phantom has also been seen within the confines of the historic structure.

Varina Davis

After his capture in 1865, Confederate president Jefferson Davis was imprisoned in a casemate within the walls of Fort Monroe. To add insult to injury, the former chief executive was shackled, a fate more common to assassins and blackguards than the head of state of a country. Following him to Fort Monroe was the former first lady of the Confederacy, Davis's wife Varina. While at the fort she may have dwelt for a while in the quarters directly across from the casemate where her beloved husband was imprisoned. It is no wonder then that late at night, some who have passed the quarters have seen, at a second-floor window, the figure of a woman peering out at the casemate across the street.

Others, who have stayed in the quarters where Mrs. Davis was housed, have reported some strange, unexplainable occurrences as well. A woman who was staying in the bedroom of the building awoke one morning to see the figure of a woman and a little girl gazing out the window toward the casemate. She arose, crossed the room to the woman, and attempted to touch her antiquated hoop skirt. As she did, the two vanished.

Is the specter at the window Varina Davis? After lobbying the powers-that-be incessantly, Varina got her husband moved from the primitive cell in the casemate to another quarters, Carroll Hall, where she and their daughter Winnie and her sister Margaret Howell stayed for the remainder of his imprisonment at Fort Monroe. Authors Polonsky and Drum speculate that while Varina Davis never lived in the building where the female ghost at the window is seen, she may have visited there.

The White Lady of Ghost Alley

There is no speculation as to the existence of an area in the fort called "Ghost Alley," so-named since the Civil War, or the specter that has been seen there for more than a century. She has been called by eyewitnesses the "White Lady," or sometimes the "Light Lady," because some people say she glows. The descriptions remain remarkably the same after so many have seen her. The story of how she became a ghost is an old one.

She was far younger than her officer-husband. A much younger officer recently transferred to the fort caught her eye, and they began an affair, meeting most often in the dark alley behind the quarters. Her husband was called out of town on an assignment, but returned unexpectedly to find the two lovers together in the act. He shot and killed his wife but the young officer made his escape, never to be seen again. So today, when they walk along Ghost Alley, passersby keep a keen eye out for a hazy, floating mist that seems to glow from within, searching, apparently, for the lover she lost along with her life.

Antietam

Like many battles in the American Civil War, the one fought on September 17, 1862, has two names: In the North it was called Antietam, after the landmark creek that winds its way through the scene of the conflict; in the South, it was named Sharpsburg, after a nearby Maryland town. Unlike other battles of the war, however, it is most famous for one thing: the rapidity of its horrific violence.

In just twelve hours of fighting, more American blood was spilled than on any other day in the country's military history. Eighteen general officers were killed or wounded during the battle. Nearly 23,000 men were killed, wounded, or listed as missing after the fighting.

The spring and summer of 1862 saw the Confederate military cause in the Eastern Theater on the rise. Thomas J. "Stonewall" Jackson had run roughshod over Union armies in the Shenandoah Valley. Confederate troops had driven the Federal forces from the very gates of the Southern capital Richmond during the Seven Days Battles on the Virginia Peninsula. Under their new commander, Robert E. Lee, the Army of Northern Virginia struck their enemy near the 1861 battlefield of Manassas. Second Manassas, in August 1862, saw Confederates so determined to win, some soldiers threw rocks when they ran out of ammunition. On a roll, they followed Lee across the Potomac River and into Maryland on their first invasion of the North.

Hoping to garner support from the citizens of the border state, Lee kept a tight rein on his men. Maryland's reception of the Confederate army was nevertheless cool. In order to open a supply route into the Shenandoah Valley, Lee needed to seize Harpers Ferry, at the confluence of the Potomac and Shenandoah Rivers.

One maxim of war is that a commander should never divide his forces in the face of the enemy. More than once Lee violated that edict during his tenure as commander of the Army of Northern Virginia. On his way northward in early September 1862, splitting his army and relying on his opponent's caution, he sent Jackson to capture Harpers Ferry. On September 13, his audacity almost cost him his army. Union commander Maj. Gen. George B. McClellan was handed three cigars wrapped in a copy of Lee's orders, discovered at an abandoned Confederate campsite, specifying the routes for the divided sections of Lee's army. McClellan could now pounce on each with his full force before they could unite and destroy the main army of the rebellion.

But instead of acting immediately, McClellan dithered. A southern sympathizer delivered the news of McClellan's finding Lee's order to Confederate cavalry commander J. E. B. Stuart, who passed the information to Lee. In response, Lee plugged the "gaps" in the South Mountains with Confederate soldiers. Savage and heroic fighting bought Lee a whole day. He was considering retreating to the Shenandoah Valley when word came from Jackson that Harpers Ferry was about to fall. (Its capture would net nearly 12,000 Union prisoners, one of the largest wholesale surrenders in U.S. Army history.) Lee sent orders to his units to concentrate at Sharpsburg, Maryland.

As it was, McClellan still managed to corner a part of Lee's army near the town behind Antietam Creek, with the Potomac River at its back. McClellan's attacks began at dawn, September 17; however, what was to be coordinated assaults struck the rebel line in piecemeal fashion.

Union attacks swept from the north and fighting rolled southward. For the next eight hours, Union soldiers fought through areas whose names would be seared into the American military psyche: the Cornfield, the West Woods, the East Woods, and the Sunken Road, soon to be christened "Bloody Lane." Lee continued to shift his troops from one endangered segment of his line to the next, barely staving off catastrophe. On the southern end of the battlefield, a handful of Georgia sharpshooters held Union general Ambrose Burnside's Ninth Corps from crossing Antietam Creek and encircling Lee's army.

When Union assaults drove the Confederates from the Sunken Road, all McClellan needed to do was send in his reserves. Confederate artillerist E. P. Alexander saw the imminent disaster: "Lee's army was ruined, and the end of the Confederacy was in sight." But true to Lee's estimation of his opponent, McClellan, believing Lee's army to be larger than it really was, exercised caution and held back.

Burnside's men finally forced a crossing of the bridge that would bear his name forever. Once again Lee's army was threatened with destruction: Burnside was about to cut off Lee's army's only retreat route across the Potomac, but he halted to reorganize his advance. All McClellan needed to do was to send in supports to Burnside. Fatally, his caution once again prevailed.

Lee had his own troubles. Looking to the south, he saw a dust cloud rising from marching troops. If they were Union troops, his army was destroyed. For what seemed like an eternity, an aide peered through a telescope and finally announced the column was marching under Confederate flags; A. P. Hill had arrived after a strenuous march from Harpers Ferry and burst upon Burnside's flank, stopping his attack in its tracks.

Dawn of September 18 around the small Maryland hamlet of Sharpsburg was nothing like the dawn of the previous day. The morning revealed fields that were strewn with some 3,650 silent dead and 17,300 moaning wounded. The two armies sat watching one another: Lee expecting a continuation of the attacks from the previous day, the next of which could be fatal to his army; McClellan seemingly satisfied he had avoided contact with what he fantasized as Lee's never-ending reserves. Lee began his retreat into Virginia.

McClellan boasted a great victory, but his main objective of destroying Lee's army went unfulfilled. The Union general assured Washington that Pennsylvania was now safe from Confederate invasion, but within nine months, the re-formed Army of Northern Virginia would be crossing the Mason-Dixon line again and marching into the Keystone State.

Politically speaking, the Union victory at Antietam did two things. First, it stymied Confederate hopes for earning recognition as an independent nation from Great Britain. Though arms would continue to be sold to the Confederacy bearing the "Tower" manufacturing stamp and run through the Union blockade, Parliament's interest in full financial and military support would wane after Antietam. Second, though Lincoln was disappointed that McClellan let Lee slip away, it gave him an opportunity to turn the war into something greater than the internecine struggle it was. After the victory at Antietam, he could issue the Emancipation Proclamation, making official one of the goals of abolishing, in the United States, the curse of human bondage.

Antietam Ghosts

As a national park, Antietam is patrolled by park rangers. While the staff may not be as large as that at Gettysburg or the Grand Canyon, they are as dedicated a group as you can find. Their job is to "protect the resource," meaning the park grounds, the modern facilities, and the historic buildings scattered throughout.

The Pry House

The Pry House had been a hospital during the Battle of Antietam and was witness to all the horrors encompassed therein. Wounds made by the soft lead (unjacketed) .58-caliber minié ball, actually a bullet-shaped cone, were devastating. If you were struck in an arm or leg, the lead projectile would flatten and shatter the bone into fragments. The only thing surgeons could do, with literally thousands of cases produced in a few hours, was amputate the limb. A Civil War hospital like the Pry House was a nonstop amputation factory. Limbs were tossed out first-floor windows until they reached the sill and were then carted away to be buried or burned. When a soldier was struck in the body, incredible damage was done. The soft tissues were known to "evacuate" from the path of the bullet, so the body would tear itself apart trying to get away from the insult. The bullet would carry pieces of the uniform, which hadn't been cleaned in weeks, into the wound. Gut wounds, with their subsequent peri-

The Pry House outside of Sharpsburg was used as a hospital during the Battle of Antietam. Union general Israel Richardson died in one of the upstairs rooms.

tonitis, were nearly always fatal. Worse, the surgeon would dip his hands into the guts of one man, pronounce him incurable, and then wipe a flesh wound of a slightly wounded soldier, who would die of blood poisoning two weeks later. Antibiotics were virtually unknown at the time of the war, so post-operative infections were rampant.

The scene at the Pry House, when Gen. Israel Richardson's wife Fannie arrived to care for her wounded husband, was no doubt frightening beyond anything she had seen before and utterly overwhelming to the senses. Although the general was considered to be only slightly wounded, infection set in and he took a sudden turn for the worse, and Mrs. Richardson would return to Michigan escorting her husband's dead body.

Another woman who was affected by the horror of the Pry House was Mrs. Pry herself, who saw her lovely dining room turned into a makeshift operating room. The Prys, like so many others in the country where battles took place, were ruined by the war. Family tradition has her dying of a broken heart. Apparently, both of the women were so affected by their experiences at the house, they have returned in spirit long after their lives ended.

In spite of careful patrolling by the rangers, sometime in the mid 1970s, the Pry House caught on fire and burned. Fortunately, the brick exterior walls remained, but the interior, both first and second floor, was completely gutted. During the fighting of the fire, something strange was reported by the firemen. According to a story in a local newspaper by Erin Julius, the Washington County firefighters were there when the fire engulfed the second floor and it collapsed. But because of what they saw at one of the second-floor windows, there may have been some discussion among them as to whether they should re-enter the building. A captain was no doubt consulted and they determined that they saw what was clearly impossible: a woman standing in front of one of the windows on the nonexistent second floor.

The story could be dismissed as a figment of the imagination, although apparently several firefighters were witnesses to the impossible scene. And a second set of witnesses emerged about a year later.

The park service eventually restored the interior of the Pry House, but before they did two rangers on patrol went out to the place one night. As they circled through the parking lot they noticed something in the gutted building: the figure of a woman standing at the window on the second floor.

Apparently there was some discussion as to whether they should check it out for a prowler—a prowler who apparently could levitate—but they decided that they could probably investigate it just as well tomorrow, in the daylight.

As the park was restoring the house, a strange thing was seen by the maintenance foreman's wife and three or four of the contractor's crew. Just after the back stairs were completed, those in the house saw an older woman with long blonde hair come down the stairs, almost as if she had been waiting for them to be completed, and pass between the individuals in the crew. She neither spoke nor acknowledged any of them, but they noticed something strange about her. As she passed by, they realized they could see each other through her translucent form.

Though she appeared once again to cause a worker to quit the job, she has since manifested herself in a more common way. Footsteps are occasionally heard going up and down the steps, unaccompanied by a mortal form to produce the noise.

Since the historic renovation of the house, the National Park Service has used it as a medical interpretive center. According to

Erin Julius, the director has heard each door slam shut individually. He went around opening them all, and it happened again, one at a time. The gentle breeze could have blown one or two on the same side of the house closed because the wind was only blowing in one direction and not swirling like a tornado.

Later, the director's twelve-year-old son came down from the second floor and reported that he had seen a woman in nineteenth-century clothing leave one of the offices by going through the wall.

There was another story Julius related about a park service interpreter who wanted to spend a night in the barn. Reports from the battle indicate that while the house was used for wounded officers, the barn held injured enlisted men. After dark he was gazing out into a field when he saw a lantern swinging through it. The odd part is that it was moving along where the original road ran from the Pry House.

Sharpsburg

The town of Sharpsburg was also filled to overflowing with the dead and dying who have left the psychic impressions of their agony. St. Paul's Episcopal Church in the town was a field hospital during and after the battle. Periodically, nervous neighbors will be awakened by screams coming from the empty church where similar cries once echoed in earnest as limbs were sawn off and tender torso wounds were probed with cold steel. Some have also seen "ghost lights," possibly orbs, floating in the belfry.

A man who started with the National Park Service with me at Gettysburg told an interesting story about the historic house he rented. He was awakened in the middle of the night by footsteps roaming around downstairs. He heard them meandering back and forth and then ascending the stairs to the second floor. He reached into his nightstand and pulled out his "little friend," as he called it, his service revolver, and walked in the dark to stand behind the wall next to the doorway leading downstairs.

He heard the footsteps coming up the stairs, but remained calm, waiting for the intruder to get close enough. The footsteps were just about at the top of the stairs when he flipped on the light and took the firing position, pointing the gun downstairs at . . . nothing.

Bloody Lane

One evening, a group of reenactors decided they wanted to sleep in the infamous Sunken Road. In spite of the fact that the park is closed after dusk, they managed to sneak their way from their cars, across the darkened fields where thousands once lay in their death throes, to one of the most blood-soaked battlefields in all of military history.

Perhaps they knew something of the crimson-stained history of the site. Along a road carved into the earth by decades of wagon traffic, Confederate soldiers under the command of Daniel Harvey Hill stayed until the last. A famous photo was made of the carnage: human bodies piled one on top of another so that the bottom of the Sunken Road could not be discerned, giving it the name Bloody Lane. Confederate general John B. Gordon's experience was probably typical. Shot in the face, he fell unconscious, face-down into his own hat, which rapidly filled up with his blood. He considered himself lucky. A bullet had previously drilled a neat hole in the headpiece and the gory liquid drained out, saving Gordon from drowning in his own blood.

Whether knowledgeable about the awful history of the site or not, the reenactors were about to get a lesson in history they would never forget.

One by one, in their uniforms, they lay down, on the earth once drenched with the blood of their ancestors, in the very space once filled by the decaying forms of dead men. One by one they began to leave, muttering about hearing whispers close to their ears, of detecting the moans of the wounded and dying echoing in the shallow depression, and of feeling a sudden cold chill sweep across them. All left but one, who laughed at them and said he would see them in the morning.

The reenactors gathered at their cars and prepared to spend the night there, still uncomfortably close to the fields of death. Within a few minutes they heard a bonechilling scream come from the area of the Bloody Lane. Across the shadowy battlefield they saw a form stumbling towards them. It was their comrade who had chosen to remain in the lane alone. He was shaking and utterly incoherent. It took ten minutes to calm him. When he did, they heard

The Sunken Road at Antietam, which came to be known as "Bloody Lane" after being the site of fierce fighting.

a story that would chase them as far away from the battlefield as they could get.

He was lying in the lane, laughing to himself at his cowardly companions. Sure, he had heard the whisperings and the moans and felt the chills, but relegated them to his imagination and hardened his determination to stay while the others left. Lying on his back, he suddenly heard a rustling in the grass next to him. Out of the corner of his eye he saw between his arm and chest, emerging from the earth, a human arm.

This was finally too much, but as he started to rise to leave, the disembodied arm and hand turned and pressed down with physical pressure on his chest, pushing him back to the ground and holding him there.

That was when his companions heard him scream and when the phantom arm and hand released him.

Those seeking an explanation for how an ectoplasmic limb could physically hold a person down must look elsewhere. But it has happened before, and may very well again, especially when one chooses to counterfeit the dead.

Fredericksburg

The Battle of Fredericksburg illustrated decisively the futility of military tactics of the past, and the innovation and horror of military tactics to come. It showed the importance of logistics and planning, and how the blunderings of an awkward military bureaucracy can bog down a campaign and decide, weeks before the fighting, the outcome of the battle. It also displayed, once again, the indomitable courage of the American soldier.

On November 7, 1862, the command of the Federal Army of the Potomac was transferred from Maj. Gen. George B. McClellan to Maj. Gen. Ambrose E. Burnside. Within three days, the new Union commander presented a plan of battle to the government. The whole plan depended upon Burnside getting his army of 120,000 quickly across the Rappahannock River at Fredericksburg in order to strike south towards Richmond, the capital of the Confederacy. Since Confederates had burned all the bridges across the Rappahannock, Burnside needed portable pontoon bridges to arrive at Fredericksburg precisely when his army did, before Robert E. Lee and his Confederates discovered the Federals' intentions and opposed the crossing.

The first of the Federals' "Grand Divisions" arrived across the Rappahannock from Fredericksburg in the afternoon of November 17. The pontoon bridges, however, had not. Lee was now tipped off

The Fredericksburg skyline at dusk.

as to where the Yankees were headed and began to concentrate his army, which would eventually number 78,000, at Fredericksburg.

The bridges finally arrived November 25. Shortly after moonset, around 1:00 A.M., on December 11, engineers from the Army of the Potomac began dragging the cumbersome pontoon boats down the slope from Chatham, the eighteenth-century mansion on Stafford Heights. Under the cover of darkness and fog on the river, the engineers got the bridges built about halfway across.

Brig. Gen. William Barksdale's Mississippi Brigade waited in rifle pits and riverfront dwellings in Fredericksburg and listened to the sounds of construction echoing through the misty night. Barksdale had determined to delay the Federals' crossing for as long as he could so that Lee could gather his forces together.

Out in the middle of the river on the unfinished bridges, the unarmed engineers and construction troops heard the bell in the clock tower of Saint George's Episcopal Church, one of the landmarks of the Fredericksburg skyline, toll 5:00 A.M. Through the rising mist, one of the Federal officers saw a line of human arms flailing up and down: the unmistakable motion of men ramming home charges in muzzle-loading weapons. A few minutes later, an engineer on the end of one of the bridges heard an ominous shout through the fog: "Fire!" and suddenly bullets ripped into the wood of the bridges and tore through the flesh of the men. Union soldiers collapsed upon the unfinished bridge or tumbled, helpless, into the icy river, weighed down by their heavy greatcoats. Those who could fled back in panic to the shore, but there was no safety there. For the rifled musket of the Civil War, the opposite bank of the Rappahannock was easily within range, and men, mules, and horses went down.

The same thing was happening across from the old city boat landing. Confederates rushed down the old ferry access, "Rocky Lane," to the end of the docks and fired into the engineers on the bridges already two-thirds across. Work on that bridge ended as the Federals ran for their lives back to the opposite riverbank.

The Union commanders decided that the Confederates must be routed by artillery, and began a bombardment of the town. By 10:00 A.M., 183 Northern cannons were firing and Fredericksburg was being blasted to pieces. When the gunners were satisfied they had done their job, the engineers returned to the bridges. Just as they began to work, the Mississippians emerged from the rubble and started picking them off again. This sequence repeated itself several times throughout the morning.

Meantime, although another bridge a mile downstream at the "Lower Crossing" was completed, Burnside refused to allow his troops to cross until the upstream bridges were complete. He feared they would be isolated without support and cut to pieces.

At the Upper and Middle Crossings, work was still stymied by the pesky rebel sharpshooters. At 12:30 P.M., Burnside ordered all available Union cannons to fire on the town, and for an hour they again pulverized Fredericksburg. In all, some 8,000 shells rained down on the city. Brick buildings suffered, but the shells merely passed through the wooden structures, leaving holes that occupying Confederates used to fire through. Sophia Street, closest to the river, looked like it had been plowed and virtually every window in the city had been broken out.

Burnside's detailed plans, established some five weeks before, were crumbling before his eyes, with his entire army held up by a handful of obstinate rebel riflemen. At that moment, Brig. Gen. Henry Hunt, Burnside's artillery chief, passed on an idea that one of the engineers had suggested: ferry a few infantrymen across in pontoon boats to drive the persistent Confederates back away from the river so the engineers could finish the bridges.

Burnside hesitated. Something like that had never been done before in the history of the U. S. Army. Could it be successful, or would Burnside be merely sentencing the men to their own execution in the middle of the river? Burnside wanted only volunteers.

Col. Norman J. Hall's 7th Michigan, when asked if they would cross the river in boats to drive out the enemy, responded with three cheers. The waterborne assault was preceded by a massive artillery bombardment beginning at 3:00 P.M. When the fire slackened, the boats would shove off.

At 3:30, the big guns fell silent and the assault troops of the 7th Michigan rushed to the boats. They had scarcely loaded when the Confederates opened on them again. Under orders not to return fire but to concentrate on paddling or poling across, the men were helpless. The boats took terrific fire until they were two-thirds of the way across, then a curious thing happened. The Confederate fire slowed to a trickle. The steep riverbank below Sophia Street hid the assault craft from the Confederates and the actual landing was made in relative safety.

But, the worst was yet to come. The landing party rushed up the slope to Sophia Street and began surrounding the houses where the rebels hid. They had been given the order, "No quarter," or take no prisoners. While some disobeyed the order, others rushed into houses and shot or bayoneted every man inside. In less than a half hour, Sophia Street was cleared.

The Confederates were not about to retire without a fight, and the battle took on a character that would become the bloody hallmark of wars of the next century and a half. A new type of tactical fighting needed to be learned by warriors—house-to-house, urban street fighting—and it began in Fredericksburg.

Confederates defended the town from the alleys and backyards behind Sophia Street; by occupying the Southern troops, the 7th Michigan was buying time for the engineers to complete the bridges. Massachusetts troops were ferried across to bolster the Wolverines, and as the bridges were completed, they were ordered to advance beyond the waterfront and push the rebels out of the town to make room for more Union solders to land via the bridges.

Federals muscled their way up Hawke Street, taking awful casualties at the intersection of Hawke and Caroline; the 20th Massachusetts lost 97 men in and around the intersection. Night fell early in December and still the fighting went on. Backyards became battlegrounds and dooryards deathtraps. One Federal broke into a second-floor room and was shot through the window by a Confederate across the street. The fighting was illuminated by musket flashes. Men were wounded by splinters flying from brick chimneys and wooden framing. The horror of not knowing from which window or doorway the next shot would come was demoralizing. Finally, with the groans of the wounded echoing through the darkened street, the lack of light brought an end to the carnage. By 7:00 P.M. most of the firing died down and Confederates began retreating from the town.

With Confederate resistance in the city of Fredericksburg quelled, December 12 was spent by Union forces crossing the Rappahannock into the city. Burnside ordered his chief signal officer to run a telegraph line from occupied Fredericksburg across both the lower and upper pontoon bridges, then to connect his headquarters with the far left flank of the army. The communicating device was a clever magnetic "pointer" system: dial a letter on the sending device and the pointer spins to the same letter on the receiver. It was claimed to be the first time the magnetic telegraph was used on the battlefield. It wouldn't be the last.

Federals drained five feet of freezing water from a canal between them and Marye's Heights, a ridge west of the city. They also began looting. Wanton destruction began in what had once been one of the finer cities of the South. Private homes were vandalized, libraries sacked, fine arts destroyed, personal treasures stolen, and businesses ransacked beyond anything that had happened in the war previously. Nineteenth-century war was not supposed to be waged upon civilians; Fredericksburg changed that.

Federal assaults were planned for dawn on December 13, 1862. Northern forces under Maj. Gen. William B. Franklin (one of Burnside's three "Grand Divisions") were to launch the attacks from the old Smithfield Plantation east of the Bowling Green Road, across the Fredericksburg & Potomac Railroad to strike Confederates under Stonewall Jackson near Prospect Hill. Franklin used Maj. Gen. George G. Meade's division and Brig. Gen. John Gibbon's division, totaling about 8,500 men, for the assault.

The morning dawned opaque and misty. The Union assault, which was to get off early, had been delayed. It was nearing 10:00 A.M. when the fog began to rise. Like ghosts, the Federal troops moved out of the haze, crossed the Bowling Green Road and headed toward the railroad. Suddenly, there were muffled artillery discharges from their left and rear. Maj. John Pelham, the twenty-four-year-old commander of J. E. B. Stuart's Horse Artillery, had used the fog to gain position and raked the Union line, halting its advance. Ordered to retire from the exposed spot, he refused, and fought, suffering serious counter-battery fire from the Federals, until his ammunition was gone. Pelham, with one gun, had managed to hold up the entire Federal assault for an hour. After Pelham withdrew, Meade continued his advance. Jackson's men waited patiently until the Federals were within 500 yards of a forested hill hiding 14 cannons, then opened fire. Gaps opened in the Federal ranks and Union soldiers dropped into whatever depressions they could find near the railroad and in the open fields beyond.

Jackson's guns drew fire from Federal artillery and there ensued an hourlong duel. So many artillery horses were shot down that the rebels renamed the place "Dead Horse Hill."

When the Confederate fire died down, Meade's men continued their advance and struck a 600-yard gap in Jackson's line that had been inadvertently left unguarded. In their drive through the Confederate line they ran into a brigade of South Carolinians. Confederate Brig. Gen. Maxcy Gregg mistook the Yankees for retreating Southerners and withheld his fire. It cost him his life. He was shot in the spine and later died.

Though Jackson had left a space in his line, he had arranged his reserves in column. During the breakthrough he launched them into the fought-out Union spearhead. The massive Confederate counterattack pushed Meade's men all the way back across the railroad and back to the Bowling Green Road. Once the Confederates got in range, they were stopped by the massed Union artillery. Both Federals and Confederates tried additional assaults in the late afternoon, but both failed. The carnage at one point was so terrible, the area was christened "The Slaughter Pen."

Burnside's overall plan was to wait for success on the southern end of the field, then launch assaults upon the Confederates at Marye's Heights, just to the west of the city of Fredericksburg. Burnside ordered the Grand Division of Maj. Gen. Edwin V. Sumner to advance against James Longstreet's Confederates.

Just before noon, Union infantry, lined up shoulder-to-shoulder, emerged from the streets of the city and began crossing the open fields between Fredericksburg and Marye's Heights. Almost simultaneously, Confederate artillery from atop the heights began lobbing shells into their packed ranks. Men remembered seeing arms, hands, legs and clothing flying into the air above their heads, the hideous result of artillery fire upon massed ranks of infantry.

In front of the Union troops lay a millrace, fifteen feet across and five feet deep, partially filled with freezing water. The only places to cross it were at bridges over three streets leading out of town. These quickly became bottlenecks as Confederate skirmishers, upon their retreat, removed the floors of the bridges leaving just the "stringers" for hundreds of Union troops to attempt to cross. Once across the millrace, the Northerners had to realign their ranks and push on. The last impediment to the Union assault was a wide-open field known as the Fair Grounds, which was swept by Confederate rifle fire from a virtually unseen enemy standing behind a chin-high stone wall in a sunken road.

Assault after assault repeated the same horrifying and deadly routine. Some of the surviving Union troops found shelter behind the few fence posts left around the Fair Grounds. Other sought relief behind the few buildings in the area: a brick grocery building called Sisson's Store, a house, and wheelwright shop owned by the

Stratton family. Men and officers piled up behind these structures, like flotsam in the lee of an island during a storm. Throughout the afternoon and into the evening the futile assaults continued.

Fifteen Federal brigades tried to pierce the Confederate line. Men were cut in two by shells, entrails flying in all directions. They were decapitated, and slumped, some still kneeling, headless, clinging to their muskets. Unbelievably, one man was seen running past an advancing column, without a head, until he tumbled into the millrace. One Confederate saw around the Stratton House that the dead were so thick you could walk on them. Holding their fire only made the slaughter easier for Confederates. Toward the end, the fallen wounded clutched at the legs of the fresh units trying to stop their comrades from a certain death.

The "butcher's bill," as the soldiers called the casualty list, was appalling. In one hour full of horror the Union army lost 4,000 men. All totaled, Burnside lost 12,600 in killed, wounded, and missing, with some 8,400 casualties occurring below the stone wall and sunken road. Lee lost about 5,300.

Fredericksburg Ghosts

Most of the buildings in Fredericksburg were scenes of deadly conflict, and the very streets were fought through. Both armies left dead and wounded strewn along the path visitors now walk in Fredericksburg. Of the hundreds of buildings here during Civil War years, some 350 remain, many perhaps holding forever the spirits of the slain. Nearly every public building and many private homes were used as hospitals.

As well, four hundred years of history has resulted in countless restless, perturbed spirits. From its Colonial heritage to the horror of being the focal point of four major Civil War battles (Fredericksburg, Chancellorsville, the Wilderness, and Spotsylvania), Fredericksburg has seen more history and more human tragedy than virtually any other city in America. Between 1862 and 1864, more than 100,000 men and boys became casualties in the fighting in and around the town; most were brought to Fredericksburg to be operated upon, recover, or perish.

The personal civilian calamities and the military terror brought on by the numerous and bloody battles may very well account for the reference to Fredericksburg as "the most haunted city per capita in the United States."

A Haunted House on Caroline Street

On December 11, 1862, after initially fighting a delaying action through the streets of Fredericksburg, the Confederates withdrew to the heights west of the city, there to repulse numerous, bloody Union attacks two days later. Union troops occupied the town, prying into private pantries, pilfering what they needed, and peering out windows of private homes, looking for the enemy, or to avoid their own provost guard.

Fast-forward to the twentieth century. According to a woman whose family has lived in Fredericksburg for well over a hundred years, renovation was going on in one of the historic buildings along Caroline Street near William Street. The new owner had spent all day tearing up old carpeting. He had finished for the day and rolled it up and placed it in the hall in order to facilitate the workmen removing it the next day. It is well known in paranormal circles that whenever there is a renovation to an historic building, there is more likelihood of paranormal experiences occurring. It is almost as if the spirits do not want their routine, their status quo, disturbed. So it was in this case.

Trash men were coming the next afternoon. As he left for the night, the owner told the workmen to remove the rolled-up carpet first thing next morning and put it by the curb. The next morning, when he arrived at the work site, there was no carpet at the curb. At first he was angry because he knew that their disobedience would cost him time, and in the construction business, time is money. He sought out the foreman and gave him a dressing-down. The foreman then took him upstairs to show him why they hadn't removed the carpet. When his men arrived to work in the morning, the carpet was no longer in the hall. He opened the door to the room. There the carpet was, laid down again, with tacks in place.

The owner was rightfully concerned and apparently felt immediately that there was something paranormal going on. He called his priest. The priest came to inspect the area. He walked upstairs to the room. He cautiously opened the door to the room in question and was greeted by the sight of several ghostly Union soldiers across the room peering out of the windows. The priest left and told the owner that he'd pray for the souls to be on their way.

Upon leaving, he said something ominous, spawned perhaps by something else he witnessed in that room, but would not talk about. He said he would also pray for the owner.

Footprints at Caroline Street Cafe

One of the tragedies of the American South before the Civil War was the forced enslavement of fellow human beings. Even in the South, slavery was considered the "peculiar institution." Many southerners emancipated their slaves long before the war; but others, with large farms to manage, realized that they just couldn't get along without slavery. Fredericksburg was part of the slaveholding South.

Of the town's 3,000 inhabitants in 1835, 1,124 were slaves. On the corner of William and Charles Streets is the auction block, which was used, among other things, for the display and sale of human beings. It is interesting to imagine that along with the ghosts of tens of thousands of Civil War soldiers who died to either free slaves or maintain a lifestyle that included slavery, that there could also be the spirits of long-dead slaves, still in bonds of a more ethereal but still unbreakable kind.

People think that ghost stories are relegated to the past. This is not true. This one comes to us from July 2005. Someone in the Caroline Street Café was looking for something. They entered an upstairs room that had been habitually sealed off since it had been last cleaned. Indeed, the person found something, but it was not what she expected. Stretching across the floor were the footprints of a large male.

They were bare footprints, and they were etched in white, walking from one side of the abandoned room to the other and back again, as if pacing, and waiting for something to happen or someone to come and release the spirit from its centuries-long incarceration. Someone in authority was called and shown the footprints.

"Well, let's wash them off," was the sentiment. But try as they might, the footprints would not wash off. The room was closed, but inspected frequently after that. Slowly, over a couple of weeks, the footprints faded from sight, returning to an unseen world whence they came.

Smythe's Cottage

On the corner of Fauquier Street and Princess Anne stands a small Civil War–era building that has been used for years as the site of several restaurants. A few years back it was called Smythe's Cottage, and according to the owners, both patrons and employees have experienced unexplainable paranormal phenomena over the years.

An employee would go around lighting candles. Returning from the other room she would see that some had been blown out. Setting tables with silverware in Smythe's Cottage before the customers came in was often frustrating: The silverware was often moved out of place. Both of these activities were known to occur when there were no other people in the room. Those and other seemingly paranormal phenomena are blamed on a woman the owners call "Elizabeth," who is believed to have committed suicide by hanging herself in the stairway leading to the second floor.

Elizabeth, according to legend, was a Union sympathizer. With Fredericksburg occupied by Union soldiers during the Civil War, one can only speculate why she would pass important information on to the enemy, although it easily could have been done. It is also rumored that the building during the war was used as a bordello, no doubt by Union troops. Whether Elizabeth was involved in this fraternization with the enemy is unknown, but the rumor is that, whatever she was doing, her husband caught her and accused her of treason toward the South and infidelity to him. The shame was too much and was the apparent reason for her suicide.

The children of the owner when the building was Smythe's Cottage had experiences on the second floor of the house. One, when he was eleven years old, watched as the closet doors began to open by themselves while he was the only person in the room. Frightened, he ran from the room. His younger brother, at age nine, saw a whitish mist begin to come out of the same closet. More recently, a patron in the back room of the restaurant saw a short, heavyset woman in a long, dark, "old-fashioned" skirt and white apron move swiftly past his table as if she had a mission in mind; she went out into the garden, which is enclosed by a tall, wooden fence. Interestingly enough, it was at the same time some ghost hunters were conducting a paranormal investigation. They rushed out after the woman. By the time the investigators reached the inescapable garden, she had vanished.

While the investigators were there, other paranormal events were recorded. In the same room where Elizabeth had been seen, a bowl containing sugar and artificial sweetener crashed to the floor and broke. No one had been in the room when it happened. The investigators caught some odd lights on tape moving in opposite directions—obviously not reflections from car lights, which would move in the same direction, over and over, as cars passed. And the closet door, which the owner's son had seen begin to open before he beat a hasty retreat, was recorded on the tape moving, ever so slightly, as if someone were trying to open it.

And most ominously, there are the reports from patrons and servers that as they pass the stairway that leads to the second floor, their peripheral vision is disturbed by a swinging motion at the top of the stairs. They look, and for a split second, they see a spectral woman floating, as if hanging in midair at the top of the stairs, swaying and then disappearing.

There is a portrait of Union general Ulysses S. Grant that used to hang next to the stairway. In a town that saw so much destruction by the Union armies, in a house that witnessed the destruction of a family by the circumstances of war, the portrait seems to be a disturbing reminder of all that tragedy. Owners of the building will come into the house in the morning to find the portrait angled. They straighten it and make sure it's still straight at the end of the day when they lock up, and for a few days it stays that way. Then, another morning, the image of the man who symbolized so much human agony for the South is tilted again. Finally, one morning, the owners entered the building after straightening the picture when they left the night before. They were shocked and confused to find the picture turned around, facing the wall.

St. George's Episcopal Church

Looking at its skyline from across the Rappahannock River, Fredericksburg seems to have an abundance of churches. Sharp steeples break up the horizon, a scene virtually unchanged since Union soldiers saw it from the same spot some fifteen decades before.

One of the larger churches in the city is St. George's Episcopal Church. It boasts the oldest congregation in Fredericksburg. In 1732, it was George Washington's church, when he lived across the river at his boyhood home, Ferry Farm. George's mother Mary Washington worshipped in the original church on the site. The present St. George's Episcopal Church, actually the third on this site, was built in 1849. Just outside is a graveyard; the oldest stone is dated 1752, and Col. John Dandridge, father of Martha Washington, and William Paul, brother of John Paul Jones, are buried here.

Uniquely, the pews in St. George's were permanently installed, rendering them immovable by hospital orderlies or Union soldiers. Some of the pews in other churches in town were cut up and used as headboards for gravesites. As well, three Tiffany stained-glass windows are set in the church walls. The church was damaged in the Union bombardment of 1862 and was used as a hospital during the campaigns of 1862, 1863, and 1864. The church remained in service for both Union and Confederate soldiers, depending upon who occupied the town during the war. During the Battle of Fredericksburg in December 1862, one wounded Northerner described what he saw outside the building along the stairs: "Dead soldiers piled on either side as high as the top step, and the fence hanging full of belts, cartridge boxes, canteens, and haversacks." The fence and the steps are the originals.

But it is what has been seen inside the church, dating back to 1858, that interests ghost hunters. The original 1858 story, found in *Virginia Ghosts* by Marguerite DuPont Lee, relates that a Ms. Ella McCarty was a singer in the choir of St. George's. She had arrived at the church at night with a gentleman and found that they were early; only the organist was present. The church was still dark, lit only by one candle in the choir loft, then located over the vestibule. The two men left Ms. McCarty sitting in the church while they looked for more candles. As she sat and her eyes became more accustomed to the dark, she saw a female figure, appearing to be dressed all in white with a veil over her face, kneeling at the rail in the front of the church, apparently in prayer. Within a short time the woman in white arose, and then, almost as if she were floating, turned to face Ms. McCarty. She looked at her with a forlorn, desperate expression. Ms. McCarty began to speak to the woman, and she then vanished.

It is remarkable to find a ghost story in a Civil War town that predates the war. More common are those more recent, such as this one from the current century. A young woman was in the church and went into the restroom. From inside one of the stalls she heard the door to the restroom open, and then the door to the next stall opened. Moments later when she was leaving, she began to realize something strange. Although she had heard someone walk into the restroom, move across the floor, and open the stall door, she heard no one leave and there was no one in the room with her. Cautiously, she pushed open the stall door and realized that she had been alone in the room.

According to the local police, their K-9 dogs are especially nervous inside and outside of the church. The dogs especially react at the door to the balcony. According to one officer, "There aren't too many police officers who haven't had an experience in St. George's." Police officers will check the doors at night to make sure they are locked—and they are. An hour or so later, they'll check again, and they will be unlocked. Officers will hear footsteps walking through the sanctuary when there is no one visible, and they will hear the benches creaking as if someone was sitting in them. The caretaker was working in the cemetery and felt someone come up behind him and touch him on the shoulder, but when he turned around to see what the person wanted, no one was there.

Certain professions produce the most believable witnesses to ghost stories. Among those are police, who are trained observers. One night, a rookie and a seasoned officer were patrolling together. They stopped at St. George's for a second time to make sure the doors were locked. The rookie said, "I'll handle this," and walked from the car to the door. He tried opening the door, which had been locked the first time they visited the church, and it was unlocked. The rookie waved for the other officer to stay in the car, indicating that he would enter the church and make sure everything was in order and then secure the building. The other officer waved his consent.

Five minutes passed. And then ten minutes passed. After twenty minutes, the seasoned officer was concerned. Just as he was about to get out of the car, the rookie exited the church, locked the door behind him, and hopped back into the car.

"Everything okay?" asked the veteran officer.

"Yep. Checked all the doors and all the rooms. Even that weird room where everything is painted red."

The veteran officer was silent and waited until a few days later to tell the rookie. There is no red room in St. George's.

The Chimneys

The Chimneys, a large historic building on the corner of Caroline and Charlotte Streets, was built around 1770 by an immigrant Scottish merchant, John Glassel. Loyal to the crown, when the Revolution broke out, he left his property to his brother and returned to Scotland. The property has changed hands many times and has assumed many reincarnations since then.

Ghosts at the Chimneys are nothing new. Although some of the stories predate the Civil War, Dr. Brodie Herndon, who owned the house in the mid-nineteenth century, contended that the house was haunted. Some of the paranormal events he recorded continue to this day, such as doorknobs being turned by invisible hands and doors opening by themselves. Apparently in Mr. Brodie's time, a woman saw her uncle standing in one of the rooms across the hall. By the time she entered the room, it was empty. This apparition was a harbinger, because her uncle died three days later.

Apparently, one of the early occupants, probably a young woman, played the harp in the parlor, for it is from that area that the sweet strains of a phantom harp are heard upon occasion, playing a melody many decades removed from the list of popular songs. Sometimes the refrain is accompanied by a ghostly singer.

Years after the harp and its player left, some occupants of the house brought a piano. One evening a young woman sat down and began to accompany herself on the piano. She heard the front door open and close. She was surprised to hear footsteps approach. She knew there were guests out front, so she asked the person obviously trying to frighten her to identify himself. The only answer was the plodding footsteps, which by now had reached the doorway. She turned apprehensively toward the sound, but as the footfalls entered the room and approached her, she could see no one. Her piano recital suddenly came to an end when someone, quite invisible, sat down on the piano bench next to her and placed an unseen, icy hand upon her shoulder.

One particular night when the Chimneys was still a residence, a woman was awakened by a chill in the air. The chill grew perceptibly colder as she approached her youngest son's bedroom. She took a blanket from a closet and entered his room. To her astonishment, there was another male child apparently asleep in the bed next to her son. She could not identify him because his face was half covered with the sheet, but she assumed that perhaps her sleeping husband had invited one of the neighbor boys to spend the night. She covered the two, and went back to bed herself. The next morning when her husband awakened, she asked who the boy was he had invited to spend the night with their son. She was met with an incredulous look and the affirmation that he had not invited anyone to spend the night. At that moment, her son came down for breakfast, by himself, and confirmed that indeed, he had slept alone that night. And while the woman's original mission was to cover her son to ward off the cold, that night—at least in the rest of the house—had been overly warm. A quick examination of her son's bed revealed to the woman that only one child—one living child—had spent the night there.

Auditory apparitions, the most common kind, also occur here. The sound of china crashing to the floor is heard, but upon inspection of the room, nothing is amiss. Heavy footsteps are detected in the hall when no one is there. Doors are heard slamming.

Occasionally, someone will see a rocking chair start moving back and forth with no one seated in it. One of the owners of a restaurant that was located in the house would come in at 4 A.M. to do his preparation for breakfast. The sound of silverware falling on the floor—with no actual silverware apparent anywhere—was so frequent, that he had to holler at the ghosts to leave him alone, because he had work to do. The ruckus abruptly stopped.

Some of the more recent activity involves child ghosts. The apparition of a little boy is seen roaming about upstairs. There is the rumor of a little boy who fell from the balcony to his death many years ago. He also apparently doesn't like a certain door upstairs to be closed, because as often as they close it and leave at night, the next morning the door is open. A little girl also walks the floor upstairs and then is seen to vanish, as well as the apparition of a grown woman. Several years ago, the owners of the bakery that was once housed in the Chimneys spent their first night in Fredericksburg in an upstairs room. They had cats—animals are often more sensitive to the paranormal than humans—and the cats did not sleep all night. As well, the two woke the next morning to find that each had dreamed all night long—of children.

Nicodemus

The stories about the famous Underground Railroad, that clandestine matrix of people, routes, and safe houses for runaway slaves in antebellum America, are as mysterious as they are romantic. Most of what we know about the system of transferring slaves from slaveholding states to freedom comes from after the Civil War, since harboring escaped slaves, throughout most of American history, was a crime, and those involved were reluctant to speak about it. In spite of that, the Virginia Abolition Society was formed in the 1780s.

That's right: the Virginia Abolition Society. So much for all the evil Southern slaveholders. As a matter of fact, only about 7 percent of all Southerners owned slaves, which makes one wonder why some eighteen-year-old Southern boy, whose family owned no slaves, would sign up to fight in the Civil War and possibly die for the rich man on the plantation to keep his slaves. He wouldn't, and he wasn't fighting just for slavery. American history is never as simple as some would make it.

Legislators representing slaveholders fought to keep the institution. In the Fugitive Slave Act of 1793, rights to slaves as property became constitutional. Regardless, by 1830, the Underground Railroad was in full operation in both the North and the South. The Fugitive Slave Act of 1850 made it a violation of Federal law to assist escaping slaves and slaves were forced to be returned to their masters, inflicting heavy fines and jail terms upon those aiding slaves' escape.

Railroad terminology was used to throw off slave-catchers: Safe houses were depots or stations located one nights' walk apart, conductors were guides to escaping slaves, agents offered their homes as day shelters for escapees, and superintendents controlled the operations in an entire state. During the day, slaves were hidden in barns, beneath floorboards, in false rooms, within the cog pits of mills, and down in damp cellars. They often waited days for forged "documents of passage" to arrive. Nighttime escapes were made on foot, in false bottoms in wagons, on the top of railroad cars, and by canoe, schooner, or steamer. The Chesapeake Bay was sought because of its access into the North, so the waterways draining into the bay, such as the Rappahannock, were desired routes. Indeed, several maps of the routes of the escapees on the Underground Railroad show Fredericksburg in the center.

At this writing, there is no documented evidence that the Chimneys was ever used as a depot on the Underground Railroad. There is, however, evidence from the other world that someone, desperate to escape, remained in the cellar of the building far too long. This is a story of two kinds of escape: one from slavery, the other from death.

On the evening of April 21, 2006, Julie Pellegrino, the spirit liaison I often use during paranormal investigations, explored the Chimneys, along with several others interested in the paranormal history of the building. After getting her impressions of several of the rooms, including the strong presence of a seafarer, Julie descended into the cellar.

The cellar of the Chimneys is currently used as a storage area for the businesses in the building. Julie approached the main area of the cellar and commented, "I feel like I can't leave, but I'm not a prisoner and I'm not locked in."

Channeling is a psychic phenomenon wherein mediums become conduits for the deceased—feeling, moving, and speaking as if they were dead people. Julie was later asked if she was channeling someone dead from the past, and she answered no, that she was merely repeating verbatim what she was hearing in the cellar that night.

According to my wife Carol, who accompanied her into the cellar, after passing through the door into the room, Julie received the name "Nicodemus." Julie's commentary went as follows.

> Don't know where I am, came with others.
>
> They got papers. They left.
>
> Can't leave without papers. Miss Hattie bring papers. Can't read, can't write, don't know what in papers. Need papers to leave.
>
> Others come, get papers, leave. Don't understand . . . .

Julie interjects at this point that she sensed that there was something wrong with his one hand, that his hand was crippled or injured in some way. When he speaks again, Julie points to some objects piled in the corner.

> I work, back strong, I carry things.
>
> I carry that . . . I work, need papers, don't understand.
>
> People in house don't know I here.

Carol asks Julie if his name is Nicodemus.

> No, just what they call me. Hattie not her name, just what they call her.
>
> Hear music, must be quiet . . . dark, Miss Hattie bring papers.
>
> More came. They got papers, left, said they'd come back for me. Never came.
>
> Music stopped, quiet . . . scared, can't leave

Julie suddenly says she thought she smelled smoke and was on the verge of tears at this point. She also had the sense that he had died there, in that cellar.

Julie's olfactory impression of a fire is interesting because the records show that in 1799 a huge fire destroyed much of the neighborhood near the Chimneys. It was rebuilt, but burned again in 1823. This may give us a clue as to which approximate period Julie was tapping into.

Carol called me into the cellar and Julie asked me to attempt to get some EVP. My technique is to ask a question pertinent to the past into a digital recorder, then pause with the recorder set on voice activation. In complete silence, the machine begins to record.

One other thing: I have never considered myself sensitive in any way to paranormal effects. Perhaps it's because I was trained as a writer to be objective; perhaps it says something about the fact that we're all different, with different sensitivities. Some of us are born with sharper hearing or better eyesight than others. Possibly it is the same with sensitivity to ghosts: some people are, some are not. I think I fall into the latter category. My mind was to change in a few short minutes.

Two sessions were attempted. The first session yielded rough, growling, staccato answers to my questions. Prior to the second session, Julie recommended that I tell "Nicodemus" that he could go now, that he didn't need his papers, and that he didn't need to wait for Hattie. I did just that. As I stood there in the darkened cellar in my short-sleeved shirt, I felt an extremely cold spot touch my right arm and remain there for about five seconds. Then it was replaced by a hot sensation, and then it returned to regular temperature. The rest of my body was normal temperature. After the session, I mentioned this to Julie. "That was Nicodemus," she said. She, too, had felt him leave the cellar. "He passed between us."

The Kenmore Inn

The Kenmore Inn was built in 1793. George Washington no doubt spent some time here. Fielding Lewis once owned the property, and Lewis most certainly would have entertained his brother-in-law George. Lewis may have lived in the building while construction of Kenmore Plantation was going on.

During the Civil War, Union soldiers used the basement as stalls for their horses. There is a garage that has been remodeled into a casual dining area, but it was used as a hospital during the battle. Employees have found bullets and buttons in the yard, as well as a whiskey flask and some vertebra that might be human.

There is a great deal of paranormal activity at the Kenmore—perhaps the unsettled spirits of the wounded who passed away at the inn during the conflict.

On Halloween 2005, one of the managers of the Kenmore, Gretchen, and two of the waitstaff were standing in the front hallway at the main entrance, where there are two chandeliers. They were talking, and Gretchen happened to mention something about ghosts. Just at that moment, the light in the chandelier over her head flashed. They all looked at each other incredulously and moved out of the room. About five minutes later, they were talking again, mentioning that the flashing light seemed kind of odd. Gretchen mentioned the word "ghost" again and the same chandelier flashed. It had never flashed before and hasn't since. Of course, Gretchen admitted that she refuses to used the word "ghost" in the hallway since the weird occurrence.

Before she started working at the Kenmore, Getchen visited Fredericksburg as a tourist. One night she was staying in Room 208. She had gone to bed, but was awakened at 3:00 A.M. by the sound of something very large and heavy being dragged down the hall past her room. It passed her room but didn't go down the stairs. At first she thought maybe it was a guest who had an argument with a roommate and was leaving in the middle of the night; however, it didn't sound at all like wheeled luggage rolling down the hall, but more like something being dragged, and upon checking the next morning, she found out that no one had left the Kenmore in the middle of the night.

She later stayed in Room 107 downstairs. She was in the bathroom and went out to the bed to get something from her suitcase. When she went back in the bathroom, the light had been turned off. She now rents that room out to guests, who report the medicine cabinet door pops open often and the bathroom door will not stay closed, even when the door is latched.

In Room 207, she hung an old picture on the wall above the commode on a nail driven into plaster. A week later a guest had reported that the picture had fallen off the wall. She never had any pictures fall off the walls because they are very securely nailed into plaster. She went and nailed it back in. About a month later it fell off again. The strange thing is that it never breaks—neither glass nor frame. It's almost as if someone gently removes it from the wall, nail and all, and places the picture on the floor.

Periodically, state inspectors have come to check the kitchen and public restrooms. A female inspector once asked to see the men's room. The manager said, go ahead, there's no one here now. The

The historic Kenmore Inn in Fredericksburg was occupied by Union soldiers and used as a stable and a hospital.

inspector went back downstairs and heard water running in the men's room. She came back upstairs to tell the manager, but the manager said, "That's impossible. I'm the only one here. Go on inside." So the inspector opened the door, and a huge cloud of what she described as "steam" came pouring out. She saw that the hot water was on as hard as it could go. But everyone in the Kenmore knows that the water down in the basement never gets hot enough to produce steam, and certainly not enough steam to create a man-sized cloud of mist. One must wonder if it was rather paranormal mist that the inspector witnessed.

The same inspector was under the dishwashing sink. She thought she'd put her hand in water because it felt so cold. Upon reflection, she said it felt like someone had put a cold hand right on top of her hand. Of course there was no water or no one—at least no one visible—lying beneath the sink with ice-cold hands. Also, periodically, Gretchen will go downstairs to the kitchen and the gas burners on the stove will be turned on full-blast.

Room 203, which is actually two adjoining rooms, had two different guests at two different times say that they felt like someone was stroking their hair. A woman was sleeping in the front room and her two children were in the back room in the twin beds. She woke up in the middle of the night and thought someone was sitting on her bed, perhaps one of her children. But when she looked up, she saw nothing. She went to see if one of her children had gotten up, but they were both still asleep.

During the winter of 2005–06, Gretchen was walking down the handicapped ramp to get some wood for a guest's fireplace. The lights on that side of the building were light-sensitive and had never worked. She hit a patch of "black ice" on the ramp and fell flat on her back. She got the wood and under her breath cursed out the owner, because he hadn't fixed the lights. The next night she went out to get wood and the light over the ramp was working. It has never worked again. She asked around if anyone had flipped a switch or anything. All said no. One wonders if the original owner of the building heard her and wanted to ensure her safety the second time.

In the fine-dining room, two of the candelabra fixtures in one of the chandeliers will periodically flicker. These are not the same chandeliers in the hallway that "flashed." The lights will go for months and nothing will happen, then they will flicker again.

Then, in May 2006, Gretchen heard something she'd never heard before in the Kenmore: disembodied voices. The first was a very deep, male voice, saying four or five words, coming from near the floor by Room 208. Then she heard a woman's voice emanating from the stairwell in the kitchen leading to the first floor. She could not understand the words, but she was sure it was female.

Several times Gretchen has used the back room as her own bedroom. She referred to the noises that older heating pipes make when the heat kicks on—kind of like a banging, metal-on-metal sound. She heard that sound coming from the floor of that room—clanking sounds, every night, coming from the floor. The room, however, is unheated and there are no pipes existing below the floor to make any sound.

Chancellorsville

After the Confederate victory at Fredericksburg in December 1862, Union general Ambrose E. Burnside attempted to maneuver Robert E. Lee out of his position. Bogged down on the half-frozen, sloppy roads, the effort was dubbed "The Mud March" and signaled to those in Washington that Burnside should be replaced as head the Army of the Potomac.

In January 1863, Maj. Gen. Joseph Hooker replaced Burnside. As soon as he took command, he reorganized the army and came up with a plan for a spring offensive that appeared to be perfect. It looked as if he would live up to the name he received when a newspaper forgot some punctuation: Fighting Joe Hooker.

Hooker would send 10,000 cavalrymen to cut Lee's communications with Richmond. While Lee was distracted by the cavalry sweep and part of Hooker's infantry attacked Marye's Heights, west of the city of Fredericksburg, the bulk of the force would march up the Rappahannock, cross it, and fall on Lee's left and rear.

Lee had sent Longstreet and his troops south to gather supplies and kept 60,000 men to face some 130,000 Federal troops. Hooker made his move at the end of April, sending Maj. Gen. John Sedgwick's Sixth Corps across the river at Fredericksburg to threaten Lee there, and fording the Rappahannock upriver with 40,000 men to land on Lee's flank. Lee, his army in a precarious trap, did what became his trademark. He took the initiative.

On April 30, 1863, Hooker's main column, now numbering 50,000, with 100 artillery pieces, emerged from the Wilderness and arrived at a crossroads called Chancellorsville where the Chancellor family tavern and inn stood. But instead of pressing the advantage and securing all the lower fords across the river, much to the dismay of his subordinates, Hooker halted and waited for reinforcements.

Stonewall Jackson arrived on the battlefield after riding through the night of May1. He ordered the first Confederates he found to attack the Yankees. His aggressiveness forced Hooker to fall back to a defensive position in the Wilderness. After planning a brilliant offensive maneuver and seeing it halfway through, Hooker was intimidated into assuming a defensive role.

That evening, a momentous war conference took place. At the intersection of the Plank and Furnace Roads, two of history's greatest commanders sat down and planned what has come to be known as one of the most perfect tactical battles in military history. Their war room was the wooded crossroads; their office consisted of two discarded hardtack boxes. For Robert E. Lee it would lead to his most brilliant victory; for Stonewall Jackson, it would lead to his doom.

The Confederate cavalry commander, Maj. Gen. J. E. B. Stuart had brought intelligence that revealed Hooker's right flank was "in the air," with no natural obstacles, such as a river, anchoring the flank to keep it secure. Officers familiar with the Wilderness area were consulted, and a back road was located that would lead directly to the Federals' flank. Sitting on his cracker box, Lee asked Jackson how many men he proposed to take. Jackson answered his entire corps—nearly three quarters of Lee's entire army—would make the dusty march along wilderness roads to find the Federal flank, strike it, and roll it up like a rug. Lee would be left with only 14,000 men to face the entire Federal army. Lee thought for a moment, realizing the dangers if Hooker attacked while Jackson was marching. Ever the gambler, and with supreme faith in his subordinate, he gave Jackson orders to commence.

Early on the morning of May 2, Jackson's column wound its dusty way past the bivouac site of the night before. Lee and Jackson spoke while on horseback one more time. It would be their last meeting.

Reports reached Hooker that a large column was moving across his front. At first he thought that Lee might be headed toward his right flank, but then convinced himself that Lee was retreating. He sent Maj. Gen. Daniel Sickles's Third Corps to attack what he thought was Lee's rear guard. The action pulled more Union troops out of the main line, in essence isolating the Union Army's Eleventh Corps—toward which Jackson's attack was aimed.

Hooker's belief in Lee's "retreat" was bolstered by Jackson turning his column away from the enemy not once, but twice. By 3:00 P.M., after a 12-mile march, Jackson's men spread out on either side of the Orange Turnpike into battle lines stretching a mile. By 5:00 P.M., he was ready, his entire corps in position to strike an unsuspecting enemy. Jackson's corps faced only two Union regiments and a few cannon pointed in his direction. The Yankees were busy cooking dinner.

The Federals were lounging with their weapons stacked. Suddenly, rabbits, deer, and other small game burst from the forest toward them. Then from the darkening woods echoed the call of bugles and the yipping rebel yell, followed by sweat-soaked, wild-looking warriors plunging into the Union campsites. Some Federals tried to resist, but they were swept away. The Eleventh Corps disintegrated.

After two hours, Jackson's assault ran out of steam and slowed to a halt. Jackson, in spite of the darkness, intended to continue his attack as soon as he could re-form his men. He wanted to cut off the Federals from their retreat routes across the river. His plan was to bag the entire Union Army and end the war here and now. He called up Gen. A. P. Hill's division. As Hill's men were replacing the exhausted troops in the darkness, Jackson and his staff rode out in front of the lines to find the Yankees. Satisfied he had found them, Jackson was returning when a nervous North Carolina regiment fired at what they thought was advancing Yankee cavalry. It was Jackson's party. Stonewall was hit by three bullets and carried off the field under fire. A. P. Hill was also wounded, and J. E. B. Stuart was called from his cavalry duties to take command of Jackson's Corps. Because of the difficulty in launching a night assault, and with very little information on the terrain or enemy, Stuart wisely postponed Jackson's planned attack until the next morning.

Stuart knew that Lee's army was still divided and in danger and so devised a massive assault for dawn on May 3 to reconnect the two wings. In the meantime, Hooker began to consolidate his lines and ordered Sickles to withdraw from the high ground at Hazel Grove. Stuart immediately captured Hazel Grove and placed thirty cannons there. At 5:30 A.M., Stuart launched his attack down the Orange Plank Road, shouting to the men from horseback, "Remember Jackson!" Confederates slammed into the Union lines until 9:30 A.M. The woods caught fire and the wounded were cremated alive. The fighting in this area was some of the most intense of the Civil War. In just five hours of combat and within just a few square miles, some 17,500 men were dead, dying, or captured.

During the fighting a shell struck one of the columns on the Chancellor House. Union commander Hooker just happened to be standing there. Though knocked senseless and, for all practical purposes, out of the rest of the battle, his final orders were clear: consolidate, fight defensively, and get the army back across the river as soon as possible. All the fight had gone out of "Fighting" Joe Hooker.

Lee's wing advanced from the south. Stuart's column pushed forward simultaneously until Confederates swarmed around the Chancellorsville clearing. Just as Lee was about to drive the Yankees into the river, word came from Fredericksburg that Sedgwick had driven the Confederates from Marye's Heights and was now closing in on Lee's rear. Lee was forced to split his army yet again and send troops to stop the Yankees. They clashed at Salem Church.

The next day in the fight at Salem Church, the rebels drove Sedgwick's men back across the Rappahannock River. Lee was then ready to finish off Hooker's army. But it was too late. The Union army withdrew across the Rappahannock under the cover of darkness on May 5, ending the fighting at Chancellorsville.

The Federals suffered 17,000 casualties during the battle. Lee lost 13,000, but it was a higher percentage of his army. The incalculable loss was Stonewall Jackson. Complications from his wounds and amputation caused pneumonia to set in and he died on May 10, 1863. It was a loss from which the Confederacy would never recover.

Lee's amazing victory at Chancellorsville against overwhelming odds gave him confidence that his army was invincible. It was a false confidence that would be betrayed less than two months later at Gettysburg.

Chancellorsville Ghosts

In 2007, my wife Carol and I took investigative medium Laine Crosby to the Chancellorsville Battlefield to get her impressions. Laine had never been to Chancellorsville before and had no idea where she was on the battlefield.

Bullock House Site

Intent on protecting their escape routes across the Rapidan and Rappahannock Rivers after Jackson's onslaught, the Federals formed a U-shaped battle line, studded with cannon, behind makeshift breastworks. The Bullock House became the apex of the final Union line at Chancellorsville. Although Lee was ready to attack again on May 6, Union commander Joseph Hooker had already retreated.

Laine's first impression at the Bullock House site was that there was a mix of people in this area: a mix of "gray and blue" and a mix of people on foot and on horses. She felt, however, that there were a lot more people on foot, meaning infantry.

Before her was a broad open field, yet she said that she felt there may have been a house here, or a barn. "There may have been a place where they piled a lot of bodies," she said. "There's an obstacle right there," she continued, pointing toward where the Bullock House once stood.

We stopped in the field before Laine could see the park service interpretive signs. Laine said she felt "a lot of confusion, a lot of things happened here. Randomness, it's mixed together. That group back there, they have bayonets. That group came from back that way," she said, pointing towards the area from which Jackson's men attacked.

"Cannons!" she shouted. "Cannons ran through here." She pointed to the intersection of Bullock Road and Ely Ford Road (Route 610), then over to Route 3. She paused to reflect some more. "They may have actually been sitting here, or pushed through here. There was more of a concentration of cannons here than out there," she said, pointing to the area of the Visitor Center, through which Jackson's infantry advanced.

"I'm seeing mostly people running through there. The concentration of cannons seems behind me. The army came and it was like, well, it's useless, because we could be shooting at our own men. So I don't think that (the cannons) were fired, (at least) not at the time that they were brought, if that makes any sense."

According to Noel Harrison in his book *Chancellorsville Battlefield Sites*, between 1866 and 1868, thirty-five bodies of Federal soldiers were exhumed from the Bullock House area and taken to the National Cemetery in Fredericksburg. No doubt the bodies were gathered—"piled," as she saw it. The "obstacle" she saw at the house can possibly be explained. On pages 13 and 14 of his book, Harrison quoted a Pennsylvania soldier: "At an angle in the breastworks lately constructed stood the White House." As far as the confusion she felt, we know of course that all battles are a jumble of confusion. But in this particular area, the Union Army literally had its "brain" scrambled. General Hooker was trying to recover from being knocked senseless by a shell striking a column at the Chancellor House. The Union commander was lying in a tent at the Bullock House.

Harrison's Pennsylvanian described the confusion, shedding some light on Laine's comments about the cannons: "Officers were coming and going in hot, important haste, some with reports, others with directions. Guns [cannons] hurried to position were crashing to their places." The final Union defensive line formed a semicircle bristling with cannons. The Pennsylvania soldier again reveals what could possibly be an amazing coincidence, or an incredible statement on a psychic's gift. He recalled what the area looked like in front of the breastworks and the Federal artillery: "The open ground in front covered about one hundred and fifty yards, dipped slightly in the centre and terminated in a sparsely-wooded crest.

"In the timber on the crest was a Union line of battle, holding its regular formation, firing and loading with deliberation and slowly retiring."

This would explain Laine's feelings about the cannons not being fired for fear of striking their own men.

Last Bivouac Site

The Last Bivouac site represents the spot where Lee and Jackson planned their most aggressive tactic of the war, which would lead to what is considered Lee's greatest victory. Sadly, it would also lead to his greatest loss: the wounding and subsequent death of Jackson. The site also represents the place where Jackson would spend his last night on an earthly battlefield. If there ever was a Civil War site overflowing with lingering emotions, it would have to be the Last Bivouac site of Lee and Jackson.

Lee and Jackson met around dusk at the junction of the Plank Road and Furnace Road. After being shot at by Yankee sharpshooters, they moved to the northwest corner of the junction, sat down on cracker boxes and discussed the battle and their options. An attack upon Hooker's right flank was one of those. Confederate cavalry commander J. E. B. Stuart arrived with the information that Hooker's right flank was "in the air." Lee and Jackson discussed the details of an attack and then retired for the night, curled up on the damp ground.

Before he lay down, Jackson unbuckled his sword and leaned it up against a nearby tree. One of Lee's aides, Col. Armistead Long, awoke before dawn on May 2 to see Jackson warming his hands by a small fire. He brought Jackson a cup of coffee and sat to talk. Suddenly, there was a clatter of metal from the darkness. Jackson's sword, so carefully placed against the tree just a couple of hours before, crashed to the ground with no human hand touching it. Apprehensively, Long picked it up and handed it to Jackson. Neither man, at the moment, said anything about it, but Long remembered it many years after the war, and knowing what he knew then of Jackson's impending fate, considered it a harbinger of ill fortune. A commander's sword falling to the ground untouched, pushed perhaps by the unseen forces swirling about a legendary Confederate commander may have changed the course of American history. It was one of those strange occurrences that men, upon retrospect, take as omens of a divine will that cannot be denied.

Laine Crosby, during a preliminary field investigation in July 2007, illustrated how mediums can retrieve information from some unknown realm by some yet-to-be-explained method. She had never visited Chancellorsville before, had never been to the Last Bivouac site, and in essence had no idea where she was, yet she came up with information that could not have been in her conscious knowledge.

As soon as we left the car she asked if there had been a dirt road here at the time of the battle. She felt that this was one of the original roads, and in fact, it was the Furnace Road. She asked if a wealthy family had lived nearby, because she saw a lot of girls, giggling and moving, as if they were going to a party. I was fairly certain that no one could prove whether there had been a party in the vicinity, until I reread the segment of Noel Harrison's book, *Chancellorsville Battlefield Sites*. I read that on December 10, 1862, some of J. E. B. Stuart's staff went to a party that Harrison thought occurred at the Alrich House, formerly located near the junction of the Plank Road and Catharpin Road, only a mile southeast of where we stood. Stuart and his staff were known to attend balls or galas and invite all the young women in the area.

Laine then said, "I'm feeling a lot of people, a lot of energy coming this way." She gestured from the intersection of the Plank Road and Furnace Road towards herself. "And they're not fighting," she continued. "They're coming to fight . . . they're going somewhere else to fight. I'm not getting fighting here. A large number of men, not hundreds, but thousands. They're on horses and on foot. They're mixed."

We were standing in the middle of the Furnace Road, in the very space Stonewall Jackson's men marched through some fourteen decades before. She described exactly what Jackson's men were doing: marching a 12-mile flanking maneuver to do their fighting somewhere else. There were some 12,000 men with Jackson. Laine also described exactly how a column of infantry and their officers would have looked traveling on this road.

Hazel Grove

Located upon one of the higher ridges southwest of Chancellorsville is Hazel Grove. The term actually refers to a homestead owned by the Chancellor family. The area became hotly contested during the fighting as the only high ground suitable for artillery use.

A story comes from a park ranger who was at Hazel Grove one evening. It was a beautiful, calm night. He was walking among the cannons placed there to show the battle positions of the Confederate artillery.

The shadows seemed to gather and play tricks with his eyes. That, in the distance, is that a horse? No. It couldn't be. The senses are fooled so easily, especially on a battlefield where so many struggled, suffered, and died. As a park ranger, he knew the vivid and horrifying descriptions of the combat at the site. Then, out of a completely calm night, a strong wind rushed past him, strong enough to rustle the leaves on nearby trees and set the branches clacking. But rustling leaves were not the only thing to be heard that eerie night.

From somewhere within that localized wind came the sound of scores of pounding horses' hooves, so near he could almost hear the squeak of leather and metallic clank of sabers. Then, as quickly as it came, the sound vanished along with the strange wind that seemed to transport the audible impossibility, and the night fell, once again, into a deathlike stillness.

I attempted to capture EVP on two separate occasions at Hazel Grove. On March 4, 2006, I was part of an investigation there and was asked to try to get some EVP. I addressed various officers and men of the Confederacy. The results were positive: I was receiving background "white noise" as well as what sounded like answers to some questions. Some unusual sounds I received were clicks, sounding like someone snapping their fingers. There was no response, other than more white noise, when I asked to hear the rebel yell. The white noise is significant. The recorder is set on voice activation mode so if I don't say anything, the recorder should stop recording. But it doesn't stop, and records something that cannot be heard.

On July 2, 2007, during another investigation, I tried contacting Maj. Pennock Huey and Maj. Peter Keenan of the Eighth Pennsylvania Cavalry, the latter of whom was killed in the fighting at Hazel Grove. Only one appeared to respond. After asking for Major Huey, a rhythmic clopping sound, like horses' hooves was heard, and then what seems to be a muffled, three-beat sentence.

Gettysburg

In the spring of 1863, after the major victory at Chancellorsville, Gen. Robert E. Lee and Confederate president Jefferson Davis determined the time was ripe to attempt a second invasion of the Northern states.

There were several reasons for the Confederate government to launch an invasion that summer, not the least of which was to draw the seat of war out of Virginia so that her farmers could have a growing season without having to feed from the Virginia soil two ravenous armies and their horses. Lee also reasoned that, during an invasion of Pennsylvania, he could send all the supplies he captured back into Virginia to help feed, clothe, and provide transportation for his army (as well as civilians) for the near future. And always, in the back of everyone's minds loomed the possibility of foreign recognition of the Confederacy as an independent nation. Lee and Davis reckoned that a big victory on Northern soil, with the possibility of capturing Pennsylvania's capital, Harrisburg, or Philadelphia would compel France and Great Britain to open full diplomatic relations. Recognition of the Southern states by the world could attract monetary investments, perhaps even military support, and possibly force the North into a negotiated peace. Morale was high when, in the beginning of June, Lee's three corps began their march westward from the Culpeper area of Virginia, got behind the screening mountains of the Shenandoah Valley, and then headed north. For nearly three weeks they marched through the lush valley, cavalry plugging the numerous gaps in order to screen their movement from prying Union eyes. By June 28, Confederates had reached Pennsylvania as far north as Carlisle and as far east as York, having marched through the small crossroads town of Gettysburg to get there. Around that same time, the Federal Army of the Potomac got a new commander, Maj. Gen. George G. Meade.

On the night of June 30, the nerve center for the Confederate invasion was Cashtown, Pennsylvania, in particular the Cashtown Inn, the largest building in the town some seven miles west of Gettysburg. Confederate generals passed in and out of the front door of the inn hundreds of times, delivering intelligence to Gen. A. P. Hill, in command of Lee's Third Corps, who headquartered there.

That evening Gen. Johnston Pettigrew brought the news that he had just been to the outskirts of Gettysburg, saw a large body of enemy cavalry, and heard drums, meaning infantry, behind them. Hill, thinking the Union Army was still in Virginia, did not believe it, somehow discarding fresh intelligence for older. Gen. Henry Heth was present and asked if Hill had any objections to him marching into Gettysburg the next morning to gather supplies, in particular shoes for his men. Hill spoke the four words that would bring on the greatest battle to be fought on the North American continent: "None in the world."

On the morning of July 1, 1863, Heth marched towards Gettysburg from the west and ran smack into Union general John Buford's cavalry stretched out along one of the ridges to the west of town. In spite of being outnumbered, the Union cavalrymen held their own, firing their breech-loading carbines rapidly from the prone position, outgunning the slow-loading infantry weapons, which were loaded from a standing position.

But cavalry can hold out against infantry for just so long. Just as Buford was contemplating how to withdraw, Maj. Gen. John Reynolds, commander of the Union Army's First Corps, arrived with his column of infantry right behind. Pleasantries were passed and Reynolds rode to watch his men spread out into battle lines. He would live only another few minutes before a rebel minié ball would slam into the back of his neck, killing him. He would become the highest-ranking Union officer to die in the battle.

At the first shots, couriers flew to scattered commands, and both Union and Confederate columns began to concentrate on Gettysburg, the Southerners approaching from the west, east, and north and the Northerners, who were attempting to shield Washington from the invasion, from the south. They spread out in parallel battle lines in the shape of two Ls facing each other.

The battle raged to the west and north of Gettysburg, with a brief noonday lull, into the afternoon. Fighting was fierce, particularly in the cuts through the ridges for a yet-to-be-finished railroad. Oak Ridge, an extension of Seminary Ridge, saw heavy fighting as Confederate brigades advanced and were repulsed. North Carolinians of Gen. Alfred Iverson's brigade walked into a virtual trap and lost scores of men in one deadly Union volley. To the north of Gettysburg, artillery shells dropped into Union ranks and musketry riddled men of the Union Eleventh Corps standing in the open fields with no protection except some rail fences.

Finally, Confederates arrived on the field from the east and flanked the Union L-shaped line, which imploded into a general retreat, through the town of Gettysburg to the hills south of the borough.

Just as this was happening, Lee rode up in time to see his hordes driving the enemy from their positions through the streets of the little town before him. Up to this point, he had not wanted to bring on a general engagement; perhaps now, seeing his men victorious, he changed his mind, because instead of retreating or waging a defensive battle, he would be on the offensive.

Overnight, the remainder of the two armies approached Gettysburg. The Federals anchored their line on Culp's Hill and Cemetery Hill and extended it south along Cemetery Ridge; their battle line began to take the shape of a giant fishhook. The Confederate Army of Northern Virginia outlined that fishhook shape curving from hills east of Gettysburg, occupying the town, and then extending down Seminary Ridge, paralleling the Union line on Cemetery Ridge at about a mile distance.

Lee reconnoitered the next morning, saw the curved Union line, and determined his tactics. With the enemy enjoying the advantage of an interior line, he would attack both ends of their line simultaneously, occupying each so one could not send troops to reinforce the other. Surely, thought Lee, one end of their line must give way and he would swarm around their flank, perhaps ending the war here.

Confederate general James Longstreet was to assault the left flank of the Union line early in the afternoon of July 2; upon hearing the sound of the cannons there, Gen. Richard Ewell would launch his attack upon the Union Army's right flank at Culp's Hill.

But Longstreet, in marching into position, thought his movement to the Confederate right flank was discovered by Union wig-wag signalmen on a small, cleared hill, later to be known as Little Round Top. He countermarched his men, found a new route, and finally got into position to launch his attack around 3:00 P.M.

The fighting during the next few hours would be some of the most savage ever encountered by either army. Longstreet's men were opposed initially by Union general Daniel Sickles's Third Corps, which he had advanced without orders. His line, in the shape of an inverted V, was blunted, then flattened, as the Confederates pushed him back through the Peach Orchard at the road to Emmitsburg, Maryland, coincidentally capturing one of the retreat routes for the Federals back to Washington.

Meade poured brigade after brigade into the area to stem the rebel tide: a wheatfield east of the Peach Orchard changed hands several times until it became the Wheatfield, a bloody landmark of the battlefield.

As the Southerners continued their advance, they ran into stiff opposition in an oddly shaped triangular field; Georgians and Texans would fight New Yorkers and Pennsylvanians for its possession. Once the Confederates captured it, they overran the jumble of boulders some locals had named the Devil's Den. But the Confederate line overlapped Sickles's line on his left; where Sickles's line ended in Devil's Den, the Confederate line swept over Big Round Top to the east. The climb to the summit in the summer heat was too much for some of the men and they stopped to rest.

Meantime, Maj. Gen. G. K. Warren, serving with the Union engineers, was observing Sickles's battle from Little Round Top, the smaller hill to the north. He thought he saw some suspicious enemy movement in the woods on Big Round Top. Looking around, he realized that he and a few signalmen were the only troops on the smaller hill, which dominated the southern end of the Union line. He immediately brought Federals to Little Round Top just in time to blunt the Confederate assault up its slopes. One of the heroes of the fighting was Col. Joshua L. Chamberlain, who ordered a bayonet charge when his men ran out of ammunition and stopped the advancing rebels cold.

From the Daniel Lady Farm and Benner's Hill, east of Gettysburg, Ewell's men listened all day as Federals built breastworks and felled trees to clear fields of fire on Culp's Hill. Even the lowliest private knew that the longer they waited, the more deadly the assault would be.

Ewell, who was to attack when he heard the sound of Longstreet's guns, for some reason, never heard the fighting begin on the other side of the field. It wasn't until Lee sent a courier around 7:00 P.M. that Ewell got his men moving. By then, there were only a few hours of daylight left, and Longstreet's assault had spent itself.

Advancing up the slopes of Culp's Hill and East Cemetery Hill, Ewell's men fought in the dusk, then into the darkness, a rarity in the Civil War. By the time the fighting died down, some of the Confederates found themselves sitting inside the Union trenches, gained with firing barely a shot. They were perplexed: Where were the Union troops? They had been pulled from their trenches by Meade earlier to help in the fighting on the other side of the battlefield. At this moment, then, Lee's plan was working. But the Confederates in the Union trenches, although only a couple of hundred yards from the Baltimore Pike and the rear of the entire Union Army, thought they had walked into a trap, and so they halted. They sent out scouts to find the Yankee enemy.

Before long the scouts came back—with Yankees behind them. Finished with the fighting on the south end of the field, they were returning to their trenches on Culp's Hill. Fighting broke out all over again. There was a lull, but then at daylight, they fought some more. Confederates were finally driven back from Culp's Hill after getting so close.

Lee had a dilemma. Supplies and ammunition were running low. He had attacked both ends of the Union fishhook, per his battle plan, and they had held. He reasoned that the enemy line must be weak in the center. Longstreet had a fresh division, Gen. George E. Pickett's, arriving on the battlefield after guarding wagons. With that and parts of two other divisions, Lee would strike at the heart of the Union line, Cemetery Ridge. Longstreet disagreed and suggested a flanking maneuver. Lee responded, "The enemy is there, and I am going to strike him."

At about 1:00 P.M. on July 3, E. P. Alexander opened with his Confederate artillery, stretching nearly the entire length of Seminary Ridge, on the Union position. Most artillery bombardments in the Civil War lasted thirty minutes; this one went on for two hours in an attempt to soften up the Yankee center. Finally, Alexander sent a desperate message to Longstreet: If Longstreet didn't send the infantry soon, Alexander's big guns wouldn't have enough ammunition to support them. Reluctantly—some say with tears in his eyes—Longstreet merely nodded his assent to launch what was to be known to history as Pickett's Charge.

Sadly, the words Pickett's Charge have also come to mean a doomed action. Some 12,500 Confederates, aligned shoulder-to-shoulder with supporting lines, crossed the open plain between Seminary Ridge and Cemetery Ridge. No sooner had they stepped off when Union artillery on Little Round Top found their range. One artillerist thought it was like shooting practice; gaps began to appear in the Confederate lines when men were driven to the ground by shells bursting overhead.

They hit the Emmitsburg Road, lined with a stout post-and-rail fence that wouldn't be broken down. Confederates began to climb over it when the massed lines of Union infantry behind a stone wall on Cemetery Ridge, just 300 yards away, stood and fired. Sons of Virginia, North Carolina, Mississippi, and other southern states crumpled into the road. Under intense fire, they halted, realigned their ranks, and continued the attack. At a spot where the stone wall makes an angle, they rushed the Yankees, driving some back. For a few minutes, Confederates held the stone wall. Brig. Gen. Lewis A. Armistead, his old black hat upon his sword as a rallying point, stood and shouted, "Come on, boys! Give them the cold steel! Who will follow me?" and leapt the wall. Three hundred survivors of the crossing followed but were met by a Yankee countersurge. Hand-to-hand fighting ensued: Muskets were swung like clubs, rocks were used as weapons, and men wrestled on the ground. In ten minutes it was over. The Confederates were driven back over the wall and began their retreat back to Seminary Ridge.

It took about twenty minutes for them to cross the fields, ten minutes of fighting, and twenty minutes to limp back. In those fifty minutes, two-thirds of Lee's attacking force became casualties. When Lee found Pickett, he asked him to gather his division for an expected counterattack. Pickett's tearful answer shocked Lee. "General Lee, I have no division."

That night and the following day, it poured rain. Under cover of darkness on July 4, Lee began his retreat back to the Shenandoah Valley and Virginia. His wagon train of wounded, as it passed the Cashtown Inn, was estimated to be seventeen miles in length.

The casualties during the three days of Gettysburg were not counted in the thousands, but in the tens of thousands: 51,000 killed, wounded, or missing. It would be the bloodiest single battle of the entire war, and the war would last nearly another two years.

Lee, for the most part, would be on the defensive in Virginia. Full diplomatic recognition of the Confederacy by the rest of the world would remain an unfulfilled dream. Years later, when the Confederacy was determined to have been a lost cause, Gettysburg became known as the High Water Mark, the closest they came to victory in the four-year American Civil War, and generations of Southerners would argue who was to blame for the defeat. Someone asked Pickett after the war, perhaps trying to draw him into the war of words and accusations, what was the cause of the Confederate defeat at Gettysburg? His answer was truer than most others: "I think the Yankees had something to do with it."

Gettysburg Ghosts

I have been writing about ghosts in Gettysburg for more than two decades and have heard many stories. Many have been published in the seven-volume *Ghosts of Gettysburg* series. Below are some of the most notable, along with a few recent ones.

The Elevator at Gettysburg College

Probably one of the most famous ghost stories of Gettysburg is the tale of two female administrators from Gettysburg College who were working late one night. The building was once used as a hospital by Civil War surgeons during the battle. Exhausted, the two women left their offices on the top floor and entered the elevator to take them to the first floor where the exits to the massive white-columned building were located.

One woman pushed the button for the first floor and the elevator dutifully announced each floor as they descended: 3 . . . 2 . . . 1. It then went past the first floor and headed to the basement.

The two women rolled their tired eyes, and the one pressed the button for the first floor again, but the elevator continued down and stopped in the cellar of the edifice. The doors began to slowly open on a scene out of time and reason.

Wounded men lay writhing in blood-dampened corners, orderlies of a century before moved about carrying crimson rags, and a surgeon stood with an uplifted saw about to amputate the leg of a semicomatose soldier lying on a makeshift operating table.

Now, not knowing into what hell they had descended, the women panicked and slammed at the buttons in the elevator to no avail. The elevator remained frozen. Just then from around the corner, not two feet from them, came an orderly in a blood-stained apron. He caught them with his gaze, pleading with his eyes to either let him on the elevator with them and remove him from the hideous scene in which he had been trapped for twelve decades, or to come with him, come off the elevator to help with his never-ending labors forever.

Slowly, mercifully, the elevator doors began to close. The women ran immediately to the security office. The officer on duty, who I interviewed, said, indeed, the women were sincere in their report. This was no hoax; they were almost literally scared to death. Yet, when he asked if they would return to the scene with him, they reluctantly agreed.

The elevator at Gettysburg College's Pennsylvania Hall sometimes delivers visitors into a Civil War hospital scene.

Perhaps it was because he had mentioned something about being able to catch one of the college fraternities, obviously conducting a stunt, that they felt less apprehensive about revisiting the scene.

Within two minutes they were back. They boarded the elevator and descended to the basement. The doors slowly opened, but to a scene of pristine cleanliness, the reams of paper and spare printer cartridges all lined up neatly in the locked cage where they had been stored, the white-painted cinder-block wall holding the electrical boxes not ten feet from the door to the elevator. Disappointed, the security guard pressed the button to ascend to the first floor. Perplexed, the women left the building wondering what had just happened to them.

In paranormal theory, what those who rode the elevator into hospital hell experienced is called a *warp*, or a tear in the fabric of time. Strictly speaking, virtually every sighting of a ghost or scene from the past could be considered a warp.

Their experience could be written off as just two tired women experiencing what is clearly impossible—a dream of exactly the same scene. Except for one thing. It happened again.

I was autographing books at the Gettysburg College Bookstore a few years back. A young couple came up and purchased some *Ghosts of Gettysburg* volumes. They said that they already owned the first book. The man leaned a little closer and said,

"You know your elevator story? We're friends with the woman that happened to."

I was interested that these two strangers and I had a mutual friend, "Oh," I said. "Then you know . . ." and I mentioned the names of the two participants in my original story. The puzzled look on their faces was disturbing.

"No. We've never heard of those people. Our friend's name was . . ." and they gave me a completely different name.

At first I was confused. "That's not the name of either of the people I wrote about."

The looks on their faces were just as adamant. They knew this woman personally; she was a solid, upright individual. She wasn't the type to make things up. I asked them what she had told them.

She had been working for an accounting firm out of Lancaster, Pennsylvania. They were doing an audit at Pennsylvania Hall because it was the administration building for Gettysburg College. Someone had asked her to go to the cars parked outside and get some papers. She got in the elevator. The elevator malfunctioned and, instead of stopping at the first floor, it descended into the basement and into a scene for which she was not prepared: men being sliced up like pieces of butcher's meat by a bloody surgeon; men in dank, rust-colored corners, quivering from shock and loss of blood; and orderlies carting piles of crimson limbs from operating table to weltering corners, dark and slick with blood.

I asked them if they were still friends and they said yes. I asked if she still lived in Lancaster and they said no. She lives in Denver, Colorado. I asked if they minded if I called her. They said no problem and gave me her number.

A few days later I called. She was pleasant and not reluctant to talk about her experience, although still, in her voice, was that tone that can only be described as questioning what exactly had happened to her that afternoon. She repeated the story I had heard from her friends almost verbatim. She added a few details that her friends had not known about. It is my experience after interviewing hundreds of witnesses to the paranormal that the events leave an indelible impression on people's minds that is usually never forgotten until death—and perhaps not even then.

This, then, makes three individuals at two separate times who have experienced a descent into what would seem to be the impossible. (At this writing I am tracking down what may be a third incident involving the elevator that drops into a man-made hell on earth.) Of course, if these separate incidents were all that has occurred in "Old Dorm," they would be enough to convince even the most ardent skeptic that something out of the ordinary was happening there.

The Blue Boy at Stevens Hall

Other stories from Gettysburg are nearly as legendary. There's the Blue Boy of Stevens Hall on the Gettysburg College campus, whose face—and face alone—hovers on cold winter nights outside the window to peer in at the young women studying on the third floor.

The fact that the youthful face levitates to the third floor is strange enough. Stranger still is the fact that it is tinged a deathly blue, as if the boy has spent too much time out in the cold. Rumors from the college hint that his countenance has been seen recently

Gettysburg College's Stevens Hall, home to the famous Blue Boy.

as well. And an experience by a family on a ghost tour places a sighting within the last year.

In 1994, I created walking tours based upon my *Ghosts of Gettysburg* books. The first route took our customers down Carlisle Street and through the Gettysburg College campus.

Nearly everyone who takes our tours wants to know: Have the guides ever seen anything spooky or heard any stories of the supernatural at Gettysburg? The answer is yes, and at least one guide on our Carlisle Street tour took the time to record a bizarre and unexplainable sighting at Stevens Hall.

During his tour he noticed a man, woman, and boy standing by the pine tree near Stevens having an animated conversation. After every other person in the tour had left, they approached the guide. The man, referring to a statement our guide had made at the beginning of the walk, asked, "You said you don't set anything up on these tours, right?" Our guide answered in the affirmative and, curious, asked if the man had seen anything. The man began to say something, then stopped and said, "No, forget it. You'll just think I'm crazy." Our guide assured him that, in our business, we hear a lot of weird things from completely sane people.

Convinced that he would not be ridiculed, the man began his story. He said that while the guide was telling the tale of the Blue Boy, he had noticed a movement in a bush at the northwest corner of Stevens Hall. He claimed that there was a face peering out from the bush. His wife concurred: She saw the same thing. Both said that it appeared to be the face of a young boy, perhaps fifteen or sixteen years old, and that the face had a strange bluish tinge to it. Interestingly (and perhaps a clue to the paranormal nature of the sighting), the man saw the figure from the waist up, yet his wife only saw the face. Whoever it was, he appeared to be playing hide-and-seek with them. Whenever they would look toward the bush, the indigo-tinged face would pull back into the foliage; when they looked away, he would appear again. The guide asked if they could see any style of clothing or hat. The husband said that he appeared to have some type of hat. The guide, who was dressed in period clothing, pointed to his own slouch hat, but the man said no, it was more like a cap. The guide was a reenactor, and the headgear the man described sounded to him like the famous short-brimmed forage cap so common to the American Civil War soldier.

The Woman in White at Spangler's Spring

Gettysburg has its own Woman in White who roams the battlefield near Spangler's Spring for some unknown reason. She seems to be searching for something known only to her. Although the original story I heard came from unknown sources, at least six others have had eyewitness encounters with the Woman in White.

One gentleman who grew up in Gettysburg recounted how, as a boy, he rode his bicycle out to Spangler's Spring at dusk and saw, across the fields, a particularly upright column of mist that would move and then seemingly collapse to the ground, then rise up again as if it were intelligently searching for something, or someone, lying on the ground around it. For several minutes, he watched the "mist" doing something he'd never seen mist do before or since.

A woman in white is said to roam the area around Spangler's Spring, at the base of Culp's Hill in Gettysburg.

Then there were the two nurses who went out on the battlefield one Halloween night in search of ghosts. They both were amused about their quest, being solid, no-nonsense individuals both by temperament and vocation. Yet when they parked at Spangler's Spring and began to see the apparition of a young, lovely woman grow from a small ball of light at the base of one of the trees, their reactions told of the strange alternate reality whose horizon they had just crossed.

One was so moved she began to cry. "She's so beautiful . . . and so sad." The other in the passenger's seat was so frightened she started the car and helped the driver, who was nearly blinded by tears, to steer out of the area.

The Phantom Battalion at Little Round Top

Another sighting that would seem to take on legendary status is the famous Phantom Battalion, or Phantom Regiment. The story was originally told to me by one of the older park rangers at Gettysburg and apparently happened to him sometime in the early 1960s, before the reenacting craze had taken hold. He was accompanying some dignitaries around the battlefield and they had stopped at the summit of Little Round Top for the view and an explanation of the fighting there. Just as they were about to leave, a unit of soldiers marched from the woods below, began a demonstration of their military skills maneuvering about the field, and then retreated back into the woods.

The dignitaries were impressed that the National Park Service thought they were so important as to put on such a demonstration just for them. When they returned to the park headquarters, they demanded to see the supervisor and proceeded to thank him vociferously for the battle reenactment he had arranged just for them.

Needless to say, both rangers were utterly confused because no program was scheduled, nor were there enough reenactors in the entire nation at that time to put on such a show, but managed to assure the visitors that they were glad the dignitaries enjoyed their "experience."

Since I heard the original story, several more have emerged, mostly centered on the same base of Little Round Top or the Wheat-

The Phantom Battalion has been seen in this area of the second day's battlefield at Gettysburg.

field area of the battlefield. The best example is the story of a family out on an early-morning battlefield tour.

A woman, her son, and their dog were on a dawn excursion. They had just turned off of the Emmitsburg Road onto the Wheatfield Road and were cresting the hill at the Peach Orchard when they saw a large unit of Union soldiers marching across the misty field. She stopped the car to watch, but something seemed out of place. Their dog was growling, apparently seeing the same thing the humans were witnessing. Impressed with what they thought was a crack reenactment unit in an early-morning drill, they watched for several minutes. The group of soldiers, in perfect alignment, wheeled, about-faced, marched around, and then did something no reenactment unit has yet to accomplish. As some joggers crested the hill, the soldiers vanished into thin air.

The dog growling at the Phantom Battalion is more important than it would seem. When humans witness a paranormal event, we do it with numerous explanations as to why what we are seeing cannot be real—something under my contacts, my imagination, I must be hallucinating, I had too much to drink, and so on. Animals, especially dogs, simply become "alert." If they are alert to something, it must be there; they must be seeing something. That is why accounts of animals "seeing" ghosts—and they are numerous—are indicative of the existence of ghosts.

The Cashtown Inn

During the off-season in Gettysburg, with the interest in ghost hunting piqued by various television programs, we conduct paranormal investigations with our team of experts in the field. We'll offer a weekend stay in one of the local haunted hotels or bed-and-breakfasts and conduct several investigations of known haunted sites.

One of the more active and perennial haunted sites is the Cashtown Inn, a restaurant and bed-and-breakfast about seven miles west of Gettysburg. It dates back to the late eighteenth century, and during the Civil War, it served as both the headquarters of Confederate general A. P. Hill and a field hospital on the Confederate retreat, so the potential for ghosts lingering there is quite high. Scores of experiences from overnight guests, former and current owners, and our investigations confirm everything that has been said about the place is true.

One night another member of our team and I placed a Bushnell infrared gamecam in the bar of the Cashtown Inn. This type of cam-

An infrared camera captured this image of an entity after closing time at the Cashtown Inn.

era was designed to take pictures of animals at night moving along a trail in the woods using infrared technology. We knew that the owner locks the bar every night after he closes, so it would be secured until morning. The nice thing about the gamecam is that you don't have to stay up all night to capture any activity. As well, everything is time-stamped. The next morning when we examined the camera, at 35 minutes after midnight, there's a bright, human-shaped figure moving past the trip zone. It's a great picture of the owner as he is finishing locking the bar. Then, at 44 minutes after midnight, there is another figure that trips the camera. No one was in the locked bar when the photo was taken. There is no explanation—no natural explanation—as to what the image is. But there certainly is a supernatural explanation.

Gettysburg & Northern Railroad Engine House

One of the other highly active spots is the Gettysburg & Northern Railroad engine house, which sits on a part of Gettysburg's first day's battlefield not owned by the National Park Service. Since the railroad is privately owned and the engine house is posted, the house is another site exclusive to our investigation team. Two-hour investigations there have yielded numerous EVPs, including communication from "Em," who was originally very loud—so loud as to make the EVP unintelligible. Finally, I asked Em if she could talk a little more quietly.

Upon playback, in front of a number of skeptical railroad executives, a female voice whispered, "I'll be quiet."

On later investigations, a road safety barrel was forcibly kicked by an unseen foot from a tire upon which it was resting, and footsteps on an engine were heard by everyone in the group. The sounds of someone invisible walking lasted for eight minutes. I asked the manager if that engine might be cooling off and contraction of the metal the cause for the noises. He replied that the engine had been parked there for a month, was cold, and had been drained of all liquids.

Ghosts of Gettysburg

Another site we investigate is the Ghosts of Gettysburg Candlelight Walking Tours® headquarters, a structure which dates back to 1834. One of the misconceptions visitors to Gettysburg have is that the ghosts only hang out on the battlefield. What they fail to realize is that the town itself was battlefield, too. Several spots in the town were fought over, such as Kuhn's Brickyard in the northeast corner of town. Confederates chased down and shot Federals on the streets visitors drive on. A chaplain was mistakenly killed on the steps of a church on Chambersburg Street. A "rubble" barricade was built across Baltimore Street right in front of the Ghosts of Gettysburg headquarters building for Confederates to fight behind.

There are several resident ghosts in the tour headquarters building, including the feisty Mrs. Kitzmiller, who bought the house right after the battle and owned it longer than anyone; several soldiers from Georgia who may have been wounded and brought to the house; and "Hank," a Louisiana soldier who goes on duty after the lights are turned off. Several people have literally "run into" Hank and all report he is "linebacker-sized." At least two children's spirits remain in the house. In a recent experiment, they moved pendulums on a rack while setting off an EMF (electromagnetic field)

The Ghosts of Gettysburg headquarters in Gettysburg, believed to be home to several ghosts.

Jeff Ritzman took this photo of a child's shadowy apparition.

meter, all recorded on video, of course. Members of our group have been pushed by the invisible children. The bathroom door handle has been jiggled by tiny, unseen hands. And three distinct footsteps coming down the wooden steps were heard by me and the group members—and everyone in the group was already downstairs! Mrs. Kitzmiller, a proper Victorian lady, tells our mediums she's upset that my wife Carol doesn't put out cookies and tea for our guests, not realizing that in modern times, without a food license, that might be illegal. After Carol put out some tiny wafer cookies as a gesture, I asked Mrs. Kitzmiller how she liked the cookies. The EVP was adamant: "I hate them," a disembodied voice said.

Finally—but not really since the ghosts in Gettysburg are continually surprising us—a paranormal research group was given permission to stay overnight in the house to see what evidence they could gather. Along with recording EVPs and taking measurements of anomalies with various instruments, around 2:00 A.M. they became the target of the children in the house.

They were in the front part of the house when they heard what they described as children laughing and playing in the back (the oldest section) of the house. They picked up their gear and moved to the back and set up their equipment, only to hear the children had moved to the front of the house. Again they chased the children, only to be disappointed again. Finally, one of the investigators set up a camera in the middle room and took a series of photos into the oldest section of the building, with excellent results.

Vicksburg

The National Park Service calls the Mississippi River at the time of the Civil War the most important economic feature on the continent. Certainly, it was a great waterway for advancing gunboats, heading north or south. Whoever held the Mississippi could split either country down the middle. And at the beginning of the war, the Confederates held the great river, cutting off the lifeblood of the Union.

President Abraham Lincoln was familiar with the geographical importance of Vicksburg, Mississippi, a major city on a high bluff overlooking a bend in the river: He had navigated the Mississippi as a youth. He thought Vicksburg was even more important than New Orleans in opening the waterway. Taking Vicksburg would reopen the Midwest to world markets; it would also complete the naval blockade by closing the loop around the Confederacy.

In the spring of 1863, Gen. Ulysses S. Grant started his army on a march down the west bank of the Mississippi River, over almost impassable terrain, creating bridges and corduroying roads when necessary. The plan was to rendezvous with the U. S. Navy at a place called Hard Times, Louisiana.

On the night of April 16, 1863, the Federal Navy under Adm. David Dixon Porter began its operation to pass below Vicksburg and meet Grant. At the big bend in the river, they were spotted by Confederate lookouts. Bales of cotton on the shore were set afire to illuminate the river and Confederate batteries opened on the flotilla. Despite the bombardment and numerous hits from shore artillery, Porter's ships made it past Vicksburg and headed toward Grant's army to the south.

Confederate batteries at Grand Gulf overlooked the proposed crossing point on the river. Despite a massive naval bombardment, the batteries could not be silenced. Grant, displaying the tenacity for which he would become known, moved his army farther south and crossed the Mississippi with 17,000 men at Bruinsburg.

The first serious Confederate threat to Grant's march inland took place at Port Gibson; however, 8,000 Confederates were no match for Grant's force of 23,000. After fighting most of May 1, victorious Federal soldiers continued their march into the heart of Mississippi.

Rather than heading directly for Vicksburg, however, Grant headed inland, determined to capture the Southern Railroad of Mississippi and cut off the major land supply route to Vicksburg. On May 12, Union forces defeated the Confederates at the Battle of Raymond and continued their march toward Jackson.

As well as being the state capital, Jackson was an important rail and communications hub. Capturing Jackson would assure that Grant could squeeze off the flow of troops in his rear. So important was Jackson to the Confederates that President Jefferson Davis ordered Gen. Joseph Johnston to take command of the city. Once there, Johnston wired Davis, "I am too late," and ordered the city evacuated. In a pouring rain on May 14, Union general James B. McPherson began an attack and drove what Southern troops remained back into the defenses of Jackson. William Tecumseh Sherman's troops were also successful in their assaults, and Jackson was evacuated. The military necessity of not wanting to leave combat troops to guard Jackson forced Grant to burn factories, tear up rails, and destroy telegraph equipment. Grant then turned his army westward towards his real objective, Vicksburg.

Every soldier knows it is better to fight a battle outside of your own perimeter than inside. Confederate general John C. Pemberton, in charge of the defense of Vicksburg, was aware of that as he marched his army to the east to meet Grant. On May 16, the two commanders engaged at Champion's Hill.

Federal troops, after hard fighting, took Champion's Hill by 1:00 P.M. Later, Confederates won it back. A renewed effort by Grant's overwhelming numbers drove the Confederates once again, and Pemberton withdrew from the field. Grant continued his march toward Vicksburg.

Grant's army defeated Confederates at Big Black River Bridge on May 17. Success after success made them seem unstoppable. Then they attacked Vicksburg's formidable defenses and, on May 19, attacked Stockade Redan. Though they planted the United States colors on the works, the Federals under Sherman were repulsed, losing 1,000 casualties.

Reconnoitering more carefully, Grant planned another assault for May 22. After a four-hour artillery bombardment, his troops advanced along a three-mile front. Federal flags were again planted on the outer works and there was a brief breakthrough at Railroad Redoubt, but the Union assault was repulsed, this time with a loss

Gun emplacements at Vicksburg National Military Park.

of more than 3,000. Grant knew that even with his resources, he couldn't sustain those types of losses indefinitely. On May 26, Grant began siege operations, cutting vital supply routes into the city and digging approaches to the Confederate lines with the plan to tunnel under them and blow them up.

By June 25, the charges were laid under the Confederate lines and detonated. Union troops surged into the huge crater formed by the explosion. Fighting raged, much of it hand-to-hand, for twenty-six hours, until the Confederates finally drove off the Federal attackers. On July 1, another mine was exploded beneath the Confederate fortifications, but no infantry assault was launched. By then, five weeks of short rations, constant bombardment, disease, mounting casualties, and a lack of reinforcements convinced Pemberton that there was no hope in sight to save Vicksburg for the Confederacy. On July 4, 1863, he surrendered the city to Grant. As Lincoln phrased it, "The Father of Waters again goes unvexed to the sea."

On that day in Pennsylvania, Robert E. Lee was preparing his shattered army for retreat after their disastrous defeat at Gettysburg. Though fighting would continue another twenty-two months, the fate of the Confederacy was sealed.

Vicksburg Ghosts

Terry Winschel, one of my housemates from my days as a park ranger in Gettysburg, became an historian at Vicksburg. A couple of years ago, my wife and I visited Vicksburg, and Terry took me on one of those unforgettable tours of the battlefield. After realizing that the fighting at Vicksburg was every bit as savage and important to the war's outcome as the fighting at Gettysburg, I asked Terry, "Why did Gettysburg get all the attention?" He said simply, "Two minutes." I shook my head, confused. What two minutes in two huge battles could have made such a great difference in the notoriety of the battlefields? "The Gettysburg Address," he said. If Lincoln had travelled to Vicksburg to deliver the address, essentially rededicating the nation to the unfinished business left before them, it would have been called the "Vicksburg Address" and the acclaim may well have gone to the city on the Mississippi.

The other thing I asked him was about the ghosts of Vicksburg. Had he heard any good ghost stories? "Mark, I've been here thirty years and haven't heard any about the battlefield. The town, yes. But not the battlefield." Then, to test a pet theory, I asked him about the geology of Vicksburg. What was below us? "About 100 feet of Mississippi River silt." Any granite? Apparently not for at least 100 feet.

As I have mentioned before, one of the theories of how human emotion in the form of electromagnetic energy can be captured and then, under specific conditions, be replayed is geologic: Quartz embedded in granite fieldstone can be affected by the burst of electrical energy when humans are killed or wounded. Most of the battlefields with plenty of ghost stories have the ubiquitous granite near the surface of the earth. Vicksburg obviously was different geologically. Yet, some have reported ghostly sightings on the battlefield.

The Illinois State Memorial

Ray Couch is one of the experts in the field of ghost research. He has hosted paranormal investigations all over the country, conducting experiments, and has visited many more sites purported to be haunted. Vicksburg was one of them. He brought about 20 people to the battlefield on October 13–15, 2006. His wife Sharon was one of them. Ray tells the story:

> On the Saturday of our weekend, we visited the battlefield with our group. We drove through the property and stopped as a group at several of the monuments. Our fourth stop was the Illinois State Memorial. As we made our way up the steps and entered the monument, everyone was respectful but in good moods. We began to read the names and I witnessed Sharon begin to become very quiet. Thinking she was having a moment, I left her alone, but shortly, I realized something was wrong. She began to seem out of sorts and began to shake. She caught herself against the wall of the monument and I had to help her back down to our car. She was actually crying and said the left side of her body felt numb. She said she saw a young soldier in her mind and saw him covered in blood. His eyes had a sad look and seemed to try to communicate with her. The feeling of his sadness stayed with her for the rest of the weekend.

What Sharon experienced was empathy, or feeling the same physical hurt and emotional sadness the spirit of the young soldier felt at the time he had been wounded. Some sensitive people are clairvoyant (clear seeing), some are clairaudient (clear hearing), but all the human senses can be involved, including that feeling of empathy, not only for the living, but for those dead who suffered greatly before they died.

The Pennsylvania State Memorial

Ray Couch's visit to Vicksburg illustrated another paranormal event that has been proven scientifically. He continues the story of his visit of October 2006:

> We visited the Pennsylvania monument late in the afternoon. We had about 15 people in our group and this was one of the last places we visited on the battlefield. We visited this location with no prior knowledge about the area. Waiting for everyone to get out of their cars, I became distracted by the feeling of being watched. We were the only people in the area, but the feeling was palpable. The feeling was coming from the wooded area behind the monument and it never left the entire time we visited here. Sharon refused to get out of the car. She felt a feeling of intense anger coming from around the monument and it shook her enough that she didn't want to leave the car. Others in our group felt similar feelings and one lady got so scared that she actually got in our car and sat with Sharon. Later that day, we bumped into some other investigators on the battlefield. They asked if we had visited the Pennsylvania monument because it was one of their favorite locations on the battlefield. I asked why and they said there were tons of stories of people feeling overwhelming feelings of being watched or feeling threatened in that area. Some people even report that the faces on the monument seem to actually watch the visitors.

Rupert Sheldrake, a renowned British biochemist who has written extensively about studying paranormal events scientifically, published a book in 2003 called *The Sense of Being Stared At*. In it he describes experiments he conducted placing people with their backs to a door in a room that had a window in it. A person would be told to relax or read. Periodically, an experimenter would look in at the person through the window. More times than not, the subject would turn around, aware that they were being stared at. Sheldrake tried it with a television camera pointed at the subject and a monitor into which an experimenter would occasionally peer. The results were the same. The subject would usually acknowledge when he was being stared at.

We've all had the same thing happen: You suddenly feel as if someone is watching you from behind, and then you turn and see your spouse standing there. What happens, though, when you have exactly the same feeling, you turn around—certain you're going to see someone—and no one is there? Is no one there, or just no one visible?

Old Court House Museum

Ray Couch related the following after visiting the famous Old Court House Museum in the city of Vicksburg:

> We visited the Old Courthouse Museum the day before we came home. Walking into the area, you just felt the history. The Court-

Several ghosts are said to be in residence at Vicksburg's Old Court House Museum.

> house is just so Southern, you almost expected to see Atticus Finch come walking down the stairs. The museum contains a large number of items from the Civil War and you will begin to lose track of time very quickly. Before we left, of course, I had to ask the staff if there were any ghosts still making themselves known. They actually had a surprising number of stories. There are footsteps that come from empty hallways. There is a Confederate soldier still seen walking around the cupola long after his tour of duty ended. Our group reported cold spots and EMF [electromagnetic field] spikes. We had to leave much too quickly, but I look forward to setting up an investigation here in the future.

The Soldier in the Fog

Finally, Ray Couch wrote of an encounter of the visual kind in early 2008:

> About two years after our first visit, I returned to Vicksburg with a friend of mine. We were only in Vicksburg for a day, but I wanted to see the battlefield. The weather was cold and it was overcast and a light rain was falling when we visited the park. We quickly decided to just stay in the car and drive through the park. We were the only people in the area and were driving along at around 5 miles per hour. We were driving up Union Avenue near the Michigan Monument when a foggy area began to move off to the right side of the road. The fog was actually moving across the road and just seconds before we were going to drive into it, it began to take a shape. I swear it looked like a Confederate soldier crossing the road. He was dressed in grayish clothing and was carrying a rifle. As we drove into the fog, he lost form and just swirled away. Goosebumps popped up on my arms and I twisted around in my seat looking back. I never saw him again. I sat in my seat and didn't say anything for several seconds, then I said, "I thought that fog looked like . . ." At this point my friend cut me off and said, "It looked like a Confederate soldier, I ran right into him. I didn't want to say anything because I was afraid I was seeing things." We drove around for another couple of hours, but never saw anything the rest of the day. That night, we were in a bar and had time to think about it. We both saw the exact same thing, including the fog just swirling apart as we drove through it. I know what I saw and I will never forget it.

McRaven Home

The McRaven Home on Harrison Street in Vicksburg is considered by many one of the most haunted houses in Mississippi—if not the entire country. Built in 1797, it was originally just a kitchen and room above. At that time it was used as a hiding place by Andrew Glass, a well-known highwayman who preyed upon travelers along the nearby Natchez Trace. One story has him wounded during an attempted robbery on the trace and brought back to his house. As the law closed in, Glass determined they would not get him, and he ordered his wife to administer the coup de grace within the walls of the tiny upstairs room.

In 1836, Sheriff Stephen Howard purchased the building to live there with his pregnant wife Mary Elizabeth. He expanded the house by two rooms—a dining room with a bedroom above. It was in that bedroom that Mary Elizabeth gave birth to their first child and then died from the complications of childbirth. The sheriff raised his child alone in the house for a number of years.

In 1849, John H. Bobb purchased the house. By 1863, during the Civil War, Bobb rented out the ground as a campsite for Confederates and saw his home turned into a makeshift hospital for those wounded during the siege of Vicksburg. The house was damaged by Union artillery and some believe that several soldiers died on the property and in the house. When Federals occupied Vicksburg, they began indiscriminant looting of gardens for food, including John Bobb's garden. He confronted them. The argument ended with Bobb using a brick on a Union soldier's head, after which they took him out and shot him several times just 300 feet from the house. His grieving wife, Selina, sold the house and moved to Louisiana.

One of the first ghost stories of McRaven comes from the *Vicksburg Daily Herald* of July 22, 1864, which reported that the spirit of a Confederate soldier who died in the house was seen by Union soldiers stationed there. He had manifested himself so clearly that the observer could see that he was "tall, gaunt, and hungry looking." He appeared to have an area around his eye that had been mutilated and his head was bandaged. He was dressed in white—perhaps his winding sheets. According to the website for *Mississippi Paranormal*

Times, he may be the same soldier who has been seen frequently "hovering" about the place more recently on the front porch and in the parlor.

In 1882, the Murray family purchased the house. One by one the Murrays moved away or died and left the house in disrepair. By 1960, the Bradway family bought the property and began restoration of the house, opening it up for tours. In 1984, Leland French purchased McRaven and was the first one to live in it since the last of the Murrays went to a nursing home. He continued the tradition of opening it up to tours.

Those who know the house well say that the room that Mary Elizabeth Howard died in is particularly active, perhaps haunted by the spirit of the young woman who was denied the opportunity of seeing her child grow up in the house. When her husband moved, he left her wedding shawl in the room where she died and those who picked it up said that it was hot to the touch, as if someone had just worn it and put it down. Others have had it snatched from their hands. Periodically visitors will see the apparition of a dark-haired teenage girl wafting down the stairway. She's been seen in other areas in the house. Lights are turned on and off, evidence of a poltergeist. Or perhaps Mary Elizabeth just wants some attention.

Civil War soldiers, many of whom were cared for or died in the house, have made their presence known in various ways in and around the house. John Bobb, murdered for defending his home, is believed to be the territorial ghost who roams the property, according to the website *Haunted Places to Go*. In addition to Mrs. Howard and John Bobb, some of the Murray family apparently still reside in the house, as well as a young slave boy and other soldiers from the siege.

Leland French apparently had some violent encounters with one or more of the spirits of McRaven. A drawer was slammed so hard on his hand that it broke his thumb. In his own parlor he was shoved by some unseen hand hard enough to make him fall, hitting his face and breaking his glasses. He needed stitches around his eye. One night he was ascending the staircase and realized someone was following him. He turned and recognized from his archive of old pictures the long-dead Mr. Murray. French realized that what was going on in his house was beyond what he could handle, and he called in an Episcopal priest to bless the house. He then bought a small house down the street and moved out.

While the house was open to tourists, one tour guide fell asleep on the couch between tours. When he awoke, the wraith of the cruelly murdered John Bobb stood glowering over him. The guide quit immediately. In spite of the house blessing, lights still flickered, doors still slammed on their own, and sightings of former owners continued. The security alarm would trigger after hours; inspections revealed that no one had entered the building. Chairs have mysteriously tipped and slammed down, armoire doors have opened and closed on their own, and beds are seen to depress as though people are reclining upon them, although no bodies are visible.

The Mississippi Paranormal Society conducted an investigation of the house, reported on their website *Mississippi Paranormal Times*. For the seven hours they remained, they were besieged with evidence of a haunting. As they moved through the house to set up equipment, doors were slammed in their faces and behind them. Two of the team actually received scratches on their skin, indicating a spirit not at all happy about having them there. In the short time they investigated, they gathered fifty EVP samples and four video clips showing paranormal activity.

Chickamauga

If the Battle of Gettysburg ended the last Confederate invasion of the North and the fall of Vicksburg opened the Mississippi River cutting the Confederacy in half, the battles for Chattanooga, Tennessee, drove a saber into the very heart of the South.

Trained, professional officers would rather maneuver an opponent into an untenable position than risk their soldiers' lives in assaults. Union general William S. Rosecrans did just that when facing Confederate general Braxton Bragg. Marching his 70,000 troops through three gaps in the mountains, Rosecrans drove Bragg's 43,000 troops into Chattanooga, then swung his troops to the south—as Bragg guarded the Tennessee River crossings to the north—and pried Bragg, in late August 1863, out of the major rail center of the mid-Confederacy.

Bragg's army reinforced, bringing 66,000 troops to the battlefield in northern Georgia that would be named after Chickamauga Creek, a Native American name that meant "River of Death." The moniker would prove prophetic.

Just after dawn on September 19, 1863, fighting broke out. The armies surged back and forth across four miles of ground, sometimes fighting hand-to-hand, staining the autumn fields with their blood. In their attempt to get between the Union Army and Chattanooga, the Confederates drove the Federals back to the LaFayette Road, which bisects the battlefield. On the morning of September 20, Bragg attacked again, but was stymied. Then, the Federals inadvertently brought destruction on to themselves. Around 11:00 A.M., Rosecrans heard from a subordinate about a gap in the Union line where a division was supposed to be positioned. The report was not true, but Rosecrans acted upon it by pulling a division from another part of his line to plug the mythical gap. His timing couldn't have been worse, because just at that moment, Confederate troops commanded by Gen. James Longstreet struck the newly created gap, routing two Federal divisions. The rout became precipitous and eventually included Rosecrans himself and two of his corps commanders. Col. John T. Wilder's brigade of mounted infantry, even though armed with Spencer seven-shot repeating rifles, could not hold back Longstreet's juggernaut.

Confederates took aim at Snodgrass Hill, to which the remnants of the Union Army retreated. Their repeated assaults were turned back by Federals desperate to hold and buy time while the rest of their army withdrew to Chattanooga. Fortunately they were commanded by a tenacious Virginian who remained loyal to the Union, Maj. Gen. George H. Thomas. For his role in repulsing the Confederates until dark, he earned the nom de guerre the "Rock of Chickamauga."

The Union Army continued its retreat into Chattanooga and Bragg's Confederates pursued, gaining seemingly impregnable positions overlooking Chattanooga on Missionary Ridge and Lookout Mountain. The two armies left behind some 34,000 casualties, making Chickamauga the second-bloodiest battle in the entire Civil War.

Chickamauga Ghosts

A Civil War battle was horrifying enough. After the first shots were fired, chaos reigned and nothing was logical. The mind reels. Time takes on a life of its own, either rushing by or slowing to a crawl. For some it stops altogether. Humans survive or are transported in an instant to that gray land we all will visit sooner or later. The aftermath of battle is not much better. Death seems to appear in its most creative forms, like some modern artist gone mad, flinging bodies and body parts hither and yon, leaving unrecognizable lumps of flesh strewn or piled across once-pleasant fields and meadows. Add to that the wounded—moaning, crying, motioning to attract attention, and trying to crawl, with Death hovering nearer always. And then time passes and the spirits seem locked to these places of suffering, such as at Chickamauga.

Women in White

To the nightmare scenario come the women: wives, sweethearts, sisters, mothers, nurses. They have heard of the battle from miles away and have come to help or find a loved one perhaps hurt in the struggle. What they find is the carnage. Searching for an individual in a field filled with hundreds, or even thousands, of dead and wounded would seem an impossible task. The heart must break every time a body is turned over and the face is not recognized, or worse, unrecognizable. Still they moved with their lanterns, like living ghosts, through the horror, stopping, bending down to try and help or to recognize a bloody, mud-covered countenance; failing, and moving on.

Perhaps this is why nearly every battlefield has a Woman in White story. And so it is with Chickamauga. She, apparently, was a young bride-to-be who lost her fiance to the hungry monster of war. No one knows if she ever found him, but if the dozens of modern sightings of visitors are true, sadly, she still seeks him.

"Who is the young lady in the bridal gown with the lantern?" visitors inquire to perplexed park employees. The answer never comes or is circumspect because she really doesn't exist—at least on this plane of life.

Old Green Eyes

One of the truly more mysterious ghost stories of any Civil War battlefield is that of Old Green Eyes from Chickamauga.

Visitors to the battlefield report seeing two glaring green dots peering from the woods. According to Georgianna C. Kotarski in

"Old Green Eyes" has been seen in the area of the Wilder Tower at the Chickamagua battlefield.

her book, *Ghosts of the Southern Tennessee Valley*, one woman who worked in Fort Oglethorpe, the town nearest the battlefield, in 1980 was taking a shortcut through the battlefield in her car. Near the famous Wilder Tower she was confronted by a pair of green eyes, level with her own, and only about twenty feet from her. Her mind raced as she went through the catalogue of local creatures it might be—raccoon, deer, squirrel—but she realized none was appropriate to what she was seeing. Whatever it was frightened her enough: She sped off the battlefield and refused to use that shortcut again.

Stories of Old Green Eyes go way back. There were rumors from the 1870s that it would kill Union veterans visiting the park. It was said that bodies of men were found mauled by some large creature.

Some theorize that Old Green Eyes might be a large cat (not the domestic variety) or a bear. Others speculate that it is one of the stone monuments come to life. There are those also convinced that the creature (or, some say, demon) predates even the battle, that some soldiers saw the ghoulish thing roaming among the dead and wounded. Old Green Eyes may have been left from the Cherokee days after they abandoned the area around the River of Death. As Kotarski sagely asks, "Was this ghoulish entity present long before the white man's madness, part of a dark past lost to history? Or was it lured to the battlefield by the unspeakable horror of new death and despair?"

According to paranormal investigator Gina Lanier, on the website *HauntedAmericaTours.com*, Old Green Eyes will sometimes approach you, and you will hear groans coming from the creature. Lanier writes that a park ranger related that in the 1970s, two different drivers crashed into the same tree in the park claiming to have seen Old Green Eyes. Lanier also gives the report of a man from New Mexico who claims that he saw Old Green Eyes on several occasions and even took a picture of the entity. He described the shape as a "black shadow-like human with a glowing face with a large nose," and added ominously, "but it wasn't human." And it had glowing green eyes.

Cryptozoologists might be interested in some of the other sightings on the Chickamauga battlefield chronicled in Kotarski's book. A man recounted his experience as a Boy Scout camping in the park. He saw something large and hairy that started to cross the LaFayette Road near the Florida Monument. He described it as between 7½ and 8 feet tall. It started walking across the road standing upright, and then it went down on all fours into a "gallop." He thought it might be a grizzly bear because it was so tall, yet grizzlies are not endemic to the park. Or, perhaps, it was the legendary Old Green Eyes.

Snodgrass Hill

Other unexplainable events have occurred within the confines of the park as reported by Kotarski. Sounds out-of-time have wafted through the woods and across the fields. Drums rattled and fifes played for over an hour to the bewilderment of some Boy Scouts on Snodgrass Hill, where the Union rear guard held their ground far longer than soldiers should have been forced to hold.

The boys investigated. As they approached the Snodgrass Cabin, a landmark on the battlefield, the martial music ceased and was replaced by another sound, just as confusing. It had started to rain, but the boys suddenly heard the distinct sound of footsteps of a dozen or so individuals rush away from them and enter the woods. One of the leaders took charge and explained that, for some reason, they were not supposed to be on that spot at that time. The boys left, their questions unanswered.

Chattanooga

After Gen. Braxton Bragg's Confederate victory at Chickamauga, disheartened Union forces retreated to Chattanooga. Confederates took positions overlooking the city on Lookout Mountain and Missionary Ridge. The Federal forces were plagued by a supply line that was far too long, over inadequate mountain paths, and vulnerable to Confederate cavalry raids. It was only a matter of time before the defeated Union troops from Chickamauga would have to face their nemesis again or be starved out of Chattanooga.

President Abraham Lincoln made several strategic moves that indicated he understood how important that section of the Confederacy was to the Union cause. First, he sent reinforcements, some 20,000 men under the command of Maj. Gen. Joseph Hooker. While Hooker had been a failure as commander of the Army of the Potomac at the Battle of Chancellorsville in May, he would soon resurrect his reputation as "Fighting Joe." Maj. Gen. William T. Sherman arrived with an additional 16,000 troops in mid-November.

Lincoln also made an important change in command. Maj. Gen. George H. Thomas replaced the demoralized William S. Rosecrans as commander of the Army of the Cumberland and Maj. Gen. Ulysses S. Grant arrived to take overall command.

One of the major problems facing the Union Army at Chattanooga was that 60-mile-long supply line. On October 27–28, in a daring riverborne assault, Union troops boated down the Tennessee River on pontoons and past Confederate batteries on Lookout Mountain to establish a pontoon bridge at Brown's Ferry, significantly shortening what the troops named "The Cracker Line," after hardtack, their food staple. With rations and supplies now readily available, Grant was ready to go on the offensive.

Grant's battle plan was to use Hooker and Thomas to threaten Bragg's left flank on Lookout Mountain and the Confederate center on Missionary Ridge. Sherman was to cross the river at Brown's Ferry and march to a point above Chattanooga, then cross the river again in pontoon boats to make the main assault on Bragg's right flank. Once Sherman dislodged Confederates on that flank, he would roll south down Missionary Ridge, sweeping it of Confederates. Hooker and Thomas would pressure them from the front.

Sherman's march was slowed by muddy roads and the assault was postponed. Grant was vexed: One Union army under Ambrose Burnside was in Knoxville, Tennessee, about to be attacked; he also heard that Bragg was about to pull out from his position. Was he going to Knoxville?

In order to ascertain if Bragg's army was still in position, on November 23, Federal forces took 100-foot high Orchard Knob, an advance Confederate picket post. They determined the main Confederate Army was still in place on Missionary Ridge.

Bragg's position was formidable. Missionary Ridge rose 600 feet above Chattanooga. His left flank appeared even more impregnable: Craggy Lookout Mountain rose 1,400 feet above the river and would require an assaulting column to climb hand-over-hand in some places. At Missionary Ridge, Bragg's men had dug in at the base in rifle pits. After Grant took Orchard Knob, they also began to dig in along the top of the ridge as well.

Sherman began his waterborne crossing just after midnight on November 24. By dawn he had two divisions or about 8,000 troops on the southern bank of the Tennessee River, just above and below where the South Chickamauga Creek empties into it. Federal engineers soon had two pontoon bridges across the Tennessee River and Chickamauga Creek. In all, four divisions would soon begin an assault on the Confederate right flank of the Missionary Ridge line. At about 1:30 P.M. the attack began.

Sherman's problems began when the men reached the summit of what they thought was the northern end of Missionary Ridge. The terrain was deceptive. Instead of being a part of the main ridge, this crest was disconnected from it with none of the expected Confederates present. Beyond a saddle was another hill and the Federals began their climb through the misty afternoon to that summit. They finally found the enemy and drove them off. But they also found that they were still not on Missionary Ridge. With only about an hour of daylight left, Sherman halted and dug in, his mission for that day a failure.

Hooker, on the other end of the line, around 9:30 A.M. on November 24, began his attack on fog-shrouded Lookout Mountain. Instead of assaulting Confederate troops head-on up the mountain, fighting the terrain as well as the enemy, Union troops advanced along the slope and struck the Confederates in the flank. The Confederates continued to fall back until they reached the Craven House. They attempted a final defense there, but as the fog lifted briefly, everyone saw that the colors flying over the breastworks at the Craven House were Union flags. Hooker's sweep down the east side of Lookout Mountain was halted by darkness and the fog rolling in again. Most on the Confederate side had reckoned the mountain a natural, impregnable position. By late afternoon, Bragg was ordering what Confederate troops were left on Lookout Mountain to retire and join the rest of the army on Missionary Ridge.

As foggy as November 24 was, the next day dawned bright and sunny, but cold. It wasn't until 11:00 A.M., however, when Sherman continued his assault on the position before him. Midwesterners under Sherman attacked troops from Texas head-on. The Confederate commander facing Sherman was none other than Patrick Cleburne, the "Stonewall Jackson of the West." He made a skillful defense of the area he named "Tunnel Hill" after the railroad passing through the mountain. Cleburne shifted his troops from one endangered area to another, utilizing the terrain to his best advantage. Cleburne's tactics were to flank the dug-in Federals, then assault head-on, driving them back through the saddle until they themselves were finally stopped around noon. Union assaults resumed, and by 2:00 P.M. it seemed as if Cleburne's defense was about to crack. Bolstered by reinforcements, he ordered an attack all along his line. By 4:00 P.M. the Yankees retreated, leaving Tunnel Hill to Cleburne's Confederates.

While this battle was raging, Grant thought he could relieve some pressure on Sherman's flank attack by occupying the rest of the Confederates on Missionary Ridge. He gave orders for Union troops to take the lowest line of rifle pits, then halt and reform to prepare for the assault upon the ridge. The mere presence of Union troops in the rifle pits at the base of Missionary Ridge, he hoped, would be enough to draw Confederates from their defense against Sherman.

The Confederate defenses looked formidable: 16,000 troops defended about three miles of entrenchments. The Union effort was to involve 23,000 attackers advancing across almost a mile of open terrain. There were those rifle pits to capture and the main Confederate force looming above.

Grant's orders were counterintuitive to some of his field commanders. To halt at the rifle pits would expose their men to fire from above and a counterattack. Nevertheless, at 3:30 P.M. the advance began. Once the Northern troops drove the Confederates from the lower rifle pits they realized one thing: The closer they stayed to the retreating Confederates, the less fire they received from above; Confederates on top of the ridge did not want to fire into their own retreating men.

As the Union troops broke from the rifle pits, Grant was surprised and concerned. He wanted to know who ordered the continuation of the attack. None of his subordinate generals had. It appeared to be a spontaneous assault by his men. It was an incentive even the lowliest Federal private understood: Follow the retreating Confederates as closely as possible to avoid being shot from above. Follow them they did, leaping from the captured rifle pits and following their colors in inverted Vs, up the rugged slope of Missionary Ridge to the summit where in brief fighting, they drove the center of Bragg's army from its supposedly impregnable position.

Grant, caught off guard by the sudden victory, had no plan to pursue Bragg. The next day he sent part of the army to do just that and another part to relieve Burnside's army in Knoxville. His pursuit of Bragg was stymied again by Patrick Cleburne in a rear-guard action at Ringgold Gap, ending the Chattanooga campaign.

Bragg's Army of Tennessee reported casualties of 6,667 men. Just as catastrophic to the Confederate cause as the loss of men was the loss of some 40 cannon. Grant lost 686 killed, 4,329 wounded, and 322 captured or missing. Strategically, Chattanooga lived up to its nom de guerre, the "Gateway to the Heart of the Confederacy." Tennessee was lost to the South.

Chattanooga Ghosts

In early June 2011, my wife Carol, author Katherine Ramsland, and I visited the Chattanooga area and stayed overnight on Lookout Mountain. Katherine's family was originally from the area; her ancestors walked the infamous Trail of Tears.

In the morning we stopped at a drugstore. Katherine asked the crew behind the prescription counter if they had any ghosts on Lookout Mountain. One of the women smiled and looked like she was about to tell us a story, but the man behind the counter gave us an untrusting scowl, and they all denied having ghosts. But a couple of published works say otherwise.

Lookout Mountain

In 2006, Georgianna C. Kotarski published *Ghosts of the Southern Tennessee Valley* and related a story the occurred near Fort Oglethorpe, the nearest town to Lookout Mountain. A woman living in the vicinity had heard that on the anniversary of the Battle of Chickamauga you could hear hoofbeats and the clank of metal of a phantom army, apparently retreating from the battlefield. She also said that she had seen a woman in early-twentieth-century clothing walk from an abandoned home above on the ridge and into her yard. The woman, she was convinced by her actions, was a phantom.

A male friend's interest was piqued and they decided to do an ad hoc paranormal investigation. At 2:00 A.M. they went out into her

Author Katherine Ramsland takes in the view of Chattanooga from Lookout Mountain.

yard. All was deathly quiet. The moon was up. At first they may have thought their eyes were playing tricks on them. But after several seconds they realized what they were seeing: From a grove of oak trees, a white orb emerged. In addition to being bright and perfectly formed, it also displayed what might be considered intelligent movement, avoiding the limbs of the trees, landing upon one, and then descending to the ground. Soon it broke into two more "ghost lights."

As they reached the ground, they transformed into three human-sized shapes standing before the man. He started to approach them and got the distinct feeling they were young Union soldiers. He saw details. They wore blue Federal uniforms and two of them were carrying another soldier who had a huge bullet wound in his stomach. But, he realized, they were all dead. The other unnerving thing: They were staring at him. He was convinced that they saw him as well, making this an "intelligent" haunting, wherein the ghost actually acknowledges the presence of the living, sometimes even speaking to the percipient. He told them aloud that they were dead, had died over a century ago, and that they needed to go to the light. The forms coalesced back into orbs and faded into the trees.

The nearby road and gap in the mountain is historic. On their retreat from Chickamauga to Chattanooga, Union soldiers limped along as rapidly as they could, fearful of being captured by the Confederate pursuit. They helped wounded friends, or when hope and strength gave out, lay down by the roadside to die.

An entire book was written by Larry Hillhouse called *Ghosts of Lookout Mountain*. Most of the stories are pre- and post-Civil War; a few are related to the battle that took place on the rugged mountain.

A small group of Union soldiers had been cut off from their comrades. Exhausted, some wounded, all lost, they began to inch their way along the east side of Lookout Mountain moving northward, running into pockets of enemy troops and unfriendly locals.

Finally, there were just a handful of them and they got lost on a dark, rainy night. They'd walked in a circle and were seen by locals passing at least three times, finally heading south into some nasty terrain with steep drop-offs, sinkholes, and caverns. There was a well-worn path below, but they apparently never found it. They simply disappeared and were never seen again.

But shortly after the war ended, people in the area began to talk about some strange noises they heard on the last rainy night. They claim to have heard voices coming through the hissing rain and the sound of marching men in the distance. Some witnesses hear cursing, crying, and even wailing, as if someone were in horrible pain.

Some actually investigated the sounds the next morning, of course, and found some interesting and unexplainable evidence. There, where the sounds came from, were boot prints in the drying mud, as if several men had marched by. But the prints were unusual: they simply started out of thin air and ended a hundred or so yards away.

Another tale of Lookout Mountain related in Hillman's book is about a dedicated Confederate sentry who took a post during the war high up on the mountain that overlooked all the roads the Union Army would have to use in maneuvering around the area. So dedicated was he to his cause that when the Union Army took the mountain, he remained hidden, coming out periodically to signal his comrades of the enemy's movements. Soon he ran out of food and water, but refused to surrender, and he died at his post. Though he passed on well over a century ago, some see his signals still. People have witnessed, at night, a light up on the mountain where no light should be. Occasionally, in the daylight, from the same spot, they will see a bright flash of light. Could it be that the sentry, with dedication to duty that can only be called supernatural, is still sending messages to an army that lives now only in the history books?

More recently, in 2009, a father posted the story "The Ghost of Lookout Mountain" on his blog *Traveling Poor*. His family was staying at an eighty-year-old hotel on the mountain. The next morning, the woman, who was staying in a separate room, was angry when she awoke and accused one of the boys of sneaking into her room and turning her heater to air-conditioning, making her room freezing. (It was December!) The child, she claimed, also turned off her TV, which she liked kept on while she slept. The young man denied it, but she claimed she'd heard him walk down the hallway, apparently to go to the bathroom, and she waited for him to return and be upbraided by her. Oddly, he never returned.

The man relating the story thought she must have been dreaming, but then remembered that he had had to get up a couple of times that night to reset his heater, which had been turned to air-conditioning as well. And he recalled that his TV also was acting strangely. It had changed channels at least five times without anyone touching the remote. Paranormalists believe that ghosts operate in the infrared realm of the light spectrum, which is why near-infrared cameras can sometimes capture images. Most TV remotes also operate using an infrared beam to the sensor on the TV. Could this explain who was changing his channels?

The next night, the children were in the bedroom watching TV. Suddenly they ran screaming into their father's room. Someone unseen had opened and closed the door to the balcony. Upon inspection, the man realized that the door would have to be unlocked and the handle turned before it could open, and would have closed against the wind. After doing some research, the man found out that their hotel was built on part of the mountain that had been a battlefield.

Missionary Ridge

Though ghost stories about the place seem to be scarce, Missionary Ridge has an interesting energy that produced some powerful EVP.

Carol, Katherine, and I had driven through Chattanooga and along Missionary Ridge. Most of the ridge is privately owned, with large to huge homes, most with a marvelous view across the city, encompassing the Tennessee River and Lookout Mountain. The ridge itself is long, high, and steep, and I again found myself in amazement at the near-superhuman endurance the soldiers of the Civil War possessed. The climb from the rifle pits below would tax the strength of any modern-day professional athlete, yet these men of our Civil War, in spite of excessive use of tobacco and consuming not nearly enough calories for the amount of work they were doing, marched themselves into good enough physical conditioning to scale a height like Missionary Ridge.

The view from Lookout Mountain looking west towards Missionary Ridge.

The monument to the Second Minnesota Regiment atop Missionary Ridge in Chattanooga.

There are reservations, National Park Service historic sites, along the ridge where we stopped and I attempted to collect some EVP. On my first attempt, I actually "cut off" someone answering my question. On the second try (#1229), whoever it was that was answering me tried to cut me off—they actually inserted some unintelligible words in an area where I paused to collect my thoughts during my question. This comes at 3.5 seconds into the recording. At 7 seconds in, I get the answer, "Men at night," and at 12 seconds there is more unintelligible garble.

In recording #1233, I ask if it was difficult climbing the ridge. I am answered with a couple of statements that don't really make any sense—and then one that might, if a soldier were tired or wounded and felt he was in the way of others attempting to climb beyond him: "Get round of me."

Finally, in recording #1234, I get four answers to my question. At 4.5 seconds, you hear three of the "clicks" like fingers snapping, and the "clink" of metal; at 8 seconds, there is the answer "yes," then birds can be heard chirping; at 11 seconds, there is something unintelligible recorded; at 17 seconds, the words "all right"; and at 20 seconds, the distinctly military "Forward!"

Richmond

In late February 1864, Union general Judson Kilpatrick led a cavalry raid on Richmond that was a failure, yet attracted more attention than almost any other raid in the war. The reason: It was considered by many in the South to be terrorism.

Though the word "terrorism" has more modern roots, the idea was the same: Strike fear into the hearts of the noncombatants by some amoral act outside the rules of civilized warfare. Because of an alleged plan described in some papers found on the body of one of Kilpatrick's subordinates, the Dahlgren Affair has stirred controversy for decades. It has also led to several ghost stories.

During the winter of 1863–64 it was learned that conditions in Southern prisoner of war camps was deteriorating rapidly. Some 1,500 prisoners were dying every month. Lincoln wanted to do something about it, especially in Richmond.

After an aborted raid by Union general Benjamin Butler launched from Fort Monroe at the beginning of February 1864, Kilpatrick won the president's ear and got his permission to raid into the Confederate capital for three purposes: The first was to free Federal prisoners from Libby and Belle Isle prisons; the second, to disrupt Confederate communications with their armies in the field; and third, to distribute amnesty proclamations to the rebels in Richmond.

On February 28, Kilpatrick and 3,600 cavalrymen left the Culpeper-Stevensburg area of Virginia and rode southeast. At Mount Pleasant the column split, with twenty-one-year-old colonel Ulric Dahlgren taking 460 troopers with him. He was to cross the James River and strike at Richmond through the weaker southern defenses. Kilpatrick was to meet him after he rode through the city and attacked the northern defenses of Richmond from behind.

It was a good plan, but it faltered when Dahlgren was ambushed north of the James. Kilpatrick, upon not finding them coming to his aid north of Richmond, abandoned Dahlgren's men to their fate. Young, impetuous Dahlgren, already missing a leg from earlier action, was killed.

Two items stained the noble cause of freeing Union prisoners. First, when Dahlgren's body was discovered by the ambushing rebels, papers were found on him. They were the draft of a speech he was going to give his men but apparently never did. In the speech was the implication that once the cavalrymen got into Richmond, they would "release the prisoners from Belle Island first & having seen them fairly started we will cross the James River into Richmond, destroying the bridges after us & exhorting the released prisoners to destroy & burn the hateful City & do not allow the Rebel Leader Davis and his traitorous crew to escape."

A second document stated, "The men must keep together & well in hand & once in the City it must be destroyed & Jeff. Davis and Cabinet killed." Finally, in his pocket notebook was written, "Jeff Davis and Cabinet must be killed on the spot."

Richmond Ghosts

Dahlgren wanted to cross the James River on March 1, and was given the name of Martin Robinson, an ex-slave who was skilled in the trade of bricklaying. The U. S. Provost Marshal's office recommended Robinson because he had helped escort escaped prisoners from Libby northward. Dahlgren promised to pay Robinson well if he found them a safe crossing point on the James River. But then he warned Robinson that if Dahlgren suspected treachery, Robinson would be hanged on the spot.

Robinson had just crossed the Rapidan River the night before and rode with confidence that he could find a crossing of the James. But when they arrived at the ford across the river, the water was too high and rapid to cross.

Robinson looked confused, realizing what this would mean. Dahlgren inquired if there was somewhere else nearby where they could cross. Robinson just slowly shook his head. Dahlgren ordered a noose and had the black man hanged from a nearby tree on the side of the road. The column rode on to its fate.

One source states that Southerners in the area allowed the body to hang for a week as a notice to local blacks what Yankees really think of them. It has been speculated that the phantom seen wandering the area at night is the spirit of poor Martin Robinson, rashly executed for something out of his control, still seeking the ford across the James that could have saved his life.

In his book *Civil War Ghosts of Virginia*, L. B. Taylor Jr. found other stories associated with the raid from local newspapers. One was of a slave named Burwell, so loyal to the Ben Green family that when Dahlgren's Yankees came to look for the family silver, he refused to tell them where it was hidden. They dragged him out of the house on Three Chopt Road and strung him up by his thumbs. The house today exhibits paranormal events that are attributed to the tortured spirit of Burwell, who for his faithfulness suffered so much pain.

Another ghost that may stem from the ill-fated raid has been heard on Cary Street Road near where a honeysuckle thicket and some woods stood near an icehouse. An officer of Dahlgren's blundered into a sniper hidden in the brush and was shot from his horse, mortally wounded. Today those who venture near the area on quiet nights have their solemnity shattered by moans, allegedly from the suffering Yankee officer.

The Wilderness

On May 4, 1864, the Army of the Potomac began crossing the Rapidan River, looking to turn Lee's right flank and then head south. Lee, without Longstreet's corps, was vastly outnumbered and realized that his only chance would be to fight Grant in the tangled, wooded area of this part of Virginia known as the Wilderness, nullifying the Northern numerical superiority until Longstreet arrived. The Confederate Army's salvation lay in audacity, which fortunately for them was their commander's hallmark.

Around 7:00 A.M., May 5, as their army marched southward, Union pickets on the Orange Turnpike saw Confederates digging defensive trenches across Saunders Field, one of the few clearings in the Wilderness. When word got to Meade that Lee was nearby, he halted his advance through the tangled forest to confront him, thereby blundering into Lee's battle plan.

By noon, Confederate general Ewell had nearly 10,000 men dug in along the western edge of Saunders Field, extending on either side of the Orange Turnpike, supported by another 4,500 men in reserve. Under orders from Lee not to bring on a general engagement until Longstreet arrived, they could only watch as columns of blue-clad infantry snaked their way across their front. A race began for the junction of the Brock and Orange Plank Roads as the opposing commanders realized its importance: If

Confederates gained the crossroads, the Union Army would be blocked from further advance.

Union general George Getty and his staff arrived at the crossroads ahead of his troops. Advancing Confederate infantry opened fire on the little group. Suddenly, from down the Brock Road came figures in blue. They swarmed into the crossroads, loosed a volley to hold the approaching Confederates, and Getty and his staff, miraculously with only one wounded, withdrew to their proper posts. When Union skirmishers pushed out, they found wounded Confederates only thirty yards from the Brock Road. It had been that close.

Finally, six hours after being ordered, Maj. Gen. G. K. Warren began his advance west on the Orange Turnpike against Ewell's dug-in Confederates. Almost immediately, unit cohesion was lost because of the tangled thickets, scrub brush, and thorn bushes. A few minutes before 1:00 P.M., the Union assault reached the open country of Saunders Field. Instead of the large force Meade wanted attacking the Confederates, a much smaller force—one quarter the size—was all that could be organized for the assault. As soon as the diminished Federal attack entered the clearing, they came under fire from Confederates some 400 yards away.

Farther south, the Union attack bogged down, literally, in a swamp near the Higgerson Farm. The units slogged waist deep in water until they veered off to several points of the compass. More than one of the soldiers believed their officers must be drunk.

Because of the repulse of those Union forces, the Federal advance units had to withdraw. This left both avenues—the Orange Turnpike and the Orange Plank Road—available for the Confederates to advance along.

The butcher's bill was growing. Saunders Field was filled with the dead and dying; those who were ambulatory, Union and Confederate alike, made it to a gully and lay down with faces to the earth to avoid the crossfire from both sides. One unit, the 146th New York, took forty-six percent casualties; Zouaves of the 140th New York suffered a debilitating fifty-one percent killed, wounded, and missing. Then, as bad as things had been, they got worse.

Discharges from Confederate muskets set the dry tinder in Saunders Field on fire. The wounded who could crawl attempted to escape from the licking flames. Those who couldn't crawl roasted. One man with two broken legs was seen watching the flames creep closer and closer, his musket loaded and capped beside him. Cartridge boxes of the crawling wounded caught fire; the black powder inside burned and popped. After the fire died out, the living noticed strange, charred, smoking lumps throughout the field—the cremated remains of those trapped in the holocaust. By 2:30 P.M., the Union attacks, like the fires in Saunders Field, had died out. They were failures because of the piecemeal, premature fashion in which they were made.

Yet another Federal attack was made north of the Orange Turnpike by fresh troops who had marched past partially burned corpses. Confederates there purposefully set the woods on fire to stall the Yankee attack. Soldiers were wounded not only by flying lead and iron, but by flying body parts of their comrades. Maj. Gen. John Sedgwick's aide was adjusting a piece of horse equipment when he was knocked almost unconscious by a human head, hitting him at nearly the velocity of the shell that separated it from its former owner and covering the aide with blood and gray matter.

By 4:00 P.M., this second round of fighting on the Orange Turnpike ended, leaving the smoky, choking, flaming maelstrom of the Wilderness the only victor.

In the meantime, Meade ordered Getty to advance along the Orange Plank Road from his position along the Brock Road. Meade

A contemporary view of the Wilderness battlefield.

assured Getty that he would be backed up by more Union troops under Maj. Gen. Winfield S. Hancock. By 4:15, without Hancock's men yet on the field of battle, Getty began his assault.

To the south of the Orange Plank Road, a Vermont brigade tried its luck against the Confederates. One regimental commander, Col. Newton Stone, was shot in the thigh, got bandaged and returned, like someone drawn inexorably to his own demise, to be shot in the head and killed. Four more commanders in the brigade were shot down. Although the Vermonters tried to attack again, it was useless, and the men lay down under fire to await support.

On the other side of the Orange Plank Road, Union units were not faring any better. Mounted upon his horse, Brig. Gen. Alexander Hays began to address one of his regiments for inspiration. The ringing speech was cut short by the eerie, hollow sound of a soft, lead bullet smashing into his skull.

By 4:45 P.M., after the collapse of a Union division, Confederates were closing in on the Brock Road and Orange Plank Road intersection. Confederates were within minutes, if not seconds, of taking the Brock Road when Hancock's lead elements entered the battlefield and, with barely enough time to align their ranks, pitched into the fiery woods and drove the rebels backward.

Around 6:00 P.M., Union assaults on the Orange Plank Road against A. P. Hill's frazzled corps were renewed. Grant had determined correctly that there must be a gap between Ewell's and Hill's corps. As Union troops drove toward the gap, only 150 men from the 5th Alabama had remained unbloodied. The unit was so small that it was being used to guard prisoners. The tiny group charged, screaming the rebel yell at the top of their lungs. In the dusky, smoky, confusing forest of the Wilderness, they apparently sounded like a massive assault. The attacking Federals stopped and fired blindly, their forward impetus blunted. The fighting along the Orange Plank Road died with the light. The two opposing lines were a few dozen yards apart, close enough to hear each other digging in, their talking echoing eerily in the hazy woods.

While the fighting along the Orange Plank Road progressed into the waning daylight, the battle to the north, along the Orange Turnpike, flared again.

Grant had received some information that Confederates were leaving the vicinity of the turnpike and heading south, toward the Plank Road. Deducing that Ewell's line must be weakened, he ordered renewed assaults. The intelligence, however, was faulty. The Union attack upon that flank failed and the woods again caught on fire.

Grant's proposed massive push against Ewell never materialized, and by 10:00 P.M., the firing along the lines died. All night the men could hear the cries of the helpless wounded and the ominous crackling of the fires creeping closer and closer to them. The groans became piercing shrieks as the flames burned the wounded to death.

Overnight Grant issued orders to round up every available soldier and put them in the ranks for a final, death-dealing blow to the Confederates. His plan was simple and massive: attack Ewell on the turnpike and Hill on the Orange Plank Road; Maj. Gen Ambrose Burnside's fresh troops would drive between the two attacking wings toward the center and divide Lee's army. On Lee's part, there was nothing to do but wait for Longstreet to come up with his corps. The fate of his army, particularly in the face of the overwhelming Federal superiority in numbers, depended upon it.

The Union attack began at about 5:00 A.M., May 6. The Confederates, expecting to be relieved by Longstreet during the night, had not entrenched. The immediate result was predictable: Confederates were driven back to the Widow Tapp Farm, where Lee had his headquarters. To blunt the Union fire, Confederates propped wounded Federals up against trees ahead of their position, reasoning the advancing troops would not fire toward their own. The unorthodox tactic worked.

By 5:15, while Hancock's Union troops were driving the Confederates back along the Orange Plank Road, there was still no sign of Burnside's force, which was to exploit the Confederate center. A Union attack from the north by Brig. Gen. James S. Wadsworth's troops upon the Orange Plank Road did materialize, however; in fact it only added to the confusion as the troops intermingled with Federals attacking from the east and jammed the battlefield with superfluous troops.

As Union units reached the eastern edge of the Widow Tapp's fields, they were greeted by the pounding of a dozen Confederate cannon—William Poague's guns—firing at a slow cadence, their shells angling across the Orange Plank Road. Overwhelming numbers, however, were with the Yankees. Poague's gunners were only buying time, and everyone knew it. Slowly the Federals began to lap around the edges of Poague's position. Each minute brought doom nearer to Lee's army.

Then, from behind the Widow Tapp Farm, came Longstreet's First Corps, having marched an unbelievable thirty-two miles in twenty-four hours. Whatever fatigue the men felt upon approaching the battlefield must have been allayed by their realization that they were saving Lee's army from destruction. Swept up by the charge that was to save his army, Lee himself started to lead it. But Longstreet's Texans would have none of it. Several grabbed his reins and tried to turn horse and rider. It wasn't until Longstreet himself rode up to assure Lee that he could stem the Yankee tide that Lee went to the rear.

The Texas Brigade paid dearly for the honor of fighting under the eyes of Lee. With no other units flanking them, they marched into a stand-up, eyeball-to-eyeball fight with a superior number of Yankees, a mere twenty yards away. It went on for twenty-five minutes. When it was over, the brigade fell back, leaving nearly 550 casualties, or almost seventy percent of their number, marking the area where they stood and fought. But they stopped the Federal advance.

In the meantime, Grant's planned 5:00 A.M. attack along the Orange Turnpike to the north was beaten to the punch by Ewell's men, who leapt from their earthworks at 4:45 and began an assault. The two sides fought to a standstill. The Wilderness again affected battle tactics: Unable to see one another, combatants merely took aim at the sound of the others' firing. By 8:00 A.M. the musketry died down

Burnside's men began their march toward the Chewning Farm between the Orange Turnpike and Orange Plank Road at about 6:30 A.M. Although already nearly two hours late, Burnside inexplicably called a halt so his men could cook breakfast and coffee. As they ate, the men could hear fighting on either side: Sedgwick battling Ewell to the north and Hancock tangling with Longstreet to the south. At 7:30, Burnside was under way to connect with Hancock.

By the time Burnside's men marched onto the battlefield, Confederate artillery began peppering them and rebel infantry loomed before their route. Burnside realized that the Confederates had taken the high ground at the Chewning Farm and called a halt to the advance.

While Burnside remained stymied, Union attacks from the north on Longstreet fizzled out. It seemed that a coordinated attack was impossible to achieve. By 10:00 A.M., Longstreet and Hancock had done nothing more than to stalemate.

Earlier, a report came to Longstreet about an unfinished railroad bed that paralleled the Orange Plank Road and then angled away from it. Longstreet devised a plan to use the bed as an avenue for an attack upon Hancock's left flank. At about 11:00 A.M., Confederates swarmed over one of the several swales between the railbed and the Union flank. The attack made it to the Orange Plank Road and beyond.

Officers on both sides continued to be shot down. Wadsworth was attempting to reorganize his troops when Federal refugees from Longstreet's railbed attack came rushing by. A rebel bullet slammed into the back of his head, showering a nearby staff officer with his blood and brains. Wadsworth's quivering, still-breathing form lay insensible near the road.

Longstreet rode in front of his column of infantry with his staff and officers. Confusion, par for the course in the Wilderness, now dealt its cruelest blow. The Confederate flanking column was just crossing the road as Longstreet and his entourage approached. Mistaking them, through the smoky air, for Yankees, they fired. Longstreet himself was hit. A large, powerful man, the bullet hit him in the neck and lifted him visibly from his saddle.

With the commander of the Confederate wing wounded and out of the action, the attacks in the sector ground to a halt. Lee's line straddled the Orange Plank Road, parallel to Hancock's Union line, both in a generally north-south orientation.

Burnside, meanwhile, had reorganized his troops to continue his assault southward. But before the attack could begin, Burnside had to have lunch! A veritable champagne picnic was presented to him and his staff, which they paused to consume. Finally, some eight hours after he began his march, he launched his attack upon Longstreet's flank. Had Hancock pushed his men out from the trenches toward Longstreet, who knows what could have been gained. As it turned out, Hancock was frozen, intimidated some said, by the disorganization wrought by his previous few hours fighting in the Wilderness.

Hancock, no doubt, felt secure behind the chest-high log earthworks his men had thrown up all along the west side of the Brock Road. They had cleared a field of fire and had artillery backup. But at 4:15 P.M., their attention was focused by the sound of Confederates, screaming their rebel yell, charging across the clearing, only to be stopped by Federal musketry. Instead of falling back, they hit their knees and slugged it out with Union infantry at thirty yards.

As the two sides blazed away at each other, the intervening brush caught fire. The wind just happened to be blowing toward the Federal line. Soon, the log breastworks flared, and the flames and choking pine smoke did what the rebels could not—drive the Yankees from their position. Confederate battle flags were soon waving above the breastworks on the Brock Road, but not for long.

Unfortunately for the Confederates, the part of the Union line they had captured was directly in front of the Union artillery. As the rebels placed their flags upon the breastworks, the cannoneers blew them off. Using double canister, their artillery provided time for Federal infantry to reorganize and attack. The fighting was hand-to-hand. For fifteen long minutes it raged until the Yankees held their breastworks again.

The Federal high command had seen that for a breakthrough all Burnside needed was for Hancock to attack with him. They had scheduled an attack for 6 P.M., but Longstreet's assault on Hancock at 4:15 had wrecked any chance for that happening. Hancock and Burnside's coordinated assault was canceled. The only problem was that nobody told Burnside. Again the Wilderness, with its dead-end trails and impenetrable lines of sight, became a player. By nightfall, Burnside's attack had been repulsed.

Most of the day, Confederate Brig. Gen. John B. Gordon had been scouting the Union far right flank, above the Orange Turnpike. From the position, he realized that the Union right and rear were exposed to him. It was ripe for a flank attack à la Stonewall Jackson. When Gordon's proposal for an attack started up the chain of command, however, it was met with undue caution. The assault was delayed until nearly twelve hours after the exposed Union flank was discovered.

Around 6:00 P.M., Union soldiers had stacked rifles, hung cartridge belts and boxes, and began cooking dinner. Suddenly, out of the dusky woods to their right rear came Confederates, howling their ungodly rebel yell. The surprised Yankees ran. Gordon's attack rolled up a good bit of Sedgwick's line, captured two Union generals, and nearly captured Sedgwick himself before running out of steam. Darkness and Sedgwick's reinforcements halted Gordon for good. For the rest of his life, Gordon would regret the mishandling of his proposal to attack earlier.

Casualty reports vary widely. The National Park Service places the figures at 8,000 killed, wounded, missing or captured for the Confederates and 18,000 total for the Federals, while other sources raise the number of Confederate casualties to as high as 11,400 and lower Union casualties to 13,948.

Historians for the most part agree, however, that the battle was a tactical victory for the Confederates, but a strategic one for the Federals. Confederates may have won the battle, but as Grant slipped southward, his men cheered. For many of his troops, the crossing of the Rapidan was the crossing of the River Styx; for others who survived, even if for a few more hours until Spotsylvania, it was the Rubicon. Either way, there would be no return.

Wilderness Ghosts

If there is any Civil War battlefield in the country where ghosts must linger, it would be the Wilderness. During the fighting, the woods caught fire from muzzle blasts. Many of the wounded, already in pain and unable to move, roasted alive. Their comrades, watching from only a few yards away, were unable to help them for fear of dying in the fires themselves. Some of the wounded were seen, as the flames licked closer, to load their weapons and place them under their chins.

There may be many soldiers who died on the Wilderness Battlefield who are still there. Early burial parties claimed they had recovered all the bodies; subsequent burial details complained about what a poor job their predecessors had done. There may still be many remains—men denied burial in consecrated ground or sepulture with a soldier's honors—scattered about the field.

Ellwood Manor

Ellwood Manor was built around 1790. During its pre–Civil War years, the large, two-story brick house was visited by James Madison, James Monroe, the Marquis de Lafayette, and Henry "Light-Horse Harry" Lee, Robert E. Lee's father.

During the Civil War, it was owned by the Lacy family. It was first occupied by Confederates after the battle of Chancellorsville and became a recovery hospital. Stonewall Jackson's left arm was amputated nearby and brought to the Lacy Family Cemetery to be buried, where it rests today.

In 1864, during the Battle of the Wilderness, the parlor of Ellwood became the headquarters of Maj. Gen. Gouverneur K. Warren, who commanded the Army of the Potomac's Fifth Corps during the battle. Grant's headquarters were nearby, and he visited Ellwood to strategize with Warren.

Ellwood is now a part of the Fredericksburg and Spotsylvania National Military Park and is open to the public on certain days. It has been restored to its May 1864 appearance by generous donations from the Friends of the Wilderness Battlefield.

Tom Van Winkle, who belongs to the friends group, was volunteering at Ellwood one afternoon and had a strange experience, which he was willing to share:

> I was volunteering as a tour guide at Ellwood, better known as the Lacy House, during the Civil War in Virginia event. Ellwood was the second home of J. Horace Lacy and family, the larger being in Stafford and known as Chatham, now the Fredericksburg and Spotsylvania National Military Park headquarters.

Now consisting of over a hundred plus acres sitting nearly in the center of the Wilderness Battlefield . . . the Ellwood site also contains the Lacy family cemetery. It is a small clearing with a couple of dead trees and surrounded by an old split rail fence in the middle of a cornfield. No headstones are evident in the graveyard, save one.

It was a clear sunny day in the Wilderness Battlefield and the corn rows were still standing. I was meeting two special guests that day, two descendants of Confederate general James Longstreet. We met and toured the house and grounds. I had explained the home's use as a hospital in the 1863 Battle of Chancellorsville, as well as its Union occupation in 1864. We then took the short walk to the cemetery past the garden and through the high corn rows out along the grassy path. There we began to speak to the lack of headstones as the family kept a Bible with locations and names of the deceased.

I then began to speak of the one and only headstone. This was the stone marker denoting the location of Confederate general Thomas "Stonewall" Jackson's amputated left arm he lost from a friendly-fire incident in 1863. Jackson was wounded on the evening of May 2, as he reconnoitered after his famous flank attack. He was brought back to a field hospital just north of the Wilderness tavern. After his amputation, Jackson's chaplin, Beverley Tucker Lacy, the brother of Ellwood's owner J. Horace Lacy, wrapped Jackson's arm in a cloth and walked the quarter mile or so to the small cemetery, where he carefully buried it.

Several years later, in 1903, the present stone was placed to mark the site of Jackson arm. This is still the only marker found in the cemetery.

As the three of us were discussing the eerily similar stories of both Jackson's and their famous ancestor Longstreet's woundings—both were shot nearly to the day a year apart and both by friendly fire—two horses appeared out of the cornfield, stopped, and looked at us over the old rail fence. One horse was bareback while the other was in full saddle. Several things were odd about this besides the strange timing. Noting that General Longstreet recovered from his wounds and would return to the war effort but that Jackson died several days later after his wounding, the dress of the horses seemed to have more meaning.

It was interesting that one man would die and one would live while one horse was bareback and the other fully saddled as if waiting for its rider to return and gallop off to another battle.

The horses stayed a mere thirty or forty seconds and then ran off. They were not seen by any other visitor at the site nor did anyone seem to be looking for a couple of strays.

Local lore has a visitor to Ellwood many years ago shooting himself in one of the upstairs rooms. Perhaps that accounts for the experience one Fredericksburg man wrote about online:

> We drove out to the spot I remembered and parked the car up the small pull off in the road and cut the lights . . . Well [,] up the path we went, gripping the flashlight and following the lighted beam that was lit before us. It led us to a large cornfield that at night pretty much freaked me out. We trudged on further into the lengthy rows of field till we arrived at the backside of the house. It was there that I turned off the flashlight and turned on the gear. I aimed the laser temp reader [a ghost-hunting tool] on the side of the house and gained readings, but no spikes to raise my attention levels. It was then that we heard it, a loud BANG inside the house. We both jumped and laughed quietly as we huddled together and then heard a noise that sounded like something sliding over a hollow wood floor. At this point we were on the east side of the house and decided to turn on the flashlight because we were afraid we were going to either fall over something or get jumped by the Chupacabra. I turned it on and the initial spot of light was at the ground displaying my sneakers in the glow. As I raised it up my eye caught a flash of light up in the small attic window. As the years went by I might have convinced myself that the flash was the reflection of my flashlight beam illuminating the dated glass of that small attic window. I moved the beam over to that window and was lowering it down the house when I heard the bang again and directed my light toward the large first-floor window in front of me. I caught a faint flash of shadows in that window rushing from left to right and quickly and instinctively followed the movement with the light till it planted its glow on the other first-floor window to the right. It was there that in a moment's notice we both saw the same thing. It was a man possibly in his 70s with wispy facial hair and dressed in a blue coat. In that quick moment of discovery I took off running. Without saying a word . . . I ran faster than I knew I could . . . around the side of the house, through the cornfield and down the path towards the car. I failed to notice that my friend was right next to me running equally as fast.

> We jumped into the car and started it and as we were heading up the road I asked what he saw. He described the same thing I witnessed in detail . . . he described the same thing I experienced. In the days after, I was trying to research what the Ellwood Manor was and how possibly we saw what we saw. It wasn't a homeless man living in the home, it wasn't park service occupying the dwelling . . . we just experienced the paranormal at the Ellwood Manor and an experience to tell for a lifetime.

The Phantom Fires of the Wilderness

A lifetime resident of Spotsylvania County told the story of strange lights that have been seen on the western edge of the Wilderness from Route 15 between Culpeper and Orange. She called them the "Phantom Fires of the Wilderness." Their source is unknown and when people go to examine them, there is no evidence that there ever were fires there—no burned wood, no scorched earth, no smoldering charcoal. (There have been other reports of phantom fires at Gettysburg and other battlefields.) Called "ghost lights," or "spook lights," they are well known in paranormal circles. As modern motorists drive along Route 15 near the Wilderness, could they be getting a glimpse back in time at the campfires of an army that had long ago marched to its dissolution and whose soldiers have decomposed along with it?

Haunted Houses in the Wilderness

The area called the Wilderness was literally a wilderness for hundreds of years before the nineteenth-century battle there. Trees there had been harvested to make charcoal, and so by the time of the battle, much of the area was secondary growth and tangled, matted forest floor. A few main roads ran through it and a railroad was attempted, but the Wilderness refused to be tamed.

Today, it pretty much remains a wilderness, except for a few private developments within the national park boundaries. The modern homes built within these developments should be nice, quiet places in the woods, but reports from residents reveal that they are not a quiet as they should be.

A woman related to me some stories about her modern home built within one of the developments that abuts the battlefield. In fact, she said, there are some of the original Civil War–era trenches, where soldiers fought and died, running across her backyard. Periodically in the evening, she will look up from her work inside the house and see through her windows vague, shadowy, humanlike forms moving across her lawn. They seem to appear out of nowhere and fade back into whatever world they came from. It has happened often enough that the family has almost become used to it.

A former law-enforcement officer, whose work is so well respected that he has been asked to appear on television, lives with his family near the Wilderness Battlefield in a beautiful, spacious, modern home. As if to remind us, however, of their ability to transcend time and space, the ghosts reveal themselves seemingly anywhere they choose.

One evening, the family had just finished dinner. Dishes were cleared and the table readied for breakfast the next morning. Casually looking down the hall, the wife was startled. There, in their modern hallway, was a man dressed in a disheveled military uniform. She knew it was a uniform of the Civil War era. The soldier was moving across the hall. She thought he appeared to enter one of the rooms, because passing through the wall was impossible. She and her husband investigated and found no one in any of the rooms along the hall, and so the impossible became the only explanation.

EVP and Dowsing Rod Findings

My wife Carol and I have visited the Wilderness Battlefield a number of times over the years. While researching this book, she took her dowsing rods to one of the temporary cemeteries there. A year before, I watched (and recorded on my cell phone) as she explored with her dowsing rods an abandoned church graveyard outside of Fredericksburg. It was fall and the gravesites were invisible under the carpet of leaves. As she walked along, the rods began to cross. Suddenly, she dropped a few inches as she stepped into one of the abandoned graves. She backed out and the rods uncrossed. She stepped into the grave several more times; each time the rods crossed. Later we read that dowsing rods will cross at the feet of the dead. Why, I don't know.

And why would the rods cross over empty graves? The only answer that seems possible is that there is still some energy left there from the human body that once occupied it.

As Carol walked among the graves, we could barely see some of the depressions. The graves were not very deep to begin with, yet each time she approached one, the rods would begin to cross. As she stepped into the grave, they crossed completely.

During an investigation of the Wilderness on July 18, 2005, I captured some EVP. In the first recording I asked some questions of the Stonewall Brigade, including who was your commander. The brigade commander was James A. Walker, but the EVP doesn't sound like that name. Perhaps the entity who answered was from one of the individual regiments in the brigade. Interestingly, the 27th Virginia was commanded at the Wilderness by a nineteen-year-old man who was killed by a bullet to the head. He had just received his promotion that morning. His name was Philip Frazer. To me, the answer to who commanded the men sounds like "Frazer."

Another EVP caught at the Wilderness is very loud. Sometimes the entities whisper and sometimes they are so loud you cannot understand what they are saying. The loud EVPs, to some, are frightening; they think the entity is angry, but this isn't necessarily true. Remember, the entity is not communicating in the normal way, vibrating air through a flesh-and-blood voice box. The physical means to produce sound has decomposed years ago. If they are using electromagnetics with which to communicate, their ability to modulate their communication is more difficult.

Spotsylvania Court House

If not for the fires in the Wilderness, Robert E. Lee might have lost the next major battle with Ulysses S. Grant, and the American Civil War could have ended a year earlier.

Unlike preceding commanders of the Union Army, Grant turned southward instead of retreating from Lee's Confederate Army after a defeat, an indication of the type of war that would be fought from now on. His objective was a crossroads that would allow his army to round the Confederate's right flank and move between them and Richmond, forcing Lee into the open to fight a battle where Grant chose. The crossroads Grant was after was Spotsylvania Court House.

Lee was under the impression that Grant, like his predecessors, would withdraw toward Fredericksburg to regroup and resupply. He was in no hurry, then, when he ordered Richard Anderson's division to begin their march toward Spotsylvania Court House at 3:30 on the morning of May 8. But the Wilderness, like some untamed entity, intervened once again in the affairs of men.

The smoldering pines and the sickening smell of the roasting bodies of men and horses drove Anderson to begin his march several hours earlier than ordered. He didn't halt his column until the last of his men cleared the fouled air. Anderson had inadvertently stolen a march on Grant. When he learned of the Union Army approaching the Spotsylvania crossroads, he was in a position to counter their move.

He sent two brigades toward the crossroads to drive back Union cavalry there and two more over Laurel Hill to intercept the Union infantry of Maj. Gen. Gouverneur K. Warren's Fifth Corps, advancing down the Brock Road. As Anderson's men crested the hill, they were met by none other than the famed Confederate cavalry commander, Maj. Gen. J. E. B. Stuart himself, who took command of the rebel foot soldiers. "Run for the rail piles," Stuart ordered. "The Federal infantry will reach them first if you don't run." In what has been called one of the Confederate cavalry's finest days, they held off Union infantry at Laurel Hill and Federal cavalry at the courthouse until more of their own infantry could arrive.

Warren, stung by accusations of tardiness and a reluctance to fight in the Wilderness, was determined to press forward this time. Thus, in a hurry, he sent his troops into battle as they arrived on the field and so ended up fighting in piecemeal fashion, one brigade at a time attacking entrenched Confederates.

Between 11:00 A.M. and 1:00 P.M., the opposing artillery dueled, but with little effect. By 1:30, Meade had ordered Sedgwick's corps to assist Warren. They did not arrive on the Laurel Hill battlefield, however, until early evening, having marched the Piney Branch Road past the burning bodies of the dead who had fought there earlier. When they finally got organized for their assault, they faced a Confederate line that had all day to dig in. The attack was repulsed.

As more of the Confederate Army arrived on May 9, their line soon resembled an inverted V, with a pronounced bulge at the apex, which the soldiers named "The Mule Shoe." Their apprehension about the position came from the fact that it could be enfiladed on either side: Bullets and shells being fired at one side would fall in the rear of the other, and a breakthrough on one side of the Mule Shoe would necessarily end up in the rear of the other side. But it did offer Lee the advantage of an interior line, whereby troops could be shuttled quickly across the area behind the lines from a safe point to an endangered one.

One of the heroes of Gettysburg was soon to fall. Maj. Gen. John Sedgwick, commander of the Federal Sixth Corps, had been warned of the persistent rebel sharpshooters in the area across from the Spindle Farm, where some artillery was stationed. Heedless of the warnings, he thought the sharpshooters too far away to be of any harm: "They can't hit an elephant at that distance," he assured some of the men who were dodging the bullets. Suddenly, there was a sickening, dull thud, and Sedgwick turned slowly and fell into one of his aides, a bullet hole just below his left eye. One of the most popular general officers in either army was dead.

The main action that day was on the Confederate right flank on the Fredericksburg Road. Maj. Gen. Ambrose Burnside sent two divisions of his Ninth Corps south on the road from Fredericksburg to Spotsylvania Court House. They were held up, however, by Philip Sheridan's cavalry beginning their ride toward Richmond. Resuming their march, they ran into Confederates at the Ni River and the ensuing battle lasted until after noon. The only result was to deny the Union Army the valuable Spotsylvania Court House crossroads again.

At about 6:00 P.M., May 10, Union colonel Emory Upton, just twenty-four years old, received permission to attack the Confederate position on the west face of the Mule Shoe. His tactics were unique: instead of lining his men up shoulder-to-shoulder according to accepted tactics of the day, he formed twelve regiments in a column, giving each a specific assignment once they penetrated the Confederate line. The "battering ram" tactics worked for a while. Upton's men pierced the rebel line almost to the McCoull House, but Confederate artillery stopped Upton's supporting troops and a counterattack pushed him back to his starting point. But Grant took notice. If a dozen regiments could break the Confederate Mule Shoe line, what could two corps do?

Preparations were made for Maj. Gen. Winfield Hancock's Federal corps to assault the "Mule Shoe" salient at dawn on May 12. Lee inadvertently assisted.

During the night of May 11, Lee began to believe that the Union Army was pulling out of its earthworks and retreating back to Fredericksburg. In order to counter the move, Lee ordered his artillery out of the Mule Shoe and started it on the road. Panicked commanders in the Mule Shoe, hearing Hancock's men preparing for their assault in the predawn, begged for the artillery to return. Lee countermanded his order to the artillery. But it was too late.

Some 20,000 Federal troops rammed into the salient, capturing prisoners and gathering booty before finally losing their momentum. By 9:30 A.M., a Confederate counterattack restored almost all of their Mule Shoe line. By then, the Federal 6th Corps had been committed to the fight and the fighting reached a crescendo of horror unsurpassed in the annals of military history.

For nearly twenty hours, in the pouring rain, the two armies battled each other, in most instances from no more than a yard or two apart. Fighting over the earthworks, men brained each other with rifle butts, stabbed at one another through the gap in the log breastworks, fired blindly over the parapets at the massed enemy, and trampled the dead and wounded alike into the mud-filled trenches beneath their feet. Men leapt upon the works, firing rifles handed to them until they were shot down, only to be replaced by others. It was called the fiercest hand-to-hand fighting of the war by an officer who struggled there.

Dead bodies were piled up for the living to lie behind as a shelter from the bullets. The 14th North Carolina began an advance, led by one Tisdale Stepp—who was firing, loading as he advanced, and singing "The Bonnie Blue Flag" at the top of his lungs. His serenade was short-lived. A Confederate musket behind him accidentally discharged, putting a bullet into the back of Stepp's skull and abruptly ending his song. The adjutant of the 30th North Carolina was so close to the enemy that he was pulled by the hair over the breastworks and captured. Even men who hunkered as close to the works as they could get were killed. The Union impetus was so great that the men in the front line literally ran themselves onto Confederate bayonets and were pitched overhead like bales of hay into the ditch at the breastworks.

Federal general Francis Barlow's aide watched as another officer tried to get his attention by waving. A shell took off the top half of his head just above the jaw like a razor. As the aide passed the body, the tongue was still moving, as if the officer were trying to convey something of the other world into which he just passed.

Confederate color-bearer Sgt. Alexander Mixon of the 16th Mississippi leapt the works with his flag, climbed the works, was driven back once, and then wounded the second time he tried. On the third try his luck ran out. A bullet pierced his head. The works grew slippery with rain, mud, and blood; Confederates, during brief lulls, pulled bodies from the trenches and flung them outside.

Federals attempted to bring artillery up, but the wheels just crushed the dead and wounded alike. For a while they were successful. At a range of about 140 feet, solid shot blasted through the Confederate breastworks. But artillery horses were doomed at such close range and soon the guns had to be abandoned, up to their wheel hubs in mud.

Confederates also used their artillery, firing point-blank into Union soldiers who were ranked eight to ten deep, cutting gaps in the tight formations and leaving nothing but a crimson mist. Still, Northerners closed those gaps, but were hindered by the heaps of dead blocking their movements.

It was soon realized that flat-trajectory artillery was a danger to the attackers as well as defenders, and so Federals brought up mortars, lofting shells high in the air to land behind the Confederate works. Their bloody effectiveness became grim amusement for some New Jersey troops who bet on what body part would be blown over the parapet next. A mortar shell landed near the 16th Mississippi's flag, decapitating one soldier whose body remained standing, blood pumping out of the neck like some surreal fountain.

Wounded were buried alive under the dead, and both sunk into the ochre quagmire at the Mule Shoe. Darkness brought a little relief, allowing Union units to withdraw under the cover of night. But firing continued past midnight. At 3:00 A.M., Confederates in the salient got the order to withdraw to a new line across the base of the Mule Shoe. It had been built with the time bought with the lives of those who now could not withdraw.

Dawn exposed evidence of what was arguably the bloodiest conflict of an already bloody war. Men were pulled out of the waist-deep mud by their extremities, still breathing. Wounded were extricated from underneath mounds of hardly recognizable, expired humanity. The dead were described as nothing but lumps of meat or clotted gore. The wounded had a chance to move out of harm's way; the dead simply were hit time and time again. In some places the dead were piled four deep. Again, from the welter an arm would wave or a hand would gesture and the corpses would be lifted and a wounded man would emerge. One man found a comrade who didn't have four inches of space on his body that hadn't been hit. His friend counted eleven bullet holes through the soles of his shoes. With the Confederate retreat, the Federals were left with the Mule Shoe, and the Confederate bodies were merely tossed into the trenches and covered over.

The final tally from May 12 was appalling: Some 9,000 Federals became casualties on that day; the rebel army lost about 8,000.

Spotsylvania Ghosts

The town of Spotsylvania is actually a T, where the road from Fredericksburg intersects with the road from the Wilderness to the road to Richmond. It doesn't seem like much, but it was Grant's route to get around Lee's army and head toward Richmond, and Lee had to prevent that from happening. The county courthouse at Spotsylvania is what made the bucolic area important to locals; the important T in the road is what made it the focus of one of the bloodiest battles in the Civil War.

The Spotsylvania Confederate Cemetery is the final resting place of nearly 600 soldiers killed in the battles throughout the Fredericksburg area.

Some of the older ghost stories come from residents of the area. Deb Pederson, who has lived in the area all her life, related that her mother had told her that when she was a teenager, she would go down to the courthouse and battlefields on the nights of the anniversary and see the armies marching in the distance. Deb's great-grandfather, she believes, was extremely sensitive to the paranormal. He claimed he could see the dead walking. Near Marye Road he saw slaves walking around their house and in the fields; many nights he would awake and say they were in the house.

Deb's grandmother may have been somewhat sensitive as well, but didn't talk about it much. There were times when she was frightened, Deb said, "due to the things she might have seen but didn't understand." She refused to go to funerals or be alone in the house at night and often slept with the lights on.

Even Deb's experiences seem to prove that something supernatural has been going on in Spotsylvania County. When she was a teenager, Deb was staying at her grandmother's house. She was the only one home. It was summer and the temperature was nearly 100 degrees. She remembers that the air was still and the big leaded window in the bathroom was being held up with a stick. She was blow-drying her hair. Suddenly she heard her name being called: "Debbie, Debbie!" At that moment, the window fell with a crash. She ran out of the house and sat in the yard until her grandparents returned, too scared to return to the house alone.

She has had candles move or fall over in the house on their own. "The best one is when things go and come back. I was missing a ring once. I stood in the middle of the floor and said, 'Look, I want my ring back, please bring it back by morning. That is all I ask.' The next morning it was laying on the dresser."

Escorts in Black

Sometimes a search for a ghost story in one place leads to a story in another place. I was interviewing the curators of the Spotsylvania County Museum, located in the old Berea Church in Spotsylvania. Located near the battlefield of May 1864, across the road from the old jail and having been there at the time, it became a makeshift hospital for the wounded from that horrendous battle.

There's a graveyard out back as well. If there were any ghost stories associated with the building, the staff was keeping mum about them.

I asked the lady minding the place if she had any ghost stories. No, she said, but she had one from Fredericksburg. She lived at the corner that would place the building right in the crossfire of Union soldiers attacking the Sunken Road and Confederates defending it. The house, however, was not there at the time of the battle. Many people believe that if the structure wasn't in existence during the time of trauma, it couldn't be haunted. Nothing could be further from the paranormal truth. Often it is the site upon which the structure sits that is haunted.

One can only imagine how many men were killed or wounded in the small footprint upon which the house was built, but from eyewitness reports, the soldiers said it was like someone poured barrels of blood out on the slope up to the Sunken Road; the grass became so slippery with gore the men had trouble walking on it.

But what the woman described was not confused or caring soldiers coming to inspect whoever was living now in the very space where they had died. It seemed to be more sinister.

She said that for about a month or more she would be awakened by this group of "beings" dressed in long black robes and black hats, who seemed to want to escort her from her bedroom. Periodically she would rise and begin to leave with them, but could only get to the door of the bedroom before they would vanish.

She said she was not the only one to have seen them. Her daughter saw them a number of times and so did a friend who slept over.

There are, in the world of the paranormal, what are called "Shadow People." They are dark figures, sometimes recognized only because they are darker than the light reflected off the dark background. There intent is unknown, but they apparently come as escorts. To where one can only speculate. Some literature has them dressed in long capes or folded robes. Rosemary Ellen Guiley, author of a number of books on witches, demons, and ghosts, adds one more telltale piece of clothing most reports have them attired in: hats.

EVP Findings at the Bloody Angle

I have been involved in several paranormal investigations in and around the courthouse area and the battlefield. One day, my wife Carol and I were the only ones at the Bloody Angle. It was so quiet that I decided to attempt to gather some EVP. I started the recorder and addressed some of the soldiers whose names were on the monuments in the area. I was pausing between questions when there was a loud noise from across the open fields in front of us. I stopped the recording, amazed at what I'd just heard. I asked Carol if she'd heard anything from the area in front of us. She said yes and I asked what it sounded like to her. "I don't know. A tree falling?"

I heard it differently. A crash, yes, but having been to many reenactments it sounded to me like the crash of musketry. I quickly replayed the recording, but it did not pick up the crash. And we did not hear any chainsaws in the vicinity.

On a previous investigation on July 18, 2005, at the Bloody Angle I captured additional EVPs. In the first, I address the men of the 15th New Jersey who fought at the angle. There is a gruff answer for the first question and no answer for the second.

During the second EVP, I addressed the men from Ohio who fought there as "Buckeyes." After the first question, "You fought here didn't you?" at 5 seconds, I hear an affirmative answer. After the second time addressing them, after I say I'm proud of them at 9 seconds, I hear a soft, "Thank you, sir."

Psychic Investigations at the Bloody Angle

Over the years we have taken mediums to the Bloody Angle. In September 2007, psychic Patty Wilson, who had never been to Spotsylvania before and knew nothing about the battle in that particular area, gave me her impressions when we visited. She said she has never seen anything so bad, and she has spent many hours on the Gettysburg battlefield. Here are excerpts from my notes during the investigation:

> Men are running, walking, stepping on bodies. . . . The leaders pushed them on. . . . Stupid moves made—bad decisions. . . . One man says that he doesn't belong here—Union—he has a head injury, his cheekbone is gone. He's from Ohio and he's not with the men

> that he started with. He was moved with 4 or 5 other guys. He's in his 30s, married, dark hair, children, from the Lake Erie area.
>
> Another young man bled to death under the tree. He's Confederate—only 17 or 18. He and his family were going to Texas (Austin) to settle and have land of their own—they made it without him. He came here to fight Meade. Patty got the name Jimmy (James) Ray. He was singing a song about Texas when he died. 39th Regiment.

According to Jeff Campbell, a local journalist who did some historical research on Patty's impressions, "fight Meade" checks out because he commanded the Army of the Potomac at Spotsylvania. Grant, as overall Union commander, chose to ride with Meade's army, and took part in planning many of its battles, running his orders, of course, through Meade. Jeff could not find any "39th Regiment" that fought at Spotsylvania. There was, however, a J. F. Wray who fought with the 5th Texas, which is listed as a unit at Spotsylvania.

> The men all fought until their bullets were gone, and then stabbed and beat each other. They couldn't stop fighting and killing. They're screaming for help and water. They still want to kill. Very little water, so many are thirsty. It was warm and the middle of day. They took canteens from the dead—some were offended by that. Some laid there for days without help. Samuel Westmont—from northern Alabama, 33rd Regiment

According to Campbell, this does not check out with the historical records.

Patty heard the name "Seth." She also got "Appleton, Portsmouth, Arkansas," but this does not check out with the records either.

Patty then sensed that one man took water from his friend who he thought was dead, but he wasn't—the friend cursed him when he took the canteen. The man felt guilty and his friend was very upset. Carol was using a crystal pendulum to verify answers, and at this point it stopped swinging and just quivered. Patty said his girlfriend's name is Elizabeth. She married someone else when he didn't return. Patty tried to help him cross over, but he wouldn't go to the light because he was too guilty about the water and couldn't forgive himself.

Another man told Patty that he wanted to apologize for frightening a little girl. Apparently the girl was a young psychic and was visiting the battlefield. She could see him, but he got too close and she could see his injuries. She ran screaming to her parents.

Patty also got the name Ralph Jacobs from Pennsylvania.

Some of the material Patty was receiving may never be verified. What can be verified, however, is her description of the soldiers walking upon the bodies of those already slain, the way they fought with bayonets and clubbed muskets, the thirst of the men who fought for hours, and the wounded lying there for days without help.

Psychic Investigations at the Old Jail House

The old jail in Spotsylvania was used to house Union prisoners of war temporarily during the battle. We did several investigations of the original old jail. Here are my notes of Patty Wilson's impressions:

> Cell on the left—man (Jack) with a French accent (1857). A con man of sorts—"he came to do business and they put him in jail." Nicely dressed. He didn't die here. He's angry that he got caught.

The Old Jail House at Spotsylvania temporarily housed Union prisoners of war.

> Cell on the right—a black woman and black man (Joseph). The woman won't speak—she's scared to death. Joseph is missing the earlobe of his left ear (he says a horse bit it). He's a free man, but she is not and trusts only him—they are connected in some way—she is his step-daughter. She's very shy. [Patty got the date 1853.]
>
> Joseph and the girl's mother live in Ohio. His wife is ill and he promised to find her daughter and buy her freedom before her mother dies. He succeeded in buying her, but when they got to Spotsylvania they put them in jail until they could verify that their papers were legitimate—they didn't believe Joseph. He's very frustrated. He didn't kidnap the girl; he bought her and is taking her home to Ohio. He is a nice, intelligent, articulate man.

When Patty asked who was the girl's master, she got the name "Warrens" or something similar.

> Joseph and his wife have tuberculosis, but Joseph is unaware that he has it. They were delayed several weeks and his wife died before they could return, otherwise they would have made it in time. Joseph is a bookkeeper—he owns his own land near the river in Ohio, in Leland.

There is currently no Leland, Ohio, but perhaps Patty misunderstood. Joseph also knew that I am from Ohio. As I always say, either our mediums have direct links to the dead or they are the most creative people since Shakespeare.

The old jail was used to house Union prisoners of war temporarily during the Battle of Spotsylvania. In my mind's eye I could see the disarmed, dirty, exhausted boys in blue filing into the little jail and collapsing along the walls, first come, first served, for a seat on the floor.

On a subsequent investigation, we brought some people interested in knowing more about paranormal investigating. We supplied some of them with electromagnetic field (EMF) meters to detect anomalies. There is no such instrument as a ghost detector. Investigators use instruments to detect the anomalies that have historically been associated with ghosts, such as cold spots or hair on the arms or back of the neck rising. Once detected, the anomalies may be photographed or recorded as EVP. One of the women began tracing an EMF where we had never found one before—along the entire wall—but only about waist-high, about the height of a man sitting down leaning against the wall. She also found an EMF anomaly on the one-foot thick windowsill that continued to move back and forth.

The first thought was to check for electrical wires; there were none. In fact, several previous investigations yielded no anomalies like the one we were seeing. A check outside for underground wiring showed overhead wires, too far from the building to affect the EMF meters.

Psychic Investigations at Spotsylvania Court House

Finally, we were allowed to investigate the courthouse itself. Although not the courthouse that stood at the time of the battle, it sits in the original's footprint. Patty Wilson again gave her impressions:

> Used as a hospital, fields all around, woods, bodies. A lot of people are coming and going, lots of energy, people all over the place. Different than Antietam or Gettysburg—more hopeless, sad, defeated, too brutal.

Spotsylvania Court House.

> Jeffrey, Henry—towards courthouse building, left to die. Henry Ward—gray clothes, leaning against the first column on right, has a gut wound, crying, lots of blood and pain. He's saying "it hurts." He's from Tennessee 14th, Company B. He was a farmer. His wife and baby boy are waiting for him. He asked "is Eliza OK?"

Cursory research reveals no Henry Ward listed in the 14th Tennessee records, but again, some impressions can be incomplete or misunderstood.

Although the courthouse is a reproduction, the builders did keep some parts of the original building and incorporated them, such as the columns along the front of the building. Could they have retained the psychic energy Patty was picking up on?

In the offices of the newer courthouse where the circuit court clerk works, there are reports from employees today of random cold spots. They also smell cigar smoke wafting through the offices when no one is smoking.

Police sometimes come in to the courthouse after-hours to complete their paperwork. Concentrating on their work, they suddenly have their eyes drawn to the door, where they will see someone pass by. Although they check it out, they know that a search of the building would be fruitless because they always lock the doors behind them when they enter the courthouse at night.

Some people have reported feeling a chill or cold spot and then, suddenly, a nearby door will open or close. There is a tunnel or underground hallway that connects the new courthouse with the old. It is used to transport prisoners from holding cells to the courtrooms. According to employees who have to travel the underground passage, it is a very haunted area. And there may be video evidence to back up that claim.

In the new courthouse basement, where deputies bring the prisoners into the courtroom, there is a hallway that is monitored by TV cameras. Officers watching the monitors have seen individuals following the deputies, but when they inquire who was behind them, the answer is always a befuddled "no one."

Cold Harbor

After the horror of Spotsylvania, where, in the pouring rain at the Bloody Angle, the wounded were trampled into the mud beneath the feet of those still fighting, only to be plucked out alive after the twenty hours of fighting ended, there were yet more horrors to come on the Virginia Peninsula.

After battling Grant as he swung eastward and southward in an attempt to get around his Army of Northern Virginia, Lee opposed him again at Cold Harbor, near the field of the Battle of Gaines' Mill, fought two years before. Grant was understandably in a hurry to get across the Peninsula, which had bogged down McClellan in its swamps. But after the nearly two weeks of fighting in the Wilderness and Spotsylvania, and the campaigning from there to the Peninsula, his men and officers were utterly exhausted. Still there was no time to be lost.

Cold Harbor, a vital crossroads northeast of Richmond, was captured on May 31, 1864, by Union cavalry under Philip Sheridan and held against Confederate infantry attacks the next day. Overnight, by June 2, the armies had entrenched along a seven-mile line; approximately 59,000 Confederates faced 109,000 Union troops. Grant, observing Confederate prisoners, was convinced the rebels were at least as exhausted as his own men and felt that his Federal soldiers could punch through the enemy entrenchments. He was wrong.

By this late in the war, entrenchments had become sophisticated zigzags with breastworks dug to enable enfilade fire into the flanks of attacking troops. No more would the soldiers stand shoulder-to-shoulder in their dress-parade lines and trade volleys, like old-fashioned duelists, as they had at First Manassas, the Brawner Farm, or Antietam. Nor would they simply use existing terrain features like the sunken road below Marye's Heights at Fredericksburg or the stone wall on Cemetery Ridge at Gettysburg. The armies had learned their deadly lessons with tuition paid in corpses. And yet, there would be, for any attacking forces, more corpses to come.

The Federals, who were about to assault the entrenched Confederates, knew their odds. This was an era before government-issued dog tags. As the follow-on troops watched the slaughter in the killing fields before the rebel trenches at Cold Harbor, they began to write their names and hometowns on slips of paper and pin them to their indigo sack coats. They wanted to make sure of two things: that when they died their families would be notified and not wonder for years whether their relative was coming home, and that their bodies would not lie in some unmarked, unknown grave.

In the dawn attacks on June 3, 1864, some 7,000 Northern men and boys became casualties in less than an hour. Total casualties for the Federals in the battle amounted to nearly 13,000; for the Confederates, about 4,600. The "battle" of Cold Harbor went on until June 12, with mortar shells and snipers taking lives for no good tactical reason. Grant himself wrote that of all the attacks he ordered during the war, the last one at Cold Harbor was the one he regretted most.

Cold Harbor Ghosts

In his book *Civil War Ghosts of Virginia*, L. B. Taylor Jr. writes of several types of hauntings on the Cold Harbor battlefield and reminds us that many spirits cling to the earthly site of their deaths because their bodies were never properly interred. Recalling the Union troops writing their names and hometowns on paper as makeshift I.D. tags, specifically so that their mortal remains would be found, leads paranormalists to speculate on the several eerie stories that have emerged from Cold Harbor.

It seems that the burial crews at Cold Harbor were not as efficient as the soldiers would have wished. A famous historic photograph of exhumations at Cold Harbor shows still-clothed skeletons thrown haphazardly onto a flat stretcher, four skulls visible, and a foot with an intact shoe and pants-leg still attached. The carelessness with which the remains were loaded onto the stretcher seems to imply that no one searched the corpses for those tiny scraps of paper bearing the honored soldiers' identities.

As well, Taylor writes that hundreds of bodies remained scattered in the area for years after the war. In 1869, "tourists" to the battlefield were treated to an exhibit no longer found on our neat National Park Service-administered battlefields: partially exposed skeletons, macabre clawed hands, and grinning skulls emerging from the earth all over the battlefield. As late as 1994, a prestigious Civil War magazine speculated that there may still be undiscovered remains at Cold Harbor.

Civil War reenactors are prone to encounters with the dead they so accurately mimic. It only makes sense: If we, the living, can occasionally see the dead, why can't they, upon occasion, see us? And if what they see closely resembles what they recall of their life—soldiers and women dressed in nineteenth-century garb milling around a campfire and tented streets, or fighting with convincing but mock ferocity—why wouldn't they be drawn to such a familiar scene? Reenactors have reported chills in certain spots on the Cold Harbor battlefield, even during the heat of summer. Hazy, indistinct forms of soldiers in the distance ducking and running for sanctuary behind some long-gone terrain feature; the cries, groans, and pleadings so familiar to Civil War-era soldiers as the firing died away and the musketry was replaced by the calls of the wounded for succor.

One female reenactor, according to Taylor, was awakened while camping on the battlefield by a pair of clammy, but unseen, hands running up her leg. She sat upright, only to be confronted by a phantom Union soldier's bearded face, which disappeared. She and her husband's visit to the battlefield was augmented later by the sounds of drums, musketry in the distance, and something heavy, like a human body, being dragged, perhaps to its temporary grave.

Others have experienced what felt like "wounds" to parts of their bodies, but the pain dissipates as they exit the battlefield. Marching sounds have been heard and one man saw a vision of a Federal soldier running at him—and then passing through him—leaving a "wave of emotions." It left him with the certainty that he must have fought at Cold Harbor in another life.

But perhaps most disturbing are the odd mists that suddenly appear and disappear on the battlefield. As quoted by Taylor, visitors to the field talk about a haze, sometimes blue, sometimes gray, that is perhaps not fog but a kind of energy that for some as yet unexplained reason manifests itself at Cold Harbor. One man thought it might even be a portal to the past, or a warp in time. A couple, William and Crystal Sykes, who have been lifelong residents of the area, may have confirmed this sighting as recently as a few years ago, according to an Internet comment post they made to an article in the *Mechanicsville Local* on March 28, 2011.

They had just exited their car and were walking down one of the pathways through the battleground when they heard what sounded like a cannon discharge very near to where they were walking. Both heard it; both were perplexed. There was no reenactment on the park grounds that day and no smoke or cannon to produce the sound.

Later, William found a trench where he wanted his picture taken. Acting like a sniper, he aimed an imaginary rifle and immediately felt a presence behind him, looking over his shoulder. He urged his wife to hurry with the photo. Suddenly the camera was "smacked" out of her hand and broke on a rock. More confused than irritated at the damage to the camera, they moved on, deeper into the park toward the Confederate positions.

As soon as they got to the Southern lines, William was overwhelmed by emotions of "anguish and pain." That's when they saw what he described as a "bubble" of fog. It wasn't like anything they'd seen on the highway at night. It started toward them, and then stopped, hovering menacingly in the killing fields. That was the final straw. They left the battlefield immediately.

I have my own weird personal story about the battlefield of Cold Harbor. Everyone who is associated with me in the paranormal field knows that I describe myself as a "psychic brick," meaning I have virtually no extrasensory powers, no ability to remote-view, no sensitivity to ghosts, none of the "clairs" (-voyent, -audient, or any other), and certainly no precognition. I test myself constantly: Every time I try to insert a grounded plug, I have to turn it over so that it goes in correctly. Very frustrating!

When I have had a personal paranormal experience, I consider it truly amazing and can remember every detail. So I remember the day I visited the Cold Harbor battlefield. It wasn't my first visit, although I don't remember seeing this particular part of the battlefield before. Perhaps the National Park Service had changed their walking tour route and it was the first time I'd taken it. I remember I was alone on this trip, which is a little unusual, because typically fellow rangers from Gettysburg and I took day trips together to see how other rangers in other parks did their talks. So I'm assuming that perhaps it was after my days as a ranger and before I'd written any of the ghost books, probably the early 1980s.

I was following a walking tour that meandered between the opposing lines. I was aware of the history of the area as a killing ground for Union soldiers. Wave after wave of Federals swept across those fields toward the well-entrenched Confederates. Revealing a fatalism only soldiers can understand, I recalled that they wrote their names on scraps of paper and pinned them inside their blue sack coats so their dead bodies could be identified.

I was crossing a wooden bridge built over what remained of the Confederate breastworks. The bridges were in place so that visitors could get close to them and peer down, but not destroy what was left by walking over them. It was a hot but clear day. That part of the battlefield, to the best of my recollection, was a broad, open plain canopied by tall, loblolly pines, typical of that area of Virginia. I got to the highest point of the arched bridge and suddenly was stopped. I didn't stop; I *was* stopped and looked to my left down into the remnant of the Confederate trench. I heard myself say, "Something awful happened to me right here." I didn't think it, I said it out loud.

I had to shake my head. "What did I just say?" I asked, again out loud. I even looked about to see if anyone else was around. I felt a little embarrassed, hoping no one had heard me. But no one was there.

Did this have some to do with reincarnation? To unconsciously blurt out that something terrible happened to me right at a specific spot where I had never been before—at least in this life—is incomprehensible to me. It was visceral, something I couldn't help myself from saying, perhaps because it was true about my *other* self, the one who may have lived in a period so bloody as to leave behind psychic imprints that affect me to this day.

Kennesaw Mountain

After securing Chattanooga and much of Tennessee, Grant was ordered to the Eastern Theater of the war to take on the seemingly unstoppable Lee. His strategy in Virginia was the opposite of previous Union generals who seemed fixated for much of the war to go "on to Richmond," and when that failed, return to the safety of Washington. Grant stated specific cities or areas of the country were not his army's objective; Lee's army was, and they would run it to the ground like a hound chasing a rabbit. Appointed general-in-chief, he was to orchestrate virtually the entire war from his headquarters in the field with the Army of the Potomac. He left the western armies to William T. Sherman, whose temperament and opponent dictated a different kind of war.

Despite his reputation as a pitiless warrior, Sherman was always reluctant to waste his soldiers' lives on the battlefield. His Confederate counterpart, Joseph E. Johnston, fought the same kind of war. Thus, much of the action in the West after Chattanooga involved strategic maneuvering.

It was obvious that Atlanta was a major hub for the war effort of the Confederacy. Its population had grown to 20,000 mainly because of manufacturing for the war. Ammunition, guns, rations, and men all flowed through to other parts of the Confederacy via the railroads that ran through Atlanta. Should the city be captured by the Yankees, they could disrupt the route from the Gulf of Mexico to the Atlantic, which would have a disastrous effect on supplying the armies and civilians of the South. And, as historian James M. McPherson wrote in *Battle Cry of Freedom*, "Because the South invested so much effort in defending the city, Atlanta also became a symbol of resistance and nationality second only to Richmond."

So, beginning on May 6, 1864, three Union armies under Sherman began their march toward Atlanta. The Army of the Cumberland, with about 60,000 men, was commanded by George H. Thomas, made famous by his stand at Chickamauga; James B. McPherson took over the Army of the Tennessee with some 25,000 veterans, once commanded by Grant himself; the Army of the Ohio, with 13,000 men, was under John M. Schofield.

Johnston's army of some 50,000 Confederates began maneuvering to gain an advantage in any coming battle. He established a defense on Rocky Face Ridge. From May 8 to June 19, 1864, the opposing armies maneuvered and fought several skirmishes and battles as Union forces masterfully flanked the Confederates, and the rebels successfully retreated before any real damage could be done. Battles were fought at Resaca (May 14–15); Cassville (May 18–19); New Hope Church, called the "Hell Hole" by the participants (May 25); Pickett's Mill (May 27); and Dallas (May 28). On June 14, Confederate general Leonidas Polk was killed during the fighting at Pine Mountain, but fighting continued on June 15 and 16 at Gilgal Church and Lost Mountain. The Confederates finally found an excellent defensive position, on June 19, along an eminence near Marietta, Georgia, called Kennesaw Mountain.

Confederates cleared the summits of Kennesaw for artillery and signalmen to work. At its highest, Big Kennesaw Mountain rises 700 feet above the surrounding countryside. Confederate lines covered the approaches to Marietta and the Western & Atlantic Railroad. Sherman began another of his flanking marches around the south end of Johnston's line.

Recent rains had turned Noyes' Creek into a swamp. What few bridges that existed had the flooring removed by Confederates, leaving just stringers for the Federals to cross on. Schofield's men made it across and established a bridgehead. The bridges were repaired and the rest of the Army of the Ohio crossed and prepared to advance.

Johnston rushed General John B. Hood's men from his right flank to his left to defend the routes to Atlanta. Instead of defending, Hood and his 11,000 men attacked on June 22 near the farm of Peter Kolb. The Battle of Kolb's Farm ended with Hood being repulsed but convinced Sherman that another end-around might not be possible.

But the fact that he had established his flanking maneuver tactic could work to his advantage. On the morning of June 27 he would make feint attacks on both ends of the Confederate line, faking his flank maneuver, and then have Thomas drive through the Confederate center toward the Western & Atlantic Railroad.

The Union feint on the Confederate right flank began with an artillery bombardment precisely at 8:00 A.M. While McPherson's attack was only to be a diversion, apparently some of the men from Illinois did not get the word: The 66th Illinois leaped into the trenches with the 1st Alabama and fought it out hand-to-hand; some Union troops nearly made it to the summit before they were stopped.

Already the temperature on this late June day was growing unbearable. The main attacks were launched around 8:15, after the artillery bombardment ceased. Burnt Hickory Road was a natural pathway to the center of the Confederate line at Pigeon Hill, and so the Federal attacking forces straddled the road. On the south side of the road some 5,500 men under Brig. Gen. A. J. Lightburn advanced over swampy, broken terrain. They scattered the Confederate skirmish line, but were stopped by heavy artillery fire from Little Kennesaw Mountain and rifle fire ahead of them. Lightburn called off the attack and began to withdraw his men. This left the Confederates to focus on the Union attack to the north of Burnt Hickory Road.

Again the terrain was ill-suited for an attack. The Confederates had strewn natural impediments among the rocks, boulders, fallen timber, and logs before their position. The slope before the attackers was steep, in some places nearly vertical. All semblance of a large, organized attack dissolved and men fought as small units. The heat, as well, was stifling. Yet some Federals managed to get within yards of the rebels. Their success was short-lived, and they had to retreat, leaving some of their comrades pinned down under a murderous, close-range fire.

Still farther north, Federals were again slowed by the unyielding terrain and withering fire from Confederates. They ran into a virtual wall of natural stone outcropping; Confederates above them threw huge rocks among the packed attackers. Only the fire of an Ohio regiments' repeating rifles allowed them, after two hours of fighting, to retreat.

The main attack was to take place against Confederate earthworks on a rise that would soon be named after its defender: Cheatham Hill. Unfortunately for the assaulting Federals, they were to attack the troops of two of the South's finest commanders. Benjamin F. Cheatham and Patrick Cleburne had their troops dug in behind earthworks protected by cannons. One spot seemed vulnerable: the Confederate line jutted out into an angle that could be attacked frontally as well as from either side. Though it appeared to be the weak part of the Southern defenses, it was protected on both sides by artillery. It would soon earn the name "The Dead Angle."

Union assaults would take the form of narrow but deep, sort of a battering ram made up of human bodies. The terrain they had to

The Dead Angle at Kennesaw Mountain National Battlefield Park.

cross, however, was open—a huge field, sloping upward to the angle—and their assaulting column would be visible and under fire the entire time. As they approached the enemy entrenchments, they would spread out into line and continue the advance.

Unfortunately for the Northerners—mostly Midwesterners from Illinois, Missouri, Wisconsin, Indiana, Kentucky, and Ohio—the Confederates had placed obstructions in the form of downed trees and brush in front of their lines, which made deployment difficult. In their confusion, the Yankees were subjected to infantry and artillery fire at a mere forty yards. As well, the heat was stifling. The first units were driven back, allowing the Confederates a free-fire zone on the flanks of other Union regiments. The attack north of the angle dissolved.

The attack upon the angle would involve a headlong assault by column on the point with units on the right swinging in an arc to attack the side of the angle. But the pivoting tactic broke down as Confederates in the trench fired as one man into the maneuvering Yankees. Half a dozen officers from Ohio went down virtually immediately, along with many more rank-and-file soldiers. Though their organized battle plan disintegrated, the Midwesterners continued up to and into the trenches, where the fighting took on a savage nature: men were bayoneted, clubbed over the head with muskets, and hit with thrown rocks and logs. The fighting was face-to-face for a while, until the Federals withdrew to a swale just thirty or so yards from the angle and attempted to dig in using whatever they had—tin plates, drinking cups, bayonets, and bare hands. The fighting had lasted less than thirty minutes. Casualties for the Union troops amounted to almost 1,800 killed, wounded, and missing.

Once dug in, the Federals faced the Confederate lines for another week. Corpses between the lines raised such a hideous odor that a truce had to be called to bury the dead.

Kennesaw Ghosts

In the broiling heat of a northern Georgia summer morning, Carol and I took a trip to Kennesaw Mountain Battlefield in June 2011. After staying overnight in a Marietta bed-and-breakfast, we took the short drive to Kennesaw Mountain. After seeing the National Park Service visitor center, we drove the first part of the battlefield tour, a winding trip up Kennesaw Mountain Drive to the parking area from which, even on a hazy day, the taller buildings of Atlanta could be seen.

We passed the Pigeon Hill site and drove on to Cheatham Hill. We walked from the parking lot around some of the best-preserved earthworks I've seen on any of our national battlefields. This area was christened the "Dead Angle" by the participants. Stone markers along the way point out the sites where prominent officers were shot in the assaults and orientation maps explain the fighting. At what appears to be the apex of the Dead Angle, the land spreads out in a sort of a huge amphitheater, a long slope down to the woodline with several loop hiking trails around the clearing. I took numerous photos into the woods around the Dead Angle hoping for the elusive orb or even more elusive full apparition, but subsequent analysis of the photos on my computer revealed nothing out of the ordinary.

However, I did attempt to get some EVP. Several attempts were made. Only one proved fruitful. Standing right in front of the Confederate breastworks I asked, "Union soldiers, men of Illinois, what was the attack like?" When I played the recording back, I got a one-word answer: "Murder."

Investigative medium Laine Crosby grew up near Atlanta on one of the battlefields over which Union and Confederate armies marched and fought. Before I met Laine, she lived a normal life in Atlanta. That is, until she and her husband visited Kennesaw Mountain Battlefield one hot July day. Laine was kind enough to write down their experience. I'll let her tell the story:

> On a typical July day in Atlanta, Georgia, the blue sky turns to a white haze and you can fry an egg on the pavement, even in the shade. This mid-July day was no different except that my husband, Chris, and I decided to go for a hike, densely ignoring the three-digit temperatures.
>
> We drove north of Atlanta to Kennesaw Mountain, two hills forming a lush respite, seen for miles around, and now owned by the National Park Service. As a native Atlantan, the great Confederate history of Kennesaw Mountain is not lost on me. As a teen, I

had given memorial services for Capt. William Allen Fuller, who chased and apprehended Union spies at Kennesaw Mountain in the great locomotive chase of 1862. And I now enjoyed my runs up the mountain trail, where Sherman's Atlanta Campaign began in 1864, ending in a defeat for the Union at this location. But as much as I liked to imagine what it would have been like to share in these fateful days, history was not on my mind as I set out for a leisurely hike this afternoon with my husband.

Upon entering the battlefield park, we drove to the Cheatham Hill parking lot and began our journey on foot. We walked about fifty yards through the woods, passing the historic breastworks, when the thick woodland suddenly opened to a bright grassy field. Although the searing breeze offered no comfort, it painted the meadow before us with different shades of green as it whipped in various directions, and surprised a hidden hare. We walked downhill, about the distance of a football field, until we reached a forest of water oaks. We rested on the banks of a trickling stream for a bit, under the shady trees, and soon decided it was too hot for human life.

Motivated by the thought of air conditioning, we walked on the slight path, through the middle of the field, toward the car. Although the park had been crowded just an hour before, we now had the meadow to ourselves. We made our way two-thirds up the hill, walking and talking, when suddenly there was no breeze. Then abruptly, Chris was silenced as we entered a bone-chilling coldness that stunned our half-baked senses. It felt like we walked into a freezer, with a temperature of not more than 30 degrees Fahrenheit.

I had a distinct feeling of being a bit off balance, as if my usual perception of the world was no longer available to me. Without looking at each other, Chris and I began to walk more briskly through the lingering chill, which followed us about thirty feet, until we simultaneously began running. We were back in the hundred degree heat, running through the woods, past the breastworks, and not stopping until our Chevy Blazer was safely protecting us—or so we wanted to believe.

We drove the half hour back to the city in complete silence that day. As we parked the car in our garage, I looked at Chris and asked, "You felt that, right?" And still without meeting my eyes, he replied, "Yes, we felt that," and we did not speak of the occurrence for many more years.

Marietta

Marietta, Georgia, is the closest town to Kennesaw Mountain Battlefield. In September 1863, Mrs. Jane Porter Glover donated part of her Bushy Park Plantation to become the resting place for twenty Confederate soldiers, victims of a train wreck north of Marietta. A few more Southern soldiers were buried there in the ensuing months. But when the Battle of Kennesaw Mountain resulted in hundreds more Confederate dead, they were brought to what is now known as Marietta Confederate Cemetery.

It wasn't until after the war that the cemetery saw its greatest expansion. In 1866, Catherine Winn of the Ladies' Aid Society and Mary Green from the Georgia Memorial Association organized women from Georgia to search for and recover the bodies of hundreds of Confederates killed at Kennesaw, Kolb Farm, Chickamauga, Ringgold, and even farther north. Eventually, more than 3,000 soldiers from every state in the Confederacy (as well as Kentucky, Maryland, and Missouri) rest in the Marietta Confederate Cemetery.

More than three thousand soldiers are interred in the Marietta Confederate Cemetery.

Adjacent to the Confederate Cemetery is the Marietta City Cemetery where generations of residents of Marietta lie buried—some not so peacefully.

One of the more interesting, if not nerve-wracking, jobs is that of sexton of a graveyard. In the past, the sexton's job entailed not only caring for the graves and tombstones in the cemetery, but often digging the very graves into which the recently deceased would lie, hopefully, for all eternity. Sextons spend a lot of time with the dead and sometimes witness things they'd rather not.

The city sexton in 1895 reported seeing ghosts in the cemetery. Sexton Sanford Gorham reported being watched as he worked in the cemetery by a man dressed in black. The man was standing in an open area of the cemetery, and so when Gorham approached him he had full view of the man the entire time. As Gorham closed on the man in black, he simply dematerialized in front of the sexton. Gorham realized that there was no place for anyone to hide and thus concluded he had seen a ghost.

And apparently, the ghosts of the Marietta Cemetery weren't through with him yet.

Several years later, Gorham had entered the cemetery on a dreary, rainy day. As he was going about his work, he noticed near a fresh grave a woman, dressed in black, standing and apparently mourning. Again he felt the need to approach the person; perhaps he could lend assistance. He walked through the dewy grass, leaving his own footprints in the moisture. But by the time he arrived at the fresh grave, the woman was no longer there. Though inured to strange things happening from working in a cemetery, it must have sent a chill up his spine to realize that it was possible the woman was contemplating her very own commitment to the earth below her feet. He looked about but saw no footprints leaving the gravesite like his own made as he approached it.

With no other evidence as to where she might have walked, the only conclusion is that she returned to her own grave.

Another Lady in Black has more tangible historic roots. In 1906, Mary Annie Gartrell, a refined musician who lived in Cobb County, Georgia, during the Civil War, died and was buried in Marietta City Cemetery. Later a lovely monument with a winged angel was erected above her grave. The cold stone carving above her grave was not the only angel associated with Mary Annie Gartrell.

Her sister Lucy, ten years younger than Mary Annie, never forgot. From the time of Mary's death, twice weekly—and sometimes more often—her loving angel of a sister visited her grave from At-

The Lady in Black has been seen around Mary Annie Gartrell's grave in the Marietta Confederate Cemetery.

lanta, always in black mourning dress. She came so often wearing that long black dress that people who didn't know her recognized her as the Lady in Black. For some thirty-eight years she visited to reflect, perhaps to play over in her head some of the favorite songs her older sister had played for her and taught her, to recall pleasant memories of growing up in Atlanta with the sister she so loved. Then, in 1954, Lucy died, and, after that, visits from the Lady in Black became more infrequent.

I say infrequent because they apparently didn't stop altogether. Occasionally visitors to the Marietta City Cemetery, while they are becoming engulfed in the rich history of the site, will look over to the winged angel statue over Mary Annie's grave. As their eyes travel down the monument, they will see, moving from behind the stone shaft, a figure gazing solemnly at the grave below. Though it may be summer and hot as blazes in Atlanta, the visitor is not dressed in light, cool summer attire, such as are worn by necessity in that part of Georgia. As the lone figure emerges from behind the statuary, it can be seen that she wears the long, black dress of one in deep mourning from a century before.

Franklin

Some historians blame the results of the Battle of Franklin in Tennessee, fought November 30, 1864, on Confederate general John B. Hood's desire to teach his soldiers a lesson in offensive moxie. Others think he's been given a bad, and possibly historically inaccurate, legacy. Whatever was on Hood's mind when he ordered the massive frontal assault on Union defensive works at Franklin may never be known. What is certain, however, are the casualties for the Confederate Army of Tennessee: six of its finest generals and 7,000 of its bravest men.

Hood had lost the use of his left arm at Gettysburg and had his right leg amputated after being shot at Chickamauga. The rigors of army life certainly presented a personal challenge. Indeed he was upset on November 30 at the fact that his officers, after receiving his orders, which would have entrapped Gen. John M. Schofield's Union army at Spring Hill a few miles south of Franklin the night before, did not follow through. Hood also realized that Schofield was only fifteen miles from the solid defensive works around Nashville, and if he made it there, he would be almost impossible to dislodge. There was little choice: attack Schofield on the afternoon of that day or watch him escape.

Some 30,000 Union troops had established a defensive line to the south of the town of Franklin, which rests within a bend of the

Harpeth River. Both flanks were anchored on the river and inaccessible to attack. They had thrown up breastworks and field obstructions in almost record time while utilizing some works that had been built a year earlier. They were sending wagons across the river toward Nashville as fast as they could.

To Hood, an immediate frontal assault was the only option. His officers objected: A large portion of the army was still not up, including much of the artillery; the late fall sun would set early, not giving them much time to follow up on any advantages they might gain; and frontal assaults against entrenchments were nearly suicidal. Hood ordered the assault anyway. As Maj. Gen. Patrick Cleburne said to Hood after receiving the orders, "We will take the works or fall in the attempt." It was prophetic.

That afternoon, some 22,000 Confederates began their march across a two-mile open plain toward the Yankees ensconced behind earthworks. For the first time anyone could remember, their bands played martial music—"The Bonnie Blue Flag" and "Dixie"—while they advanced.

There was an irregularity in the defensive disposition of the Union line. Two brigades were positioned in a V shape about 1,500 feet ahead of the rest of the Union line, with the apex on the Columbia Pike facing the attacking Confederates. At first it was supposed to be temporary, but soon orders came to hold the position to the last man; file-closers were to fix bayonets and those leaving the ranks would be shot or bayoneted. The men frantically began digging in. Soon they realized that both flanks of the V-shaped line were exposed. As the flank would be exposed in the middle of the field, the men feared a tragic mistake had been made. As well, if the Confederates overwhelmed the first line and the Union soldiers began to retreat toward their main breastwork, they faced the distinct possibility of being fired upon by their own men if they got intermingled.

As the long lines of Confederates advanced, it must have felt to these two brigades that they were supposed to hold out against the entire rebel army. As it was, they fired only five or six shots before the Union soldiers at the salient near the Columbia Pike attempted to engage in hand-to-hand combat, but were driven back by the sheer weight of numbers. The rest of the line crumbled and began to race the Confederates back to the main line. That was when the Confederates got a good look at the defensive line they were supposed to overwhelm.

A Tennessee sergeant observed that a "chevaux-de-frise" made up of locust bushes with sharpened limbs was laid out about forty feet in front of the Union breastworks. The works themselves consisted of a ditch in front with the excavated dirt thrown up to make the works capped by head logs of green timber with a space through which the men could fire without exposing themselves. The Confederate attackers, mingled with the few Union soldiers from the advanced line who couldn't outrun them, were a mere hundred paces from the main line when the Federals stood almost as one and fired.

Cleburne was seen riding his horse diagonally from left to right, through the lines of men when his horse was killed. His momentum took Cleburne almost to the outer ditch of the breastworks. An aide gave him his horse, which was killed by a cannon shot coming from

The office at the Carter House in Franklin is still pockmarked with bullet holes.

near the Carter cotton gin. Cleburne continued forward on foot, waving his cap. Shortly after that he was killed.

Confederate Brig. Gen. Hiram B. Granbury was midway between the advance line and the main entrenchments when Cleburne's aide heard him from ten feet away encouraging his men: "Forward, men; never let it be said that Texans lagged in the fight!" They were the last words he said.

The weakest point in the Union line was where the Columbia Pike entered it. It was here that the Confederates broke through. The problem for them was that there was yet a third Union line about 200 feet away, just in front of the Carter House and along the line of the Carter office and brick smokehouse.

Some made it to the Carter outbuildings and hid behind them. A few tried to cross the garden but were shot down. A Federal hid in the smokehouse and claimed he counted seventeen separate Confederate assaults attempting to break the Union line. One Union officer noted that a rebel body was lying between the barricade near the outbuildings and the main house

In the meantime, the fighting at the second line became savage. The opposing forces held the opposite sides of the same earthworks. The men were packed so closely that the front rank did nothing but fire weapons that had been reloaded by the rear ranks and handed forward. Union soldiers tilted their muskets over the head logs and pulled triggers; Confederates on the other side took bayoneted muskets from their comrades and threw them, spear-like, into the packed Federals on the other side of the head logs. Bodies piled up on either side of the earthworks until men stood on the dead and dying to fight.

To the east of the Columbia Pike, Carter's cotton gin, 240 feet from the road behind the Union entrenchments, represented a landmark on that section of the battlefield. In that area two Union regiments were armed with breech-loading repeating rifles; one company carried the sixteen-shot Henry Rifle. Once the Confederates gained the ditch, they were subjected to that flank fire from the Federals. Participants remembered seeing opposing rifle muzzles pass each other and fire; Union soldiers who lifted their rifles above the parapet to fire had their hands shot off. Osage orange

Heavy fighting raged around the smokehouse on the Carter farm.

bushes with thorns were used as impediments to attackers. Confederates who had gotten hung up on these chevaux-de-frise were shot over and over, hundreds of times, according to one observer. Officers who went down wounded were shot again and killed. Many of the unwounded Confederates, once they reached the ditch, were too exhausted to go forward. Retreat across the plain was suicide.

The men in the ditches in front of the Carter House sector continued taking enfilade fire from the Federals near the cotton gin where the Union line was bent back. The Confederate dead piled up by the score.

Some Federal officers later told Confederate prisoners that they had checked their watches as the rebel attack began, and from the time they began their advance until the firing ceased was one hour and forty minutes; but the most savage part of the fighting, once the Confederate infantry swarmed over the advanced entrenchments, was only forty minutes. Darkness normally brought on a cessation of hostilities during the Civil War. Communication between units was difficult enough during daylight; at night it was virtually impossible. But two more Confederate units arrived on the field, and Hood put them in to attack west of the Carter House and the firing continued after dark.

Most reports have the heavy firing ending between 9 and 10 P.M. Overnight, the Federal Army slipped across the Harpeth River. Hood, apparently ignorant of the incredible losses his army had suffered, brought up all his artillery and planned to renew the attack at 9:00 A.M.

Night brought additional horrors to Franklin. Capt. Theodrick "Tod" Carter was shot nine times in the arms and legs with a minié ball lodged in his brain above his left eye. Going into battle he gazed upon his boyhood home with its familiar brick smokehouse, wooden office, and garden, which he hadn't seen in almost three years. One of the last things anyone heard him say was, "Follow me boys, I'm almost home." The Carter family found him facedown in the fields just 150 yards southwest of the smokehouse and brought him home to die.

Dawn brought the horrors of the night before to light. A Confederate artillerist who had come to see the aftermath claimed he'd never seen the carnage so thick as at the gap in the Union line where the Columbia Pike entered. He thought there were 2,000 Southerners piled in the gap. Another visitor noticed that nearly all of the Union dead, because of the nature of the head logs, were shot in the foreheads.

The wounded were gathered in town. Forty-four buildings, from the female institute and college to the courthouse, businesses, churches, and private dwellings became hospitals.

The Confederate dead were buried in long trenches on either side of the Columbia Pike. The 3rd Missouri, for example, buried 119 of their men in one grave between the cotton gin and the pike. Some graves were marked, many others were not. Dead Federal soldiers in the ditch had the earthworks pulled over them for their burial. The battle was fought on a Wednesday; on Saturday it rained. On the outside of the breastworks, where so many were killed, the water literally ran red.

A large number of Confederates were later exhumed and taken to Carnton, the plantation home of the McGavock family, and buried in land donated by them. Hood visited the battlefield after the Federals had retreated. Witnesses say that he wept upon seeing the carnage. Some 2,500 Federals became casualties. The real horror was reserved for the Confederates. At least 7,000 (a sign on the battlefield indicates 9,500) Southern soldiers became casualties. Out of twenty-eight Confederate generals who participated in the fighting, fifteen became casualties. Sixty-five field-grade officers went down, and some units lost 64 percent of their strength. The Army of Tennessee was ruined.

Franklin Ghosts

Franklin has been called "Tennessee's most haunted town." If mass carnage and futile death are contributors to human spirits lingering in one area, Franklin certainly must live up to its reputation. Ghost tours of Franklin are available, presented by *Ghosts of Franklin* author Margie Gould Thessin.

Carter House

In winter of 2008, a man and his father were touring the Carter House, apparently the last of the day to do so. The tour was finished and their guide locked up the house. As they were walking to the welcome center and exit, they suddenly heard a door slam at the house. They looked back, but all the doors were closed. Then they saw a figure dressed in a Confederate uniform appear near the building walking slowly away from the house. A reenactor? Not likely. As they got a better look at him, they realized that he was missing his head.

Poltergeist activity in the house has been attributed to Annie Carter, who has been identified by visitors from her photograph. She was seen by employees running across the upstairs hall and down the stairs. Staff has had clothing tugged, and a worker has heard her own name whispered in her ear, not once, but a number of times. While a tour was being conducted, a visitor saw a statue bouncing around on a dresser behind the guide.

Other strange sightings have occurred in the Carter House. The staff has repeatedly seen the apparition of a little girl. Others have seen the wraith of a little boy who apparently died tragically in the house. Soldiers have been heard marching outside, and wounded soldiers have been seen inside. Perhaps most disturbing was the vision seen in the room where Tod Carter breathed his last. He was seen, more than once, sitting up on the edge of the bed in the room, apparently healed of all the hideous wounds he had taken during the battle. He sat for a few seconds and then vanished.

A woman who was a guide and later became director of the Carter House was closing for the night when a young man dressed in brown woolen pants and suspenders approached the door and asked for a tour. As Alan Brown relates in his book *Haunted Tennessee*, she was giving her tour when the young man corrected some of her facts about the Carters and the house. She was a little miffed at being interrupted by someone who thought he knew more about the house than she did, but she continued the tour. They were about to descend into the cellar, where the Carter family spent their time as the battle raged outside, when the young man said, "We can't go down there." She turned to tell him that they were allowed into the cellar, when he promptly vanished before her eyes. Later, she was going through old photos of the Carter family and came upon the image of the young man to whom she'd given the tour. She suddenly realized why he knew so much about the history of the house and family. The young man was Tod Carter, who had lived and died in the house.

Carnton Plantation

It seems that General Cleburne's spirit has not been at rest either for the last 150 years. At Carnton Plantation, where his body, along with three other Confederate generals, was laid out on the back veranda, heavy riding boots have been heard pacing the second floor of the rear porch while confused visitors and staff listen apprehensively. There seemed to be much activity during the 1980s when a security guard's watchdog began to growl and bark at someone behind the house. As he searched with his flashlight, it finally illuminated a figure on the second floor of the porch. The guard saw that the man wore a long gray coat, much like those in the photos of Confederate officers he had seen. Of course, that would make him a ghost, and the security guard knew there were no such things as ghosts. He called to the man to halt and come down. Instead, the officer dematerialized.

A local resident was driving up the driveway one night. As he approached the house, he saw a man in a long coat and hat sitting on the porch with his head drooped over the railing. As the driver watched, the man disappeared. The staff, while reluctant to talk about their ghosts, has named the recurrent shade "The General." He has forced them to remove a key from a door, because if given access to the key, he locks the door. Others have seen Confederate soldiers meandering about the property when no reenactors are present.

When standing at the graves of two brothers in the Carnton Cemetery you may have your ankles tickled or grabbed. The sound of a small hand running along the fence is attributed to the ghost of a little girl, perhaps one of the children, who died during the long history of Carnton. Some have seen soldiers in the cemetery, apparently guarding the graves. They follow visitors around until they leave.

EVP Findings

During a paranormal investigation in August 2011, I collected EVP near the site where General Cleburne was shot and killed on the southern edge of Franklin. During one recording (#1354), I ask, "General Cleburne, are you still here?" At 5.5 seconds into the playback you can hear a quiet "Yes." Later I ask, "General Cleburne, do you regret fighting for the Confederacy?" At 15 seconds, you hear a two or three syllable answer that sounds like "____ever." Does he say "Never"?

In a second recording (#1355), I say "God bless you and your men, General Cleburne," and at 10 seconds into the recording a woman's or child's voice says, "Let's do this . . . for him."

Prisons

At the beginning of the Civil War, the opposing sides were little prepared for the unexpectedly large number of killed, wounded, or captured. For those captured in battle, a prisoner exchange system was implemented, first by field commanders immediately after battles, then as a formal government-sanctioned practice. It was eventually realized by the Union that the manpower-short Confederacy benefited from having their soldiers returned to fight for the cause again. The exchange system was halted by the Federals, resulting perhaps in a shorter war, but the policy increased overcrowding and suffering for those stuck in the prison pens.

Johnson's Island, Ohio

Over the years, Johnson's Island, in Sandusky Bay, Ohio, has been a privately owned island, a pleasure resort, the site of a quarry operation, and a development for private homes. But its most notorious use was as a prisoner of war depot for Confederate soldiers during the Civil War.

During the summer, the island can be a comfortable place to live, with water views readily available. Recently, the old quarry was opened to the surrounding Sandusky Bay, which itself opens into Lake Erie, and luxurious homes were built on the cliffs above the quarry. Private docks usually go with the homes, turning the quarry into a protective cove for sport fishermen and boaters who want to venture out on the Great Lake.

But winters in northern Ohio, especially near Lake Erie, can be brutal. Icy winds can howl in off the lake, which itself can freeze out several miles from the shoreline. If you're not used to the climate, the winter can be as effective a killer as any bullet; or, in Civil War parlance, it is as effective a killer as any minié ball.

In 1862, Leonard Johnson leased forty acres of his island to the U. S. government, anticipating the internment of Confederates captured during the war. The fall of Fort Henry and Fort Donelson provided the first prisoners at the island on April 10, 1862. Early in the war, prisoners were treated relatively well, with adequate food and well-kept living quarters. Sutlers set up shop within the prison and sold food and other items that weren't provided by the government. There was even a prisoner exchange system between the Union and Confederate governments, whereby a certain number of privates

More than two hundred Confederate prisoners of war were buried in the Johnson's Island Cemetery.

could be exchanged for an officer. But by 1864, the exchange system virtually ceased, and Johnson's Island, like other prisons around the country, rapidly became overcrowded. The U. S. War Department cut rations by half and limited what was available through the sutlers.

Twenty-six Confederate generals and generals-to-be were imprisoned at Johnson's Island, the longest internment being that of Maj. Gen. Isaac Trimble for fourteen months. In the spring of 1865, as the war was coming to its conclusion, some of the men signed an oath of allegiance to the United States and gained early release. Some chose to escape rather than "swallow the eagle." Security was lax after the war, and some prisoners escaped by simply dressing as guards and making their way south. Yet by September 1865, when the prison was closed, some civilian prisoners and true-blue Confederates had to be moved to other prisons in the east.

Over the course of its existence, some 9,000 prisoners were confined on the island. More than 200 Confederates will never leave: they rest in the Confederate Cemetery on the island.

Johnson's Island Ghosts

Beginning in 1902, rock for breakwaters in Cleveland and nearby Cedar Point was quarried from the island. The workers had a small village with a school, post office, chapel, and tavern. Most were of Italian ancestry and spoke little English. They had their traditional songs, games, and entertainments from the Old Country, and being on an island with their own village, they maintained their traditions.

As the story goes, one day a supervisor was observing the men leaving the quarry. On their way out they were humming a tune in unison. The supervisor stopped them and asked them where they had heard the tune. The quarrymen looked at each other and shrugged their shoulders. They had heard someone singing from the woods across the road from the quarry where the old prison camp used to be. They liked the catchy tune and adopted it. The supervisor was stunned, because it was something they never would have heard in their native Italy. It was "Dixie," the old minstrel tune from the South.

A story appeared in the *Cleveland Plain Dealer* by Grace Goulder recounting the experience of some of the Sicilians who worked

Upscale homes now line the edges of the former quarry on Johnson's Island.

in the quarry on Johnson's Island. A thunderstorm blew in off Lake Erie with howling winds and driving rain. The workers were in the vicinity of the Confederate Cemetery and found shelter on the lee side of the monument erected by the Daughters of the Confederacy to the soldiers who must lie for eternity in Northern soil, far from their beloved homeland.

As they crouched behind the monument, suddenly they heard something odd rising above the screech of the wind: a bugle call. Their attention was directed to the cemetery behind the monument, where they began to see the impossible: Soldiers in gray and butternut, with shouldered muskets, rising from the graves. They formed ranks, and as they had braved the storm of Yankee musketry many years before, began to march off silently into the storm of wind and rain to vanish from view.

The next day, those who witnessed the mustering of the dead rowed across Sandusky Bay and told their story to any who would listen. Some scoffed, but the fact that the workers refused to go back to the island convinced quite a few that they must have experienced something not of this world.

Shadowy single figures have been seen in the cemetery and in the tree line near the old camp. A paranormal research group witnessed the figures during an investigation of the cemetery. They also took photos with what appears to be a misty figure in the background.

On certain nights voices have been reported to have been heard emanating from the woods where the old prison camp once stood. In paranormal circles it is well known that when a historically significant site or building is being renovated, paranormal activity increases.

Perhaps, with the building of modern homes on the edge of the old quarry and the archaeological dig across the street, the spirits of the Confederate soldiers who once suffered through the bone-chilling winter nights of northern Ohio have returned to manifest themselves.

Point Lookout, Maryland

In 1830, the first lighthouse was built at Point Lookout, Maryland, a peninsula created by the confluence of the Potomac River with the Chesapeake Bay.

Point Lookout, Maryland, was the site of the largest Federal-run prisoner of war camp.

After the Civil War broke out, Hammond General Hospital was established at Point Lookout in 1862 to care for ill and wounded Union soldiers. By 1863, it was determined that the point would be a good site for a prisoner of war camp. Camp Hoffman would be established and remain open until the end of the war, eventually passing as many as 52,264 Confederate prisoners through its gates. Of those, some 4,000 died of disease and malnutrition. It was the largest Federal-run internment camp in the North.

After the war, the lighthouse was rebuilt in 1883 as a two-story, 40-foot-high edifice, the structure that exists today. And, although the current lighthouse was not there at the time of the prison camp, it has gained the reputation as the most haunted lighthouse in America.

Point Lookout Ghosts

Hans Holzer, the famous ghost hunter, did an investigation of the structure and recorded some twenty-four different voices (EVP) including the phrases, "Fire if they get too close to you," seemingly from the prison years; "Let us not take objection to what they are doing," an apparent endorsement for the investigation; and a woman's voice saying, "My home," attributed to Ann Davis, the first female lightkeeper. Ann Davis has also made herself known as an apparition. A woman has been seen at the top of the stairs dressed in a white blouse and a long, blue skirt.

More than one occupant has detected a foul odor, like rotting meat, emanating from one of the upstairs rooms. In addition, there have been more common auditory events heard, such as laughter, singing, snoring, and footsteps.

I had an opportunity to work on a television production with Laura Berg, a former resident of the lighthouse who had experienced a number of the supernatural happenings while living there in the late 1970s. I was a talking head, brought in to give the historical background of the Battle of Gettysburg, which contributed to the overflow of prisoners in 1863 at Point Lookout prisoner of war camp. Laura then told her experiences in the lighthouse, which were chilling. I remember her talking specifically about the basement.

The Point Lookout Lighthouse is alleged to be home to a number of ghosts.

She had heard, upon moving in to the lighthouse, that strange things went on inside and outside. Gerry Sword, a park ranger who later became superintendent of the park, had lived there when he first came to the park. He had experienced lights turning on and off, doors banging, a wall in the kitchen begin to glow and remain glowing for ten minutes, someone invisible walking up and down the hallway and the stairs, loud disembodied voices coming from outside, and his dog being released from an outdoor pen while the pen, upon inspection, was still locked. It was Sword who invited Holzer and his team.

During three other investigations, multiple witnesses saw a figure standing in the basement against a back wall. EVP was recorded that either asked for help to be let out or ordered the team out. Investigators have heard breathing and been pushed by an entity in the lighthouse.

A number of shipwrecks have occurred off Point Lookout. The steamship *Express* was out of Baltimore when she ran into a gale. One Mr. Haney attempted to row to the Point Lookout Lighthouse for help, but his tiny boat capsized and he was drowned, his body washing up on the rocks the next morning. Someone living in the lighthouse reported having seen a man at the door in "old-fashioned clothing," who when the door was opened "floated" across the yard toward the Chesapeake Bay.

Gerry Sword heard snoring coming from, of all places, the kitchen (which may or may not have been a kitchen to the entity who snores.) One night he saw figures moving through the house.

In March 1977, a park ranger who had just been hired was out near the lighthouse checking weather instruments located there. A short distance away he saw an elderly woman walking around, looking at the ground as if she had lost something in the grass. He approached her and asked if there was anything he could do to help. He remembered some details: "She seemed very distant and our conversation was very brief. I only remember three points she made: she did not need my assistance, she lived up the beach a-ways, and she asked if I knew where the gravestones were that used to be where we were standing."

He continued, "About five minutes later, while I was walking back to my truck, which I had left parked near the river, I noticed that the woman had disappeared. It was then that I realized the adjacent parking lot was empty. Furthermore, from my vantage point since our conversation, I would have had to have seen any cars entering or leaving the area. None had."

Later he spoke to Gerry Sword about the strange woman and her virtual disappearance. Sword told him that at one time the Taylor family had their family graveyard in that area. The exact location is now not known, but its former existence is indisputable. One of the individuals buried in the graveyard was named Elizabeth Taylor. Apparently, someone had once found her missing burial plot and stole her headstone, dooming her grave to oblivion. Later, the gravestone was found in a local hotel by a vigilant park ranger.

The same ranger reported seeing someone running from the location of the campground, across the road to the woods off park property. He has seen the figure several times, always in the daylight and always in his rearview mirror. Other rangers have seen the figure as well at different times of the day and different times of the year. The area from where the figure emerges is near the Confederate cemetery for victims of the smallpox epidemic that struck the camp. The figure would have been running away from the smallpox hospital adjacent to the cemetery.

Historians claim that Confederate prisoners, in an effort to escape, would tell their captors they had the symptoms of smallpox. The guards would hurry them to the hospital, whereupon the "sick" soldiers would miraculously be well enough to run away towards the woods. Apparently some indeed had infected themselves by going to the hospital, and died in the woods. Could this be the entity rangers see dashing across the road?

Andersonville, Georgia

Andersonville prison was built in early 1864 to alleviate the crowded conditions in the prisons near Richmond, Virginia. It was open only fourteen months, yet its legacy of privation is as raw today as it was in May 1865 when it closed. In all, more than 45,000 Union soldiers were interned within the 26.5 acres. Men were jammed cheek to jowl even after it had been expanded from its original 16.5 acres just six months after it opened. Of those who were confined within its 15-foot-high stockade, some 13,000 died from exposure to the elements, disease, lack of sanitation, or starvation.

Beginning in February 1864, prisoners arrived by train at the rate of 400 a day. In June, 26,000 were encamped in a space meant for 10,000. By August 1864, the stockade held its highest number—32,000 in nearly unbearable conditions. One trickling stream, Stockade Branch, ran sluggishly through the camp and was used for washing, a latrine, and—unbelievably—drinking. The bakery and cookhouse were located upstream, outside the stockade, and added to the pollution.

Newly arrived prisoners, after being marched the short distance from the railroad depot in the town of Andersonville, entered the stockade through two doors. The outer door was closed and the inner door was opened to reveal what many thought was a vision of hell. There were no permanent shelters, only what the soldiers called "shebangs," bits of cloth, wood, or branches set up as lean-tos, the only shelter from the savage Georgia sun. The new men

The springhouse protecting Providence Spring at Andersonville.

were called "fresh fish" and often became the victims of the more seasoned inmates, relieved of any valuables they may have brought with them. They were shown the "dead line," a single-railed fence 19 feet inside the stockade wall, the crossing of which meant death from an armed sentry overhead in a "pigeon roost."

Not only were the prisoners guarded night and day inside the prison, there were eight earthen forts containing artillery surrounding the camp to discourage Federal attempts at freeing the prisoners.

Soon the Stockade Branch was inadequate to supply water for all those interned. In August 1864, a heavy thunderstorm—some swore it was a lightning strike during that storm—uncovered another spring, which the prisoners named "Providence Spring," just outside the dead line. In an act of kindness, Capt. Henry Wirz, the commander in charge of Andersonville, allowed the men to divert the water via a flume into the camp.

In time, a new horror plagued the prisoners. A group of savage bullies known as the "Raiders" began to rob men of clothing, food, and other valuables, some essential to life itself in the prison. A police force known as the "Regulators" was formed, rounded up the

Raiders, and put them on trial. Captain Wirz recognized this as legitimate and when the trial was over had six of the Raiders hanged. They lie buried in the Andersonville National Cemetery, but segregated from the rest of the men who died there.

The camp was finally liberated in May 1865, but not until 12,914 of the men held there had died. Careful attention was made upon each burial to record a number on a wooden marker and a corresponding name in a register book. Still, some 460 are unknown, men who gave not only their freedom, lives, and futures for their country, but their very identities. With their signature on an oath of allegiance to the Confederacy, they could have been released. They chose death instead, some wondering at the end, after the prisoner exchange system was halted, whether they had been forgotten by the country for which they suffered so much.

At their liberation, photographs were taken of some of the emaciated prisoners. When the public saw them, they demanded justice. And while the cessation of the prisoner exchange system was part of the cause for the overcrowding in all the prisons, North and

Nearly 13,000 men died at Andersonville. Many are interred at Andersonville National Cemetery.

South, someone must pay. When Union soldiers arrived to liberate the camp in May, the entire staff had fled—all but Captain Wirz, who was promptly arrested.

Wirz was taken to Washington, tried, and hanged. Some of his accusers perjured themselves by accusing him of beating and shooting prisoners during August 1864. The fact that Wirz was on leave because of sickness that month didn't seem to matter. As he stood on the gallows awaiting his death, Union guards around the yard chanted over and over, "Wirz, remember Andersonville." He died a scapegoat.

Andersonville Ghosts

If human suffering and the expenditure of emotional energy are two of the reasons why spirits are bound to a specific area, it is not surprising that prisoner-of-war camps have ghost stories associated with them. That must be particularly true of Andersonville, Georgia, where some 45,000 men suffered humiliation, starvation, brutality, disease, and lack of water for the fourteen months the prison was open. For the nearly 13,000 men who died during that same time, the near certainty of death became a stark, terrifying reality as life slowly ebbed away. And for at least one spirit, it is the utter unfairness of his situation that perhaps causes him to still walk the road outside the camp, many decades after his execution.

One of the continuing sightings on some of the roads that lead to Andersonville National Historical Site is of a Confederate officer. He is, in contrast to any prisoner's ghost one might see there, impeccable in his dress. It certainly is strange for motorists driving along Route 49 to see what they must think is a reenactor walking alone along one of the less-travelled roads in that part of Georgia. Besides the historic site, which is usually closed by 5:00 P.M., the citizens of the small town of Andersonville would have heard about a prankster in their midst who likes to dress up and risk his life by prowling the roads at night. If it is a prankster playing a ghost, it is one who has passed his avocation down through several generations, for this is one of the oldest legends associated with Andersonville.

The apparition of the officer has been, to the satisfaction of most who have seen or heard of him, identified. He is the former commander in charge of Andersonville, Capt. Henry Wirz, who was taken to Washington after the war, tried, and put to death by hanging for his role in running the camp.

One woman who lives across the street from the old prison camp posted her experiences on the *Ghosts of America* website. Along with her husband, she has seen uniformed men moving across their property. Voices and calls of distress emanate from the surrounding woods. Frighteningly, the activity is not confined to outside the home. Inside, doorknobs shake on their own and shadows can be seen moving about. Not surprisingly, the woman occasionally gets a feeling that makes her exceedingly uncomfortable.

Another woman who visited Andersonville some three decades ago also posted on the *Ghosts of America* site. While she and her family were listening to a ranger talk in the old visitor center, she glanced over to a corner and saw a young man standing there. She was "shocked" by his disheveled appearance and wondered why someone would visit a historic site dressed in such ragged clothing. Then she realized that he "did not exist below the knees." The floating wraith then realized that she had seen him and responded by giving her a weak smile before simply vanishing before her eyes.

The stories she heard during the family visit to Andersonville gave her nightmares for days after their visit. It took twenty-five years for her to return. Expecting to see the young man again, she was disappointed, but still felt the overwhelming sadness of the place once conveyed by the soldier.

Visitors to the site, in addition to seeing shadowy forms move about the area and hearing disquieting cries from the nearby woods, have had their olfactory senses assaulted. The stench of the camp, in reality, must have been overpoweringly nauseating: human waste floating down Stockade Branch; bodies and clothing soaked with perspiration, unwashed for months on end; the dead piling up in the heat waiting to be taken to the cemetery. Perhaps that is why one veteran at Andersonville, according to Daniel Cohen in *Hauntings and Horrors*, was reminded of his days in the service and the ungodly smell of a military field hospital. The only problem was this was a veteran of the Vietnam War, and the smell was coming from a camp that had been closed over a hundred years before his visit.

While human suffering is a known cause for a haunting, intense human compassion can also trap souls in an area. This may explain the several sightings of a man, dressed in a black frock and carrying an umbrella, moving through the camp site and then vanishing. According to Alan Brown in *Haunted Georgia*, he has tentatively been identified by park officials from the descriptions of eyewitnesses as Father Whelan, a priest who visited the ill and dying within the camp. Prisoners remembered he often carried an umbrella to shade himself from the blistering Georgia sun.

Carol and I visited Andersonville on the afternoon of June 7 and again in the morning of June 8, 2011. The heat was stifling; it came in waves up the gentle slope from the lower area where Stockade Branch and Providence Spring ran. I couldn't imagine living with that heat day and night for months on end.

The first visit I attempted to gather EVP twice. The first attempt I asked "What did you think of this place called Andersonville?" The answer, at 3 seconds into recording #1629, sounds to me like a male voice and whispers ominously, "Life breeds in hell."

The next day I asked several more questions, mostly for the Raiders at their gravesites, which yielded little. Perhaps it was because I was disgusted with their activities to take advantage of their fellow prisoners who were weaker. My questions were along the line of "Were you proud of what you did?" and the like. It's a technique for getting EVP called "enticement." Perhaps I sounded too threatening or disgusted. They were mostly silent or gave unintelligible answers.

We returned to the camp site and Providence Spring. Referring to the spring, I asked, "Men of Andersonville, did it quench your thirst?" At 4 seconds into recording #1208, I hear a voice say three separate words: "Oh . . . yes . . . indeed."

One other attempt at capturing the voices of the spirits of the men of Andersonville yielded results. Carol, using a pendulum, got the name George from New York. So I asked, "George from New York, were you captured at Gettysburg?" Perhaps George was not from New York, or had moved away to Wisconsin. Perhaps there are no reasonable answers for the information we get during EVP sessions. At 4 seconds I hear, "Hell no." At 6 seconds into recording #1214, I hear, "Died, Milwaukee."

Savannah

Savannah, Georgia, is not just one of the great cities in America; it is also one of the most haunted. And both its greatness and ghostliness come from the fact that it is also one of the oldest and most historic.

Savannah was founded by Gen. James Oglethorpe and a group of settlers from England in 1733. After the American Revolution, Savannah boomed. Rice and cotton flourished in the rich soil and the large plantations were worked with slave labor. The Africans brought to the area the rich Gullah culture, unique to the Low Country region. The increased wealth and trade allowed the citizens of Savannah to build impressive homes, churches, and other public buildings. But like so many old cities, Savannah was vulnerable to fire. Two of the most devastating occurred in 1796 and 1820, but it was the yellow fever outbreak of 1820 that was particularly brutal to Savannah, filling the city's cemeteries with about 10 percent of her population.

The coming of the Civil War brought radical changes to the city. Though Fort Pulaski, outside of the city, fell to Union forces in 1862, Savannah itself wasn't captured until Sherman marched to the sea in December 1864. It was one of the few towns along his route he spared from the torch. It is said he was so impressed with its beauty, he couldn't bring himself to order it burned. Instead, he gave it as a Christmas "present" to Abraham Lincoln.

Because of the Union blockade and the ravages of the war on the South in general, post-war Savannah suffered economically. Revival came slowly, with the lumber and cotton industries. But, like every American city, Savannah had its ups and downs. The Great Depression took its toll, but in the 1950s a movement to preserve and restore Savannah's historic buildings began. The Historic Savannah Foundation was formed and preserved buildings such as The Olde Pink House, site of Georgia's first bank; the Pirate's House, setting of the beginning of Robert Louis Stevenson's *Treasure Island*; and the birthplace of Juliette Gordon Low, founder of the Girl Scouts.

And something more than brick and mortar was preserved in those houses. According to witnesses, the spirits of early inhabitants, especially those associated with the Civil War, also remain ensconced within the walls.

Savannah Ghosts

Ray Couch, founder of the paranormal investigation group Southern Ghosts, has done extensive research on the Civil War ghosts of Savannah for his ghost tours. The Riverfront is one of the ghostly hot spots he has identified.

Riverfront Shops

The Riverfront was once the busiest place in Savannah, the Savannah River being a major artery for business and trade. Many of the old warehouses have been repurposed into bed-and-breakfasts, stores and restaurants.

Down Bay Street where it crosses over Martin Luther King Jr. Boulevard is the route of the retreat of the Southern army from Savannah as Sherman approached in December 1864. Shortly before the surrender of the city, the Confederates gathered every boat they could find in Savannah and made a pontoon bridge spanning the Savannah River for their retreat into South Carolina.

Nearly every restaurant, shop, and bed-and-breakfast seems to have a ghost story associated with it. A few years ago, Couch was invited to view a security video that was taken in one of the gift shops. On the video a small ball of light, an orb, can be seen moving around the shop and finally stopping in front of the cash registers, where it begins to rotate. The light then moves back towards the camera and underneath it. It was almost as if the light anomaly moved with a purpose, an intelligence. The next day when the owner arrived, she found all of the T-shirts and some broken souvenir glasses on the floor. No source was found to explain the mess.

Another shop owner reported being called by his security alarm company advising him that someone had triggered the alarm inside the store. When he investigated, he found no one inside. Later he reported that this seems to happen several times a month, yet no one is ever found to have broken into the shop.

Moon River Brewing Company

Moon River Brewing Company is one of the more famous haunted places in Savannah, having been investigated for some major television programs. Ray Couch and Southern Ghosts have investigated the brewery a number of times and have gotten substantial evidence of ghostly activity.

During the Civil War, the building was used as a hospital for both sides. Waitresses and waiters have been touched by unseen hands, even pushed out of the way just as a passing breeze was felt. Bottles have been thrown and silverware has been seen pushed off the tables onto the floor. One woman from the 1820s has made at least two appearances. First she was seen by a manager at the top of the stairwell. Doing his job, he asked if he could help her. She stared for a moment and then vanished. Another time, a woman in the same dated garb was seen walking across the crowded barroom. As she approached, the bartender thought she was a visiting reenactor about to order a drink. When she reached the bar, however, she simply dematerialized. The entire bar suddenly went silent, having witnessed the seemingly impossible phenomenon. Then they realized where they were.

During a paranormal investigation of the Moon River Brewing Company in June 2011, Libby Oxenrider, one of the mediums on the investigation, mentioned that she felt presences in the back room of the cellar, an area used for storage and meetings. Five pictures in a row were taken with a Nikon digital camera. The first picture contained nothing except a small orb; the next picture showed a large orb moving at the ceiling; the third showed an orb down the hall; the fourth captured a large orb on the floor; and the last was clear of all orbs.

Juliette Gordon Low Birthplace

The house that became Juliette Gordon Low's birthplace was built for the mayor of Savannah in 1821. Ten years later, William Washington Gordon I purchased the home. He was the founder of the Central of Georgia Railway. His son, William Washington Gordon II, called "Willie" by the family, inherited the house.

Although Juliette Gordon Low is renowned as the founder of the Girl Scouts, she has a Civil War connection—and a ghost story associated with her family and the house.

Perhaps the most hotly debated theory in paranormal circles is the contention that some remnant of our personality survives death, which would indicate that our mind, or consciousness, might maintain an existence separate from our physical, flesh-and-blood brain.

Many reported activities of ghosts indicate that this is so. Ghosts indicate playfulness and mischievousness by moving physical items around or removing objects, then returning them after being asked to do so. They have been known to communicate emotions to their percipients, while some other ghosts are humorless and merely appear as an emotionless image, a mere residual image of the live person. And many mediums will attest that, while some houses are not haunted, most people are, by the caring ghosts of their dead relatives. So, to some paranormalists, it seems that the strong bond of love does not die with the body, and that the emotion may reside someplace other than the heart or the head.

Juliette's mother, Eleanor "Nellie" Lytle Kinzie, and her father, William "Willie" Washington Gordon, formed an acquaintance in 1853 in a rather unique way. They met when Nellie slid down the banister of the Yale Library and landed on Willie's hat. Nellie was not hurt. The hat didn't fare so well.

Willie fell immediately in love with the vivacious young woman. They were married and Juliette "Daisy" Gordon was born on Halloween night in 1860.

Nellie was caring and protective of her husband. Although he became a member of the local Savannah militia unit when they moved to the city, it must have pained her to see him go off to the Civil War. The family was influential and Nellie was headstrong. She once enlisted her friend Gen. Robert E. Lee to find her husband in the field and make sure he was all right. Willie was wounded during the battles for Atlanta, but survived the war.

During the war, Willie was a supply officer for Confederate general Joe Wheeler's cavalry unit. Although the Savannah family was obviously pro-Southern, Nellie had once been a pen pal of William Tecumseh Sherman. Union generals Sherman and O. O. Howard would both visit the Low home during their time in the Savannah. Once, four-year-old Juliette noticed Howard's missing arm and asked how he lost it. Howard told the little girl that a reb had shot it off. Juliette said "I wonder if my Papa didn't do it. He's shot lots of Yankees!" Those present said that nobody laughed louder or harder than Sherman. Sherman, after the war, recounted many times a story of little Juliette, how she sat on his lap and began to inspect his head. He asked her what she was doing and she replied that she had heard her neighbors refer to him as "That old devil Sherman," and she wanted to see his horns.

After the Civil War, Willie served the United States Army in the Spanish-American War as a brigadier general of volunteers. Nellie and Willie never lost their spark and they remained passionately in love for the rest of their lives.

Willie died in 1912. Nellie was devastated and never fully recovered from the loss. She died on February 22, 1917. While she was on her deathbed, she suddenly rose up and opened her arms, then lay back and passed away. Margaret, Nellie's daughter-in-law, was in the room but glanced out into the hallway to see Willie wearing his dress-gray uniform. He was smiling and seemed to glow as he looked into the room where the children were sitting with their mother. He turned and slowly walked downstairs. Margaret told the family about seeing Willie but they all dismissed her until they went downstairs and saw the butler with tears streaming down his face. He said he had seen the master of the house come down the stairs in his general's uniform. He was smiling as he walked out the door. He said he looked young, handsome, and happy and believed that the general had come back to get his wife at last. The people in the death room said that as she died Nellie's face seemed to take on the glow of a bride.

Fort Pulaski

Construction on a fort to protect access up the Savannah River was begun in 1829 and took eighteen years to complete. It was to be a part of the coastal defense system conceived after the War of 1812. At the time it was thought to be impregnable. But by 1860, it still was not armed or garrisoned and, as it turned out, would not be occupied by United States troops until after they had conquered it by siege.

Two weeks after South Carolina seceded from the Union, in January, 1861, the Georgia State Militia occupied the fort named after

Fort Pulaski near Savannah was captured by Federal forces in 1862. Its walls still show the damage from the bombardment.

the Polish hero of the American Revolution who died defending Savannah. Two weeks later, when Georgia seceded, Fort Pulaski was turned over to the Confederate States of America.

The summer after Fort Sumter fell, President Abraham Lincoln ordered the Navy to blockade Southern ports. In November of 1861 a combined army and navy expedition had arrived about fifteen miles north of Fort Pulaski and established a base at Hilton Head Island. From here they could conduct operations all along the South Atlantic Coast, including against Fort Pulaski.

Once the Federals had captured Hilton Head, Confederates abandoned Tybee Island. It was a tactical mistake, handing over the only place from which Fort Pulaski could be taken. Union troops moved to Tybee Island and cut the fort's communication with the mainland.

Thirty-six Federal guns and mortars were soon aimed at the brick fort from batteries on Tybee Island. Confederates refused the formal request for surrender and the Union gunners opened up on April 10, 1862. At first, Confederates thought they were safe: the fort was a mile from the smoothbore cannon whose effective range against fortifications was half that distance. Unknown to the Confederates was that ten of the bombarding guns were new, experimental rifled cannon whose spiraling projectiles could bore into the brickwork.

Soon large gaps in the walls appeared. By noon on the second day of the siege, the powder magazine was nearly exposed. The young Confederate commander, Col. Charles H. Olmstead, was afraid of what a direct hit on the magazine would do to his men, and so surrendered the fort and its 384-man garrison after only thirty hours. Federal troops held the fort until the war's end.

Like many of the coastal forts after the war, Pulaski was abandoned to a caretaker and lighthouse keeper. Soon, they also left. But the island was declared a national monument in 1924 with restoration efforts beginning in 1933. The fort today still bears much of the damage inflicted upon it during the bombardment leading to its surrender and stands as a symbol of an era of a bygone military theory of impregnable fixed fortifications.

Visitors to the fort can explore the interior of the structure and climb the staircases to the parapet and examine exhibits of some of the larger guns used in the Civil War. Apparently, they are accompanied by other, unseen visitors to the fort.

According to Margaret Wayt DeBolt in her book, *Savannah Spectres and Other Strange Tales*, during World War II, a young woman was returning with a soldier one night from visiting Tybee Island. As a full moon emerged from behind a cloud, the fort loomed dark and ominous in the distance. They were under the impression that the fort had been abandoned, but there, on the parapet, were men in uniform marching guard duty atop the walls. They watched for a while, and they then continued their drive.

It would have helped if they had recognized what kind of uniform the men were wearing since the Navy did have a presence at Fort Pulaski during the war. But since there were few, if any, Civil War reenactors at that time, noticing a kepi or slouch hat on one of the guards would have been—no pun intended—a dead giveaway.

Not all ghost experiences are visual. According to DeBolt, a young man and his friend who decided to do some relic hunting near the fort one night had an auditory experience. They took a boat from

The interior of Fort Pulaski, where several ghost sightings have been reported.

Tybee Island and were walking around the fort in the tall marsh grass when they heard someone else walking alongside of them on the other side of the grass. They stopped and the footsteps also stopped. They began to walk again and the sounds of someone paralleling their path started again as well. They were coming to a clearing and were anxious to see who else was out in the marsh that night. As they emerged from the high grass, so did the sound of the footsteps, but unaccompanied by any physical form. As they watched, they could see the grass compressing before them as the sound passed and continued out into the marsh. They abandoned their relic-hunting plans and ran as fast as they could back to their boat.

Reenactors provide an authenticity to motion pictures that Hollywood just can't muster. Often, Hollywood will also turn to original historical sites as backdrop for a number of history-related films. Savannah is one of the most popular places outside of Hollywood to film and Fort Pulaski has been the filming location of a number of feature films, most notably the 1989 movie *Glory*.

According to a story on the website *Military Ghosts*, while acting as extras in the movie, a group of reenactors, on their way to a set, stopped by the fort to visit the historic site. In Confederate uniform, they must have added to the ambience of the fort itself. As they wandered around in a group, they were struck by a nattily dressed young Confederate lieutenant striding across the parade ground. Often, reenactors will remain "in character" just for the fun of it. They will speak in the vernacular of the Civil War era amongst themselves and even when answering modern visitors' questions. If they are depicting a certain period in time, say, the Confederate occupation of Pulaski, they will claim to know nothing of happenings after the fall of the fort. There is no Union victory yet, no Gettysburg, no Sherman's March, no Appomattox. So, when the lieutenant approached and upbraided them for not saluting him, they all figured they knew what was going on.

They saluted the young officer and he ordered them into line to prepare for the upcoming Yankee attack. Some of them must have smiled, at least inwardly, as he gave them very authentic-sounding commands. He ordered them to about face, placing him at their backs. When no other order came, some of them looked back. To their astonishment, in the middle of the parade ground, there was no sign of him. He had simply vanished back into that misty veil from which he had suddenly emerged.

Some former employees also get uncomfortable feelings on a certain stairwell where it is known that a young soldier, doomed to die after being wounded in the bombardment, was carried. Others disdain going into Colonel Olmstead's quarters after the sun sets, haunted by eerie feelings of despair and regret. Considering what an agonizing decision the twenty-five-year-old commander faced before the surrender, it is no wonder.

Fort McAllister

Fort McAllister was key in defending the city of Savannah against Union gunboats on the Ogeechee River after the fall of Fort Pulaski in 1862. Confederates placed obstructions in the river and allowed only friendly ships in and out. In July of that year, a blockade runner sought refuge behind the obstructions. Union gunboats needed to silence the guns of Fort McAllister before they could sink the blockade runner, but four separate attacks on the fort in 1862 yielded little.

For five hours on January 27, 1863, the Union Navy monitor U.S.S. *Montauk* lobbed eleven- and fifteen-inch shells into the fort. The earthen construction absorbed any damage, unlike Fort Pulaski's brick and mortar walls, which were breached by artillery fire the year before. There were no casualties.

On February 1, 1863, *Montauk* bombarded Fort McAllister again. This time they killed the commander, Maj. John B. Gallie, apparently decapitated by a shell. On February 28, the big monitor was finally able to sink the blockade runner. On March 3, Union gunboats again shelled the fort for eight hours, but McAllister withstood the bombardment. After that failure, the Union Navy gave up on trying to destroy the fort.

In December 1864, when Sherman approached Savannah, he realized he couldn't bypass Fort McAllister, because he needed the Ogeechee River open to supply his army. He ordered Gen. William B. Hazen's division to cross the river and assault the fort from the land.

Union forces finally captured Fort McAllister in 1864 after several unsuccessful attempts.

At 4:45 P.M. on December 13, Hazen's three brigades, vastly outnumbering Maj. George W. Anderson's 230 Confederates defending the fort, attacked. By 5:00 P.M., the Yankees had swarmed over the earthworks capturing the fort. Union losses amounted to 134, or 24 killed and 110 wounded. Confederates loses were 14 killed, 21 wounded, and 195 captured. During the fighting Confederate captain Nicholas Clinch was called on to surrender by the Federal soldiers. He responded by attacking them with his sword. Before he surrendered he suffered three saber wounds, was bayoneted six times, and was shot twice.

The fort was abandoned and nearly forgotten until Henry Ford purchased the site as part of a larger tract. Ford did some restoration of the site. The state of Georgia acquired Fort McAllister and now maintains it as an historical park.

According to an administrator of the park, during the restoration of the fort, workmen stayed on-site overnight to prevent vandalism. Apparently, they were never able to spend an entire night at the fort.

Strange, otherworldly sounds were heard across the parapets of Fort McAllister, all attributed to the former defenders of the fort.

Current lore has the sources of the haunting narrowed down to the casualties during the naval bombardment of the fort in 1863. One of the more famous casualties was garrison mascot Tom Cat, a tabby that was killed during the March 3 bombardment. His death was recorded in the official report sent to Gen. P. G. T. Beauregard. He has his own metal interpretive sign and was buried with military honors inside the fort. As we know, living cats are capable of making some strange noises; who knows what is heard from Tom's ghost.

It would also seem that Captain Clinch, who sacrificed and suffered so much for the defense of the fort, would have left some of the superabundance of energy he expended. Yet the specter most associated with Fort McAllister is Major Gallie. On particularly dark, quiet nights a shadow can be seen moving about the ramparts, apparently checking on the now-invisible defenders, making sure they are ready for the bombardment that now will never come. Who

An orb is seen in this photo from the powder magazine at Fort McAllister.

might it be? The answer becomes apparent when you get a better view: the figure is missing its head.

In June 2011, Carol and I visited Fort McAllister, took some photos, and tried to capture some EVP. The photos taken inside the reconstructed magazine were interesting. The first photo shows an orb at the end of the gallery on the right just above the barrels of powder. In the second photo it appears to have moved towards the camera and is just in front of the second-from-last column on the right. Enlargement of this photo shows several more smaller and lighter orbs scattered about. A third photo shows a strong orb located against the horizontal white log above and to the right of the wooden cases. In the final photo, taken within seconds of the previous one, the orb has moved to the top of the wooden case.

I attempted to capture four EVP. The first one contains an answer to my question but is far too faint to understand and partially obscured by the wind. In the second EVP, I ask Major Gallie, "It was near this spot where you were struck, wasn't it?"At 6 seconds into the recording, there is a voice that responds, "Was it?"

Petersburg and Appomattox

Appomattox Court House was not the end of the American Civil War. Fighting continued in the Western Theater for a few more months until the final land battle at Palmetto Ranch near Brownsville, Texas, on May 12 and 13, 1865. The Confederate commerce raider C.S.S. *Shenandoah* didn't get word of the collapse of the Confederacy until August 2, 1865.

But Appomattox was the symbolic culmination of the South's struggle for independence. It came just a week after the breaking of the ten-month's siege of Petersburg.

After the fighting at Spotsylvania, Grant began a pursuit of Lee's army southward. A horrific battle at Cold Harbor, Virginia, with its numerous, seemingly suicidal Federal assaults, had the despondent Union soldiers writing their names on pieces of paper and pinning them inside their jackets so that their bodies could be shipped home and not lie in unmarked graves. Grant admitted in his memoirs that the last charge at Cold Harbor was the only one in his career he regretted.

Between June 15 and 18, Grant assaulted partially built Confederate lines around Petersburg, twenty-five miles south of Richmond. Petersburg was a rail hub for five rail lines, a depot for trains coming from the deeper Confederacy and feeding Richmond with supplies and troops. His assaults, however, were delivered piecemeal and no advantage pressed by his commanders. Lee arrived to command the bolstering of the Petersburg defenses on June 18, and Grant began siege operations, as he had at Vicksburg.

Grant adopted the strategy of launching an attack upon Richmond every time he sent one against the lines at Petersburg. It stretched the Confederacy's manpower to the limits. In addition, Grant used his 110,000 men to continually creep westward, forcing Lee to burden his 60,000 men with holding ever-lengthening lines.

Like a noose about to come full circle around the Confederates at Petersburg, the long, blue line eventually outstretched the Confederates. At the end of March 1865, battles along the White Oak Road and in Dinwiddie County relentlessly pushed the fighting front westward. At a major crossroads called Five Forks, the Confederate line finally snapped on April 1, 1865, and Richmond and the lines around Petersburg had to be abandoned the next day. A footrace between the armies ensued.

During a week of running fights, the Federals finally cut off Lee's army outside of a little village on the Southside Railroad near Appomattox Station, where Lee was headed, hoping to find supplies waiting. However, hard-riding Union cavalrymen captured the trains at 8 P.M. on April 8 and drove off the Confederate artillery stationed to guard them.

Believing all that was ahead of them was Gen. Philip Sheridan's Union cavalry, Lee ordered an attack to the west on the morning of April 9. As the attack matured, Confederate general John B. Gordon soon realized that there was more than just cavalry before him. Grant had force-marched his infantry overnight in an attempt to encircle Lee's army—and did just that. By 11:00 A.M., with no reinforcements to send to Gordon, Lee called off the attacks and sent out flags of truce. There was only one thing left for Lee to do—speak to Grant about surrender—and, as he said, "I would rather die a thousand deaths."

Petersburg and Appomattox Ghosts

The Dodson Tavern

The Dodson Tavern on High Street in Petersburg, Virginia, was built about 1753 by John Dodson. Needless to say, because of the long history of the building, many historical figures have stepped through the door and refreshed themselves with food and drink. British redcoats were quartered in the tavern during the American Revolution. Vice President Aaron Burr was a guest at the tavern, as was Confederate general Robert E. Lee.

In an article titled "Community Spirits," by Kiran Krishnamurthy, published in the visitors' guide for Petersburg Virginia, he related a story that the owners in 1994 reported items in the house vanishing and then mysteriously reappearing. A visitor to the house once passed a mirror and suddenly stopped, frozen in front of it. There, in the looking glass, was a figure—not the guest's reflection, but someone else, dressed in garb completely out of another era.

Another time, a young granddaughter was spending the night. The next morning she asked her grandmother why she kept peeking in on her at night. Of course, the grandmother had not. She then insisted that a woman was watching over her while she slept in an upstairs bedroom.

One of the owners of the tavern, on her first night in the house, heard the front door open and shut from an upstairs room. Almost immediately after she heard the door, she heard three heavy footsteps behind her and what sounded like a heavy duffle bag drop to the floor. She turned, looked around a corner, and saw no one. It wasn't until the next day when they met their new neighbors, who asked if they knew the house was haunted, that she began to suspect the real source of the noise.

In the early days of its existence when Dodson Tavern was a boardinghouse for travelers and occasional ne'er-do-wells, some overnight guests would indiscreetly brag about the large sums of money they were carrying. It was fatal for at least one of them. In the middle of the night, he had his throat cut for the bag of gold he carried. A slave was blamed, perhaps by the perpetrator, for the murder and lynched from a tree behind the tavern. The real thief escaped. The slave's ghost, seeking to avenge his earthly self, purportedly roams the grounds.

High Street

High Street seems to be a mecca, of sorts, for other spirits who, for one reason or another, refuse to move on to a higher plane.

Individuals passing the 400 block of High Street will periodically see a Confederate soldier still walking the post he was assigned a century and a half before. At another home on the block a female wraith has been known to toss curtains about the room and even unhinge doors. Other residents of High Street have also had bizarre, unexplainable experiences.

In one instance a pet dog was found upstairs in one of the houses when the owners had locked the creature in a downstairs room before they had left. The lock to the room where the dog was kept was on the outside of the door. Another homeowner was pleased to find coins piled in a corner of one of their rooms, until he realized the supernatural nature of their appearance. He removed the coins, only to find more piled in the corner the next day.

Near the intersection of Market and High Streets, the Baltimore Row Houses have seen their share of bad luck. Fires and deaths seem to plague that area more than others in Petersburg. A poltergeist must roam the area, for residents have reported hearing doors slam when there is no one present and the wind is calm. Coins are occasionally found in the corners of rooms there, too.

Center Hill

Center Hill, an imposing architectural gem of Petersburg, dates back to 1823. After Petersburg and Richmond fell, Abraham Lincoln visited one of his generals, G. L. Hartsuff, at his commandeered headquarters at Center Hill. In 1950, it was opened as a Civil War museum and was eventually turned over to the City of Petersburg to become a tourist attraction. Of course, with the building, the city also received Center Hill's ghosts.

Marguerite DuPont Lee, author of *Virginia Ghosts*, was born in 1862. She moved to Washington with her husband, a Virginian, at age eighteen, and so had an opportunity to gather firsthand many of the stories in her book, first published in 1930. In 1885, she interviewed Mrs. Campbell Pryor, who lived in Center Hill for a decade. She claimed that virtually every evening at dusk, those passing Center Hill could see, seated at the second-floor window above the front door, "a beautifully dressed lady." The reports came in for many years.

One morning, her six-year-old daughter sat down for breakfast and asked, "Mother, where is that pretty lady who came and sat on my bed last night? She held my hand and talked to me. I do not see her." She described in detail what could only have been the spirit seen at the window so many times before.

Mrs. Pryor told of a melodeon, which stood in one corner of the room they used as a library. She said that very often they would hear the melodeon playing a familiar tune. When they entered the room to see who was playing, the room was empty.

Her husband slept in a small room on the first floor near his office, but just for a short time. Tucked in for the night, sound asleep, he would be awakened by the bedcovers ripped from his body and thrown into a heap in the middle of the floor. No one was in the room with him.

L. B. Taylor Jr., the dean of Virginia ghost tales, related the most famous story of Center Hill in his book *Civil War Ghosts of Virginia*. It is very unusual for ghosts to keep a strict schedule. (The Woman in White at Chatham Manor in Fredericksburg is supposed to appear every seven years on June 21. The Phantom Regiment, for ten years, apparently kept as tight a schedule.) But on every January 24, at precisely 7:30, the door of the home's library was heard to open and the tramping of marching feet, accompanied by the distinct clank of sabers confirming a military unit, was heard. The unseen soldiers made their way up the stairs and their cadenced footfalls faded into the room above the library. Twenty minutes later, they were heard to retrace their ghostly steps, back down the stairs and into the library where the door was slammed shut. The soldiers were so punctual, the Pryors invited guests to witness the supernatural event.

Appomattox Court House

Lee's retreat from Petersburg to Appomattox is well-documented and can be followed by automobile from Petersburg. With his army in a race for supplies, they passed through a number of small villages and crossroads, like Sutherland Station, Amelia Court House, Jetersville, and Deatonsville, on their way to a devastating battle at Sailor's Creek, where Lee wondered if his army had been "dissolved." Though their dissolution was to take place less than a week later, it seems they may have gathered together again . . . sixty years later, almost to the day.

James R. Furqueron in a 1994 article for *Guide to Historic Richmond, Fredericksburg, and Petersburg*, recalled a discussion an elderly gentleman had with his grandfather near Burkeville, Virginia. In April 1925, the farmer was living in Amelia County, Virginia, and was up early one morning working in a field near Deatonsville. It was just beginning to get light and it was, as he put it rather ominously, "quiet as a tomb." He was in a hollow on the north side of the road to Rice, Virginia. Suddenly, he got that feeling that he was being observed. Turning, he saw a horseman at the top of the hill just off the road. The fact that a horseman was out that early was not unusual, but, he admitted, there was just something about the man that made him uneasy. The horseman made no sound, but slowly lifted his left arm and gestured to the west. He turned his horse's head and disappeared over the hill.

The farmer admitted that the scene frightened him some, but his curiosity got the better of him and he walked toward the hill where he had seen the horseman. At the top of the rise, he looked to see where the man had gone and was shocked by a sight out of time and reason.

There, before him, as far as the eye could see, was an army filling the road. Soldiers with rifles slung, cannons and caissons with artillerymen riding upon them, wagons and horses, and the red battle flags of the Confederate Army flapping above the column moved before his astonished gaze. He was not more than fifty feet from the undulating column and yet he heard not one sound coming from the multitudes. He watched for ten minutes as the thousands of men passed and although it was a chill April morning, he was bathed in sweat. As he summed it up later, "They kept on a movin' without a sound, and I knowed it was the passin' of the dead."

Washington, D.C.

According to John Alexander's classic book, *Ghosts: Washington's Most Famous Ghost Stories*, the capital of the Northern states during the Civil War is the home to literally hundreds of restless spirits from the earliest days of the republic to modern personalities who once lived there.

George Washington has been encountered by men who are themselves now long dead. John C. Calhoun was visited once by the country's first president, who warned the secessionist of the dangers of breaking apart the union of states. Washington has also been seen riding his horse toward his home in Mount Vernon.

From the specters of soldiers of the Revolutionary War and the ghost of Dolley Madison to the spirit of Woodrow Wilson, ghosts have been documented roaming the environs of the nation's capital. But it's Civil War ghosts we are interested in here, and they are numerous.

Daniel Sickles

Gen. Daniel Sickles was a political general in the Civil War, which means he had enough money and influence to raise his own brigade from New York, the Excelsior Brigade, and be appointed its commander. Although never having had any formal military training, he rose in rank and responsibility, eventually commanding the Army of the Potomac's Third Corps. At Gettysburg he was at the center of a great controversy.

He had been in the tactically poor position of occupying low ground with his command in earlier battles, and when he found himself with unoccupied high ground before him at Gettysburg, he took matters into his own hands and advanced his corps to secure a peach orchard on that high ground. In so moving, however, he made two mistakes: First, his line ended up in the shape of an inverted V, meaning bullets and shells fired at one wing would fall into the rear of the other; and second, his line was not long enough to connect with the rest of the Union forces, leaving a gap of about a quarter mile.

Union commander George Meade was furious when he saw what Sickles had done without orders. Meade was also nearly killed by an exploding shell as Confederates under James Longstreet began their assault upon Sickles's salient before he could get back into position.

Sickles's line eventually was driven back to its original position after suffering many unnecessary casualties. If it wasn't for the lucky Confederate shell that struck Sickles in the leg, shattering it and forcing an amputation, he might have been court-martialed. Instead, he was hailed as a hero by none other than President Lincoln himself.

When asked by the surgeon before going under the influence of chloroform what to do with his amputated leg, Sickles told them to save it, and he later donated it to the Army's National Medical Museum to be displayed there.

Even before his Civil War adventures, Sickles had a tumultuous life. In 1859, he was a congressman from New York and married to the much younger Theresa Bagioli, daughter of a famous Italian music teacher. While wining and dining other women back in his district in New York was acceptable to the congressman, when he discovered his wife had been seeing one Philip Barton Key, he was enraged. Key was not just some casual fling. He was Washington's district attorney as well as the son of the author of the "Star Spangled Banner," Francis Scott Key. He was also quite the ladies' man of Washington. He had set up an apartment near the Sickles home as a trysting place, and he and Theresa had established a handkerchief-waving signal when the coast was clear.

When Sickles confronted his wife with the accusation of adultery, she calmly replied, "Oh, I see I am discovered," and implored him to spare her. Instead he had her write out a confession, explicit in detail as to how many times she and Key had met and how he had "disrobed" her.

After a week of stewing over his wife's infidelity, Sickles saw Key waving his handkerchief outside his house and exploded in rage. As Key returned from his visit to the Washington Club, Sickles rushed into the street brandishing firearms and, despite Key's begging for mercy, shot him three times. Key died soon after.

Sickles was tried and acquitted using a previously untried defense: "temporary aberration of the mind," or, in modern parlance, temporary insanity.

Key, though gone and buried, apparently returns periodically to Lafayette Square, scene of the violence. His shade has been reported for more than a hundred years, with newspapers printing descriptions of the ghost by scores of people who have seen it. He's also been seen leaving the Washington Club where he visited last, and in Lafayette Square, evidently attempting to complete his rendezvous with Mrs. Sickles.

Sickles himself had been seen, long after his death in 1914, visiting the leg he lost but saved in the Army Medical Museum. The accounts are the same: a fat, obese, or rotund shadow floating along the hallway. Oh yes, and the shadow is missing its leg.

Sickles, with his influence after the war, had a wrought-iron fence brought from Washington and installed to separate the National Cemetery at Gettysburg from the Gettysburg Evergreen citizen's cemetery. That the ghosts of Philip Barton Key or Dan Sickles have never been observed reenacting their tragic and murderous roles near that fence at Gettysburg is surprising; it once surrounded Lafayette Square in Washington and was witness to one of the more infamous crimes of the nineteenth century.

Henry Rathbone

The people and events surrounding the Lincoln assassination seem particularly prone to tortured lives and traumatic deaths and, consequently, living on and on as ghosts.

When Ulysses S. Grant and his wife could not make the date to accompany the president and his wife to a play at Ford's Theatre, Maj. Henry Rathbone and his fiancée, Clara, daughter of New York senator Ira Harris, were invited by the Lincolns to attend. Perhaps to their eternal regret, they accepted.

After the sudden, explosive violence of seeing his president shot in the head by the famed actor John Wilkes Booth, Rathbone, in an attempt to stop the perpetrator, was slashed viciously in the arm and about the head with a large knife Booth carried.

Though he recovered from his physical wounds, something about the night and his inability to protect the president ate at him. Or perhaps he was already prone to whatever mental aberration it is that causes one to lose touch with reality. Nevertheless, the end was tragic.

Despite his increasing moodiness after the assassination, Clara married him in 1867. It was a fatal mistake.

Rathbone resigned from the Army and was offered an appointment as U.S. consul in Hanover, Germany. Perhaps in an effort to escape the demons haunting him from that April night in 1865, he accepted and moved with Clara and their three children to Europe.

But the move proved no panacea and his decline culminated just two days before Christmas in 1883. He shot and killed his wife, tried to kill his children, and finally attempted suicide. When the police arrived to subdue the bloody Rathbone, he tried to explain to them about the people hiding behind the pictures in the room. The rest of his life was spent in an asylum for the criminally insane in Germany. After he died in 1911, his body was committed to a plot next to the wife he killed. In 1952, however, because of lack of family interest and recent activity, the management of the cemetery "disposed" of their remains.

Apparently, the paranormal theory that a violent demise and an unconsecrated burial may lead to a perturbed and restless spirit also extends to a disturbed burial site. The former Washington home of the Rathbones at Number 8 Jackson Place on Lafayette Square has had a reputation over the years of events that have forced passersby to cross the street rather than walk in front of the house and experience them.

The most disturbing of the phenomena are, on certain nights, the incessant, heartbreaking sobs emanating from the house. They have been identified as those of a man inconsolable to the seemingly out-of-control life that began at Ford's Theatre on the evening of April 14, 1865.

Lincoln in the White House

Of all the United States presidents, none has presided over a more tumultuous time in our history than Abraham Lincoln. And, arguably, none wrestled more with his own demons.

Melancholy was steeped into Lincoln's personality, from the time of his birth-mother's death when he was four years old, to the loss of Ann Rutledge, his first love, to witnessing the deaths of two of his four children, his life was crisscrossed with personal tragedy. Then came the schism in the nation, which many Southerners argue was precipitated by Lincoln's election and subsequent actions.

While living in the Executive Mansion, the Lincolns sponsored and participated in several séances. In 1863, medium Charles Shockle held a séance there. Medium J. B. Conklin passed a cryptic message he said had come from Lincoln's close friend Edward Baker, killed leading Union troops at the Battle of Ball's Bluff: "Gone elsewhere," Baker allegedly said, and added, "Elsewhere is everywhere."

Nettie Colburn Maynard, a medium who had conducted séances with the Lincolns in and outside the Executive Mansion, wrote a book about it called *Was Lincoln a Spiritualist?* In it she recounted the Lincolns witnessing the spirits levitating a piano with a man sitting on it.

Like so many mothers and fathers in mid-nineteenth-century America, when 620,000 of their boys had died, the Lincolns may have been drawn to spiritualism in an attempt to reconnect with their two sons, Eddie and Willie, who had died. The great bloodletting of the Civil War may be the reason for the renewed and increased popularity of spiritualism during the period.

Mary Todd Lincoln certainly seemed fascinated by the subject; whether her husband bought into it, as Maynard's book title suggests, is arguable. One thing that is beyond argument, however, is

Lincoln's continued presence in the Executive Mansion, as well as the presence of the spirit of one son.

Some of President Grant's family believed that they could contact the dead, and one was reported to have spoken with little Willie Lincoln's ghost. Lynda Johnson Robb, daughter of President Lyndon B. Johnson, felt sure that it was in her room in the White House that Willie had died. Her mother, Lady Bird Johnson, while watching a television special on Lincoln, suddenly got a chill when the program talked of the importance to Lincoln of the very room she was sitting in. She immediately got an uncomfortable feeling, as if Lincoln were there, behind her.

Theodore Roosevelt, survivor of an assassination attempt himself, was perhaps speaking metaphorically when he claimed he was very much aware of Lincoln's presence in the White House some four decades after his death: "I see him in the different rooms and in the halls."

President Calvin Coolidge's wife, Grace, claimed she saw Lincoln dressed in black wearing a shawl across his shoulders, something Lincoln was known to do. He apparently was standing at a window with his hands clasped behind his back, gazing thoughtfully out across the Potomac. It wasn't the last time she would see him.

Harry Truman, as no-nonsense a president as we've ever had, was awakened one morning by two solid knocks on his bedroom door. He rose and opened the door to find no one. But he felt a freezing cold spot before him that began to accompany footsteps as they moved down the hall.

Perhaps it was the straits the country found itself in during the Great Depression and World War II, but the Franklin D. Roosevelt era was one of the most active for Lincoln re-visits to the White House. One of the most famous personages that Lincoln's wraith visited was Queen Wilhelmina of the Netherlands, who was staying in the Rose Room. This episode possibly occurred during her visit to the U.S. between June 24 and August 11, 1942. It was late when she heard the knock on her door. Thinking it may be some urgent state business, she answered it, only to be confronted by the six-foot, four-inch form of Abraham Lincoln. The next thing she knew, she was lying on the floor after blacking out from the shock of seeing the American president killed during the last century.

Winston Churchill, during his visits in the 1940s, never liked sleeping in the Lincoln bedroom and would be found, in the morning, in the room across the hall. During one visit, after taking a hot bath (accompanied by a glass of scotch and omnipresent cigar) he emerged from the tub and strolled naked into an adjoining room where he ran right into Lincoln, who was leaning on the mantle above the fireplace. They looked each other in the face. Churchill was embarrassed. Lincoln simply vanished.

Various employees in the White House saw the sixteenth president during the Roosevelt administration. Mary Eben, Eleanor Roosevelt's secretary, passed Lincoln's bedroom once and saw a tall, thin, dark man sitting on the bed pulling on his boots. At seeing the former occupant of the White House, dead at that point for more than seventy-five years, she screamed and ran from the second floor. FDR's personal valet, Cesar Carrera, once ran completely out of the White House screaming that he had just seen Lincoln's ghost. Perhaps more interestingly, the Roosevelts' little dog Fala would react to unseen entities in the White House.

Mary Surratt

The most pathetic spirit said to haunt the White House is that of Annie Surratt, daughter of executed Lincoln assassination conspirator Mary Surratt.

There is much controversy surrounding the Mary Surratt execution. In the frantic search for the assassins after Lincoln's murder, a roundup unprecedented in American history occurred. No one really knew how far-ranging the conspiracy was and a vast dragnet was thrown out. Everyone from Confederate president Jefferson Davis to every lowly private in the Confederate Army was suspected by Secretary of War Edwin M. Stanton, who personally took over the case. Eventually the suspects were narrowed down. Eight men and one woman were suspected in the conspiracy.

Mary Surratt was in her teens when she married John Surratt. He was an alcoholic and they had trouble keeping land for farming, which he constantly had to sell off to pay his debts. They had three children and tried to educate them at the several Catholic schools in the area. John and Mary finally settled at a crossroads tavern and post office, and the town soon became known as Surrattsville. Although Mary was a devout Catholic, she and John held slaves, and her political sympathies lay with the Confederacy. By the time John died in 1862, Surratt Tavern had gained a reputation as the hub of a rebel spy network, with John Jr. allegedly one of the spies.

Though she kept ownership of the tavern, she and her daughter Annie moved into Washington, buying a townhouse on the 600 block of H Street. It, too, became somewhat of a safe house for Confederate sympathizers.

After her husband's death, Mary may have taken a more active role in supporting clandestine Confederate activities. In fact, at least one author, Donald E. Markle, in his book *Spies and Spymasters of the Civil War*, lists her as one of the "Confederate spies executed by the Union."

Her association with John Wilkes Booth has been documented. Her own son brought Booth to the Surratt boardinghouse for meetings. Lewis Powell (aka Lewis Paine), who would be involved in the attempted assassination of Secretary of State William Henry Seward, blundered into the boardinghouse a few days after the assassination, and by his presence, indicted her while she spoke with the police. But at the time Booth was meeting at her house, the plan was to kidnap President Lincoln and haul him into Virginia to hold as ransom for a negotiated peace favorable to the Confederacy. Did Mary ever know that Booth's plans changed to murder just before the assassination? Perhaps we'll never know.

She was incarcerated along with the other coconspirators and tried through the spring and hot early days of summer 1865. Whenever they were moved about, the conspirators were forced to wear thick, sweltering hoods, and at least one report states that Mary Surratt was not allowed a change of clothing for the entire period of her imprisonment until her execution.

In spite of an attempt to gain her presidential clemency, and her daughter Annie's pounding on the White House doors to speak with President Andrew Johnson, in July 1865 she became the first woman executed by the United States government, along with three other coconspirators.

Mary Surratt has been blamed, long after her death, for the pacing footsteps heard over the years on the second floor of the Surratt Boarding House, which still stands on H Street.

The Old Brick Capitol, once used as the seat of Congress during the War of 1812, formerly stood where the United State Supreme Court Building now stands in Washington. At the time of the Civil War, it was used to house Federal prisoners, including the famous Confederate spy Belle Boyd, Andersonville prisoner-of-war camp commander Henry Wirz, and accused Lincoln assassination coconspirator Mary Surratt. It was also used as the headquarters for the National Women's Party, the Suffragettes, beginning in 1922. John Alexander interviewed a former resident who showed him old newspaper clippings documenting some of the supernatural events that went on in the building. Though the inmates and cells were long gone, the women would still be kept awake at night by disembodied weeping, moaning and sighing, and an occasional "maniacal scream" ripping through the darkened halls, or the cold-metal sound of a cell door being slammed. While Boyd's ghost is blamed for the peals of bitter laughter once heard echoing through the building, the sounds of footsteps pacing incessantly coming from what was once a cell are thought to belong to the tortured spirit of Captain Wirz, who paced and paced the last few hours of his life away before climbing the gallows.

Also disturbing, according to Alexander's interviewee, were the agonized cries from what could only have been a female spirit, a remnant of paranormal energy they attributed to Mary Surratt when she learned her fate would come at the end of a rope. Particularly unnerving is the report that on the anniversary of her death, July 7, a vague female form was seen at a window sobbing eternally. A closer look revealed deathly white fists clutching black iron bars where bars no longer existed.

The wraith of Mary Surratt has also been seen floating around the courtyard of Fort Leslie McNair where the gallows from which she swung were located. Eerily, shortly after the executions, a boxwood tree grew out of nothing but bare ground where the gallows once stood. Legend claims that Mary caused it to bloom, a living testament to her innocence.

A spirit seen moving aimlessly along Brandywine Road near Clinton, Maryland has been attributed to Mary. Clinton was once named Surrattsville, her home in better times.

Perhaps the saddest of all the specters associated with the murder of Lincoln is the lithe, young female ghost that is seen pounding periodically at the doors of the White House pleading for clemency from the president for her mother, doomed to drop those few fatal feet until stopped abruptly by the hangman's noose. Those who have seen it and know their assassination history have identified it as the image of Annie Surratt, still heartbroken after all these years.

Ford's Theatre

Ford's Theatre, where John Wilkes Booth struck, is one of the museums in Washington administered by the National Park Service. After the assassination, it was closed as a theater and used for government offices. Rumors of it being cursed swirled after the brick façade collapsed in 1893, killing twenty-two and injuring another sixty-eight people. In 1968, it was reopened as a theater and still serves as one. It has also been the scene for some unexplainable events. Before its renovation between 2007 and 2009, reports emerged of phantom footsteps rushing to the box where Lincoln was shot. Some claim to have heard again the gunshot, the screams of horror, and Mary Todd Lincoln wailing, "He's killed the President!"

Before the renovations, actors would avoid certain spots stage left, below the fatal box from which Booth leapt. If the actors hit the spot where Booth landed and broke his leg, they stumble over their lines and forget where they are in the play no matter how well-rehearsed they are. A chill welcomes them to the spot; some have become nauseous and begin to shake uncontrollably.

According to *TheCabinet.com*, some people claim to have seen the spirit of the assassin himself hurriedly limp across the stage, attempting to escape again, this time through the other world.

One of our guides at the Ghosts of Gettysburg Candlelight Walking Tours, Amanda Beck, works at Ford's Theatre. I asked her about any otherworldly presences, and she only recalled one recurrent supernatural event. She and several of the staff, while walking through the lobby and gift shop, have heard whispering in their ears. She heard it so distinctly a number of times, she actually turned to see who it was. No one was in sight. While seemingly innocuous, it is still unnerving. Whoever whispers to her is unseen but apparently knows her intimately, because the word she hears whispered so close to her ears is her own name.

Bibliography

Books and Articles

Alexander, John. *Ghosts: Washington's Most Famous Ghost Stories*. Washington D.C.: Washingtonian Books, 1975.

Blue & Gray Magazine's Guide to Haunted Places of the Civil War. Columbus, OH: Blue & Gray Magazine; The General's Books, 1996.

Brown, Alan. *Haunted Georgia: Ghosts and Strange Phenomena of the Peach State*. Mechanicsburg, PA: Stackpole Books, 2008.

———. *Haunted Tennessee: Ghosts and Strange Phenomena of the Volunteer State*. Mechanicsburg, PA: Stackpole Books, 2009.

Cohen, Daniel. *Hauntings and Horrors*. New York: Dutton Children's Books, 2002.

Coleman, Christopher K. *Ghosts and Haunts of the Civil War: Authentic Accounts of the Strange and Unexplained*. Nashville: Rutledge Hill Press, 1999.

Daniel, Larry J. *The Battle of Shiloh: National Park Civil War Series*. Fort Washington, PA: Eastern National, 1998.

Davis, William C. *The First Battle of Manassas: Civil War Series*. Fort Washington, PA: Eastern National, 2008.

DeBolt, Margaret Wayt. *Savannah Spectres and Other Strange Tales*. Virginia Beach: Donning Company, 1984.

Furgurson, Ernest B. *Chancellorsville, 1863: The Souls of the Brave*. New York: Vintage Books, 1993.

Furqueron, James R. "Lee's Ghostly Soldiers . . . Still on Their Last March," *Guide to Historic Richmond, Fredericksburg, and Petersburg* III, no. 7 (October 1994): 1.

Guiley, Rosemary Ellen. *The Encyclopedia of Ghosts and Spirits*. 3rd ed. New York: Facts on File, 2007.

Harrison, Noel G. *Chancellorsville Battlefield Sites*. 2nd ed. Lynchburg, VA: H. E. Howard, 1990.

Hennessy, John. *The First Battle of Manassas: An End to Innocence July 18–21, 1861*. Lynchburg, VA: H. E. Howard, 1989.
Hillhouse, Larry. *Ghosts of Lookout Mountain*. Wever, IA: Quixote Press, 2009.
Kelly, Dennis. *Second Manassas: The Battle and Campaign*. Fort Washington, PA: Eastern Acorn Press, 1983.
Kinney, Pamela K. *Haunted Richmond*. Atglen, PA: Schiffer Publishing, 2007.
Kotarski, Georgianna C. *Ghosts of the Southern Tennessee Valley*. Winston-Salem, NC: John F. Blair, 2006.
Lee, Marguerite DuPont. *Virginia Ghosts*. Rev. ed. Berryville, VA: Virginia Book Company, 1966.
Logsdon, David R., ed. *Eyewitnesses at the Battle of Franklin*. Nashville: Kettle Mill Press, 2000.
Markle, Donald E. *Spies and Spymasters of the Civil War*. New York: Hippocrene Books, 2000.
Marietta City Cemetery and Confederate Cemetery (brochure). Marietta, GA: Marietta City Cemetery.
Martin, David G. *The Second Bull Run Campaign: July–August 1862*. Cambridge, MA: Da Capo Press, 2003.
McPherson, James M. *Battle Cry of Freedom: The Civil War Era*. New York: Oxford University Press, 1988.
Miller, William J. *The Battles for Richmond, 1862: Civil War Series*. Eastern National, 1996.
Nesbitt, Mark. *Ghosts of Gettysburg*. Gettysburg, PA: Thomas Publications, 2001.
———. *The Ghost Hunter's Field Guide to Civil War Battlefields: Fredericksburg and Chancellorsville*. Gettysburg: Second Chance Publications, 2005.
———. *Rebel Rivers: A Guide to Civil War Sites of the Potomac, Rappahannock, York, and James*. Mechanicsburg, PA: Stackpole Books, 1993.
O'Reilly, Francis A. *The Fredericksburg Campaign: Winter War on the Rappahannock*. Baton Rouge: Louisiana State University Press, 2003.
Polonsky, Jane Keane, and Joan McFarland Drum. *The Ghosts of Fort Monroe*. Hampton, VA: Hoiston, 1972.
Rhea, Gordon C. *The Battle of the Wilderness: May 5–6, 1864*. Baton Rouge: Louisiana State University Press, 1994.
———. *The Battles for Spotsylvania Court House and the Road to Yellow Tavern, May 7–12, 1864*. Baton Rouge: Louisiana State University Press, 1997.
Roberts, Nancy. *Civil War Ghost Stories and Legends*. Columbia: University of South Carolina Press, 1993.
Schultz, Duane. *The Dahlgren Affair: Terror and Conspiracy in the Civil War*. New York: W. W. Norton, 1998.
Seabrook, Lochlainn. *Carnton Plantation Ghost Stories*. Franklin, TN: Sea Raven Press, 2010.
Sheldrake, Rupert. *The Sense of Being Stared At, and Other Aspects of the Extended Mind*. New York: Crown Archetype, 2003.
Taylor, L. B., Jr. *The Big Book of Virginia Ghost Stories*. Mechanicsburg, PA: Stackpole Books, 2010.
———. *Civil War Ghosts of Virginia*. Williamsburg, VA: Self-published, 1995.
———. *The Ghosts of Virginia*. Vol. 13. Williamsburg, VA: Self-published, 2009.

———. *Haunted Virginia: Ghosts and Strange Phenomena of the Old Dominion*. Mechanicsburg, PA: Stackpole Books, 2009.

Wilson, Patty A. *Haunted West Virginia: Ghosts and Strange Phenomena of the Mountain State*. Mechanicsburg, PA: Stackpole Books, 2007.

Online Sources

"Andersonville, Georgia, Ghost Sightings." *Ghosts of America*. www.ghostsofamerica.com/3/Georgia_Andersonville_ghost_sightings.html.

Carter House. www.carter-house.org.

"Chickamauga, Georgia Ghost Sightings." *Ghosts of America*. www.ghostsofamerica.com/3/Georgia_Chickamauga_ghost_sightings.html.

Coleman, Dorcas. "Who's Afraid of Ghosts." *Maryland Department of Natural Resources*. http://dnr.maryland.gov/naturalresource/fall2001/ghosts.html.

"Dark Destinations: Ford's Theater National Historic Site." *The Cabinet*. http://thecabinet.com/darkdestinations/location.php?sub_id=dark_destinations&letter=f&location_id=fords_theatre_national_historical_site.

"Fort Pulaski: The Commander's Spirit." *Military Ghosts*. www.militaryghosts.com/pulaski.html.

"Ghost of Lookout Mountain, The." *Traveling Poor*, February 18, 2010. http://travelingpoor.wordpress.com/2010/02/18/the-ghost-of-lookout-mountain.

"Haunted Places in Georgia." *The Shadowlands*. http://theshadowlands.net/places/georgia.htm.

Lanier, Gina. "Chattanooga Ghosts." *Haunted America Tours*. www.hauntedamericatours.com/ghosts/Chattanooga.php.

"McRaven House." *Mississippi Paranormal Times*. http://msspiparanews.wordpress.com/2011/06/22/mcraven-house.

Sears, Stephen W. "The Dahlgren Papers Revisited." *Historynet.com*. historynet.com/the-dahlgren-papers-revisited.htm.

Sykes, William, and Crystal Sykes. "Reader Comments," March 28, 2011, with Amy Condra, "Looking for Ghosts at Cold Harbor." *The Mechanicsville Local*, May 13, 2008. www.mechlocal.com/index.php/news/article/looking_for_ghosts_at_cold_harbor.

Taylor, Troy. "The River of Death." *American Hauntings*. www.prairieghosts.com/chick.html.

"Vicksburg's Haunted House: The McRaven Home." *Haunted Places to Go*. www.haunted-places-to-go.com/haunted-house-2.html.

Villani, Denise. "Haunted Lighthouse: Point Lookout Light." *Articlesbase*, March 1, 2008. www.articlesbase.com/religion-articles/haunted-lighthouses-point-lookout-light-347766.html.

Acknowledgments

Thanks to Cathy Adams, Fredericksburg Hampton Inn & Suites, Fredericksburg, Virginia; Marilyn and Elliott Bardsley; Amanda Beck; Jeff Belanger; Jeff Campbell; Paul Chiles; Guy W. Condra; Ray and Sharon Couch; Fiona Crawley; Laine Crosby; Gretchen Dugan; The Kenmore Inn, Fredericksburg, Virginia; Dale Kaczmarek; Brett Keener; Fredericksburg Convention and Visitor's Center; Fredericksburg Police Department; Gettysburg & Northern Railroad; Rosemary Ellen Guiley; Jennifer Henise; Thomas Longstreet; Frank May; Gregg and Carol McCrary; Jackie Mullen; Helen Myers; Jack and Maria Palladino; The Cashtown Inn; Sharad Patel, Windsor Hotel, Americus, Georgia; Deb Pederson; Darla Peightal; Dale Phillips; Greg Platzer; Katherine Ramsland; Ed Raus; Jeff Ritzmann; Jennifer Suroviec; L. B. Taylor; Troy Taylor; Kyle Weaver; Patty Wilson; Terry Winschel; and Tom Van Winkle.

Index